AMA Physicians' Guide to Financial Planning

by

PAUL H. SUTHERLAND

Author of *Twelve Steps to a Carefree Retirement*

Vice President, Business Products: Anthony J. Frankos
Director, Editorial: Mary Lou White
Director, Production and Manufacturing: Jean Roberts
Senior Acquisitions Editor: Suzanne Fraker
Developmental Editor: Lisa Chin-Johnson
Copy Editor: Mary Kay Kozyra
Director, Marketing: Pam Palmersheim
Marketing Manager: Erica Duke
Senior Production Coordinator: Boon Ai Tan
Senior Print Coordinator: Ronnie Summers

© 2008 by the American Medical Association
Printed in the United States of America.
All rights reserved.

www.ama-assn.org

No part of this publication may be reproduced, stored in a retrieval system, or transmitted in any form or by any means electronic, mechanical, photocopying, recording, or otherwise, without the prior written permission of the publisher.

This book is intended for information purposes only. It is not intended to constitute legal advice. If legal advice is desired or needed, a licensed attorney should be consulted.

Additional copies of this book may be ordered by calling 800 621-8335 or from the secure AMA Book Store web site at www.amabookstore.com. Refer to product number OP230107.

Library of Congress Cataloging-in-Publication Data

Sutherland, Paul H.
   The AMA's guide to financial planning / by Paul H. Sutherland.
     p. ; cm.
   Includes bibliographical references and index.
   Summary: "A resourse to help physicians in debt management, insurance, tax planning and real estate"—Provided by publisher.
   ISBN 978-1-57947-875-9 (alk. paper)
   1. Physicians—Finance, Personal. I. American Medical Association. II. Title. III. Title: Guide to financial planning.
   [DNLM: 1. Income. 2. Physicians—economics. 3. Investments. W 79 S966a 2007]
   R728.5.S867 2007
   610.68'1—dc22

                                                                                                            2007040421

The authors, editors, and publisher of this work have checked with sources believed to be reliable in their efforts to confirm the accuracy and completeness of the information presented herein and that the information is in accordance with the standard practices accepted at the time of publication. However, neither the authors nor the publisher nor any party involved in the creation and publication of this work warrant that the information is in every respect accurate and complete, and they are not responsible for any errors or omissions or for any consequences from application of the information in this book.

The ideas and opinions expressed in this book do not reflect the views or the official policy of the American Medical Association (unless otherwise specifically indicated). The ideas and opinions provided in this book are only intended to provide guidance and should not be used as a substitute for independent professional advice and personal judgment. It is the responsibility of the individual investor/physician and/or his or her advising financial advisor/s, relying on personal and independent experience and knowledge of financial matters, to determine the best investment course for the investing physician. The American Medical Association and author do not assume any responsibility for any loss and/or damages to persons, relationships, investments, or property arising out of or related to any use of the material contained in this book.

ISBN 1-57947-875-1
BP37:06-P-041:12/07

This book does not constitute an endorsement by the American Medical Association for any company, service, financial instrument or investment strategy, expressed or implied, mentioned herein.

CONTENTS

Dedication   ix

The New Yorker cartoon   x

Author Bio   xi

Acknowledgments   xii

Introduction   xv

1   Financial Stewardship   1

Developing a Productive Relationship with Money   1

Your Money's Financial Future: A Mission Statement   2

Career Cycles: Early Enthusiasm, Mid-Career Burnout, Mellow Maturity and Choices   4

Medicine for Medical Burnout   8

The Role of Money in Your Life   13

Planning Finances with the Family   15

2   Risk Management   22

Prudence, Intention, and Fiduciary Obligations   22

Keeping Promises   24

Debt Management for Risk Reduction   31

Risk Management Strategies   38

Pre-Nuptial Agreements   42

Income Protection Insurance   45

Life or Death Insurance   51

Insurance on Children   61

Financial Privacy   62

3   Homes and Real Estate   68
Houses versus Homes   68

Double Your Pleasure Triple Your Pain with Debt   70

Selling Your Home   71

4   Childran and Education   79
Saving for College   79

529 College Savings Plan   80

Cows Plus Ice Cream Equal College   85

Death and Dying   96

5   Retirement   104
To Work Or Not To Work?   104

First Step: Visualize   107

Second Step: Retirement Budget After You Have Visualized Your Lifestyle   110

Third Step: Estimating How Much You'll Need in Retirement Assets   110

Fourth Step: How Much!?   113

Retirement Chapter's "After Five" Stops   116

$10,000 Windows, $1,000 Chairs and $20 a Month for Starving Kids   117

Estate Planning: Event-driven dispositions   119

Budget Busters   121

Synergy and Tax Planning for Retirement   122

Retirement Plan Specifics   123

Investment Options for Retirement Plans   133

It's Simple   134

Retirement Planning   135

Tax Strategies   136

Tax Deals   137

Fixed Immediate Annuities   140

In God We Trust; Others Provide Data   145

6   Invest Wisely   152

Investing with Confidence and the Paradox of *If*   152

Bottoms and Tops   156

Indexing? Asset Allocation? Run!   159

Diversification Demystified   160

Hedge Funds   162

Hedge Funds: "Regulation Light"   164

7   Guided Do It Yourself Portfolio Management   169

The Importance of an Investment Philosophy   169

Sustainable Portfolios   173

Doing It Yourself   175

Asset Classes   185

100% Funds   190

Pulling It All Together   193

Not Leaving It to Chance   198

Appendices   202

Glossary   229

Index   261

Dedicated to all those kids that said,
"Someday I want to be a doctor!"

"... and now in this next scene you've graduated from medical school and become the most famous neuropathologist in the world."

© The New Yorker Collection 1948 Peter Arno from cartoonbank.com. All Rights Reserved.

AUTHOR BIO

Paul H. Sutherland, CFP®
Financial Advisor, Portfolio Manager
President

Paul Sutherland, married to Amy Sutherland has two children: daughter Akasha age 15 and son Keeston age 13. Since 1975, Paul H. Sutherland has worked in the investment and financial advisory business. Paul is president, founder, and the chief investment officer of Financial & Investment Management Group, Ltd. (FIM Group), and the manager of Utopia Funds. FIM Group is a fee-only financial planning and money management firm. FIM Group serves an international clientele from offices in Michigan, Wisconsin, and Maui, Hawaii. FIM has over 35 dedicated employees serving clients. FIM Group manages the Utopia Funds no-load, no 12(B)1 mutual funds. Paul is a member of NAPFA (National Association of Personal Advisors), an organization with strict fee-only and practice style standards.

Paul is the author of four financial books: *Financial Strategies for Physicians* (published by W.B. Saunders of Harcourt Brace Jovanovich, 1988); *Physician's Financial Sourcebook* (1998); *Zenvesting: The Art of Abundance & Managing Money* (1999); and *Twelve Steps to a Carefree Retirement* (published by the American Medical Association, 1999).

Over the past 25 years, Paul has been a contributing editor and writer for magazines such as *Business Ethics, Financial Planner, National Psychologist, Physician's Management, Dental Management*, and *Publishing Entrepreneur*. Paul has been interviewed by *Barrons, The Wall Street Journal, Wall Street Transcript* and *Money Magazine*. He's also appeared on the local NBC affiliate's "Money Watch" program. Paul received his MBA from Lake Superior State University. He has spoken to the Kansas Medical Society, World Future Society, Baylor College of Medicine, Northwestern Michigan Osteopathic Physician's Association, National Library of Singapore, and other organizations such as CPA associations, churches, service groups, medical groups, colleges, in addition to sitting on expert panels as a professional investor for Beijing business people and investment forums throughout the USA.

ACKNOWLEDGMENTS

WHILE NATURALLY IT IS appropriate to thank all my colleagues at FIM Group and Suzanne Fraker and the delightful staff at the AMA, really this book's energy has come from the people I have served over the years. Their stories have given me the motivation to write this book.

In my conference room sits a young widowed doctor. He has a fourth grader at home, tons of debts, in his second marriage, and both he and his wife worked because they needed to. No wills, no trusts, asset ownerships and beneficiaries were set up before the marriage. The emotional grief was horrendous for this young man, a child to take care of, patients, and a financial mess that sadly could have been avoided by, in medical terms, something as simple as getting the shots and anti-malaria drugs before going to less developed countries. A few hours with a competent financial planner could have made such a difference. Reading a book on financial planning could have made such a difference. His first wife, statistically should be alive today; statistically, he would not have ever needed to wonder about those beneficiaries, he should have died first. Statistically, the yellow fever, meningitis, hepatitis A and B, and tetanus shots I get so I can travel to Ethiopia, Cambodia, and Guatemala, probably are not necessary, but I have them. Stomach medicine and antibiotics are always in my backpack, along with my opened-only-once first aid kit (a Band-Aid and antibiotic cream were used for a kid's sliver, gotten on a dock on a small island in Australia's barrier reef).

The young doctor knew he should have planned, "but you know kids, work, marriage, practice, no time to play, and besides that you guys cost money," he lamented.

Hundreds of physicians have chatted with me over my career in my conference room, on the phone, through emails, after speeches or seminars. Most have shared the raw details of their [financial] lives; they have been my testing ground for the advice in this book. Early in my career the advice was from my head and mechanical—get a will, get life insurance, set up a retirement plan, get disability. Now it is from my head and heart—protect your children, allow them to have a good education, don't leave a mess if you die or get disabled, realize that if you speculate with borrowed money that its consequences can be quite uncomfortable. I believe we can have it all in life—the key is defining the "all." Creating financial security for you and your loved ones is easy but it's not automatic, hopefully, this book will guide you to make great choices. My colleagues: Judy McCorkle, Barry Hyman, Suzanne Stepan, Zach Liggett, Alice Vanni, Linda Brzezinski, Kevin Russell, Jeff Lokken, and the project manager, Katie Hall, made this book possible. I am especially grateful to my clients who saw me or chatted with me a bit less because I was working on the book, but of course they now say they would rather talk to Zach, Suzanne, Kevin, Robin, Linda, Meredith, Jeff, Barry, Alice, or Judy anyway.

In our lives we sometimes have people that we mesh with and feel are "kin," as automatically as we know that newborn baby is "my child." This is my second project for Suzanne Fraker of the AMA and I am so grateful to have an excuse to chat with and work with her. Working with Suzanne has been delightful. Suzanne's kindness in extending my deadline twice on this book was a great blessing for my children, co-workers, and me.

Thank you to Glen Mathison and Joanne Cuthbertson, both from the AMA Corporate Communications. *Twelve Steps to a Carefree Retirement* was my first book with the AMA. My past experience working with my editor, Jean Roberts, and how well the designer, Steve Straus, pulled the prose, charts, graphs, quotes, and sidebars into a cohesive flow (on *Twelve Steps to a Carefree Retirement*) made me know working with the AMA on this book would be great.

Chuck Schwab's staff and colleagues also must be acknowledged, including Scott Rister, Services for Investment Managers; Susan Campbell & Darin Lott with the AMA; and Jeff Holzbach, from Schwab Financial Planning Group. I do not work for Schwab, but they have been very helpful in providing support service for my clients, and have allowed our no-load Utopia Funds' mutual funds to be available no-load to their investment clients and retirement plans. I have worked with them for 15 years or so and have the experience of working with dozens of firms. I must admit that Schwab, due to their care, pricing, service and integrity, has kept them as a fine partner in serving my clients.

This book would not be complete if it were not for the content about happiness and children, which was greatly influenced by Martin Seligman, MD, author of *The Optimist Child* and other books. I am so blessed to have been introduced to his work by my daughter's physician 8 years ago. His comments about how inheritance can influence children's lives and attitude, on page 94, adds soul to this book.

INTRODUCTION

Common Sense, First Things First, and You Don't Know What You Don't Know

"Physicians are busy. They don't have time for all this financial stuff," I explained to the new American Medical Association (AMA) team members assigned to the *Physician's Guide to Financial Planning*. I went on to explain that the primary goal of our book is (1) to help physicians make better decisions so they can have better financial outcomes, and (2) to help them avoid mistakes.

Unique to this book is explanation of how to use the many resources available to physicians and how to find the best help and resources. The book takes a cost-effective approach and is designed to be a valuable resource for AMA members and their families, financial advisors, and other physicians.

Financial planning is simply managing and arranging your income and assets to accomplish life goals. It requires you to know yourself enough to know what your goals are, even if a goal is as simple as, "I want financial security and to manage my affairs efficiently." If you are without goals, any solution might sound good.

Thousands of salespeople driven by commissions are striving to get a piece of physicians' income flow or assets, disguising that desire by offering "a solution for you." I am amazed that anyone still buys variable annuities, load mutual funds, expensive wrap programs, or commissioned cash-value life insurance and when retirees with $100,000-plus annual incomes succumb to a slick salesman and purchase nursing home policies that are not necessary or appropriate.

Agents and financial consultants backed by the marketing muscle of the insurance and investment industry with their sketchy and self-serving charts, graphs, and facts can make such products sound like the ideal product for today. Like the healthy-looking cigarette spokesperson of old or the athlete or model pushing alcohol today, there is only one goal: to hook you on the product early when you are naive and susceptible to *endowment behavior* (see glossary for explanation of this behavior). You see, you don't know what you don't know! For example, most people do not know that low commission, cash-value insurance, and variable deferred annuities were an okay, acceptable deal two or three tax reform acts ago, but today they are near-toxic in their inefficiency as financial tools.

It is common sense to understand that as financial markets and the economy change, financial products and solutions change too. Often, inefficient, obsolete products are redesigned to look new. Advertising, design, brand, and brand identity can make or break companies or their products. We need to get past the hype and glitter to evaluate true worth. This is where common sense can be priceless.

Common sense comes from good education and up-to-date information combined with wisdom from experience. Investments get expensive and should be sold when that happens; insurance needs will change; budgeting priorities will flex with your career, family needs, and income—all are common-sense statements that are addressed in this book.

Adding efficiency is what this planning stuff is all about, helping you to make wise choices that can help you retire with confidence, educate your children with ease, and avoid the pitfalls that cause setbacks. None of the financial advice will have much value unless it is consistent with your goals, commitments, priorities, values, intentions, and life circumstances. The "My Way/Our Way Life Plan: Balancing Current and Future Needs" tool on page xviii is designed to help with the process of first figuring out what you want and then how to get it. Note the Middle Eastern proverb, "Blessed is the man who gives advice, but a thousand times more blessed is the person who takes this advice and uses it." Please take everything in this book and process it through your own common-sense filter! It should make sense to you; if it does not, run it by a well-recommended fee-only advisor. This book is about method and practical things you can do now.

I firmly believe that by reading this book, you will have better financial outcomes in your life; feel better and be more apt to choose appropriate insurance coverage; have a fundamental understanding about investments and be better able to communicate with and choose an investment mutual fund for your portfolio, and feel comfortable with the lingo of investing. When it comes to debt management, insurance, tax planning, home buying, and budgeting, you will be powerfully equipped to make good choices.

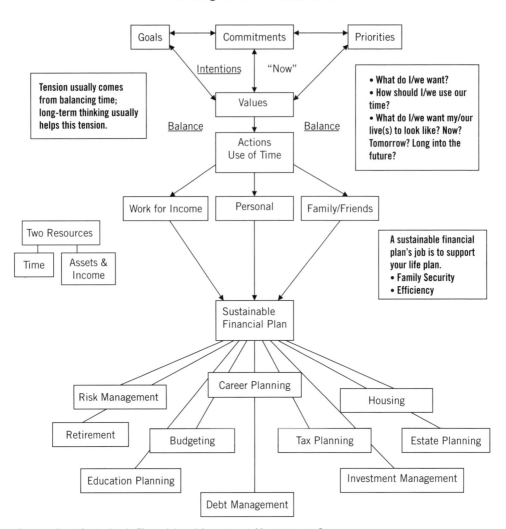

Source: Paul Sutherland, Financial and Investment Management Group.

CHAPTER 1
Financial Stewardship

Developing a Productive Relationship with Money

"Doctors don't know %#& about money! I know, I'm one of 'em!" said the 55-year-old internist sitting across from me at a business luncheon. I smiled as he said, "We also don't know anything about business and managing people. They don't teach it to us in medical school; we have to make a lot of mistakes to learn. Why don't you write this stuff in your book to help keep us from [messing] up?!" My hope is that this guide will do much more than keep the reader from [messing] up but that it will allow you to relax and enjoy life, confident that your finances are on solid footing.

We work to produce income and, presumably, because we enjoy it. We trade time for money, and although time is limited, money is not. We can work and work to pile up money or things, but because our time is finite, first we should be good stewards of that. If we can manage our time, the rest will fall into place. Money's only role in your life should be to support your and your family's goals, commitments, and intentions and to support priorities consistent with your values. Your work should help to support your life, and ideally, you find work fulfilling.

Work can be separate from your monetary goals. Talk with Doctors Without Borders (www.doctorswithoutborders.com) physicians or research doctors earning one third of what they could earn if they said "yes" to the group practice that gently hints they could use another partner. Balancing a wonderful work environment with a wonderful pay environment is one of the trade-offs many make in their careers.

For any physician, getting rich fast is as easy as working extra shifts, working where you can earn the most, living simply, and, of course, saving and investing. The key is to have a life that is rich in joy, good relationships, security, and fulfillment and that allows you to relax, knowing you are moving toward your financial goals while comfortably balancing your current needs. (See the top box in the "My Way/Our Way Life Plan: Budgeting Time and Money" chart on page 14.)

Tension comes from finding and trying to maintain a balance between current and long-term goals. The key is to be aware of the trade-offs you make and to get buy-in from those who are affected by those decisions, including partners, spouses, children, parents, and so on. Balance is the key; great tension can come if your spouse is trying to fit a nice second car into the budget while you want to pay off the student loans as fast as possible, start funding a 529 plan for your first child, or simply slow down. We all make choices, and we as individuals have control of the choices we make. We only have so much time; how we use it is up to us.

Your Money's Financial Future: A Mission Statement

After tests, boards, residencies, fellowships, and, finally, landing a good job, a young physician should sit back, relax, and say, "What do I really want my life to look like over the next 50 years?" This "life visioning" can be daunting, but it is the most important step in the financial planning process. Add a spouse, parental expectations, children, and other responsibilities to this life vision and you can get caught up in an "I think I'll read charts or go play tennis" avoidance technique.

A financial vision statement does not have to be written down, but it is helpful to do so. A vision statement will help develop a mission statement and goals that are beneficial when creating your financial plan. The "My Way/Our Way Life Plan: Budgeting Time and Money" on page 14 is a flowchart to help you see the complexity and importance of first understanding what you want before you get to the easy part of financial planning. If you do not know where you want to be or what you are willing to give to get there, you will be prone to use your assets and income inefficiently—chasing cure-all programs or drifting along without financial direction.

The following desires are easy to place in a vision statement:

I/we want financial security.

I/we want to live in a nice home.

I/we want our children to be in good schools.

I/we want to have a healthy, balanced lifestyle.

I/we want to be able to retire someday without financial worries.

I/we want to use our talents to help others.

I/we want to enjoy my/our career(s).

I/we want time to enjoy our children.

I/we want a big, wonderful life outside my/our career(s).

General Vision Attributes

As you think about what you want your life to look like, your "vision" ideas will coalesce into a tangible philosophy based upon your intentions, values, commitments, and desires. Following are some sample attributes:

Personal: Health, happiness, fulfillment, contentment, ability to express love through a committed relationship, honest friendships, family, children.

Family: Raise responsible, happy, healthy children in an education culture; be in a marital relationship built on trust, love, and commitment; be married to someone who takes care of the home, the children, and me; be married to someone I can talk to, who accepts my love as I wish to express it, who wants to grow together, and who is a good listener and communicator.

Lifestyle: Be where I/we can swim, walk, hike, boat, play tennis, golf, allow the dogs to run, have horses; be near our church, family, friends, work, great restaurants, museums, university, good airport, great schools; be in a safe environment; travel, do mission work, volunteer, have time for spiritual practice.

Possessions: Car, boat, ship; home with great views, home in woods, home in city; home with swimming pool, tennis courts, near health club; home has a great soaking tub in master bath, well-equipped kitchen, game room, entertainment room; second home, cottage, travel, an island, retirement plan account, investment accounts, real estate in this or another country; separate investment account set aside so I/we can take a year off to live in another country; house for parents or in-laws—apartment or cottage—at your home; art collection, antique collection; farm, jewelry; ability to give to charities, religious organizations, help people.

Later chapters educate you in this visioning process and take you on a ride down life-cycle lane, helping you to see your life over many years. Life planning works best if you have a long view. A long-view plan allows you to be patient with yourself and those around you and live in the moment, confident that things are moving ahead as you wish.

The ultimate goal of all these chapters is what I call "financial ease," in which your finances are arranged to support you comprehensively, comfortably, and easily. So when your child needs college money, you can just write out the check; when retirement comes, you can just turn on the income; when health issues hit you, insurance or the cash falls into place and you can count on getting well without worrying about income security or bills.

Career Cycles: Early Enthusiasm, Mid-Career Burnout, Mellow Maturity, and Choices

I have worked with physicians for over a quarter of a century. Earlier in my career, physicians wanted to retire "someday." Now, physicians come into my conference room and ask, "How fast can I retire?" Many professions have work weeks of 60-plus hours; however, physicians are three times more likely than members of any other professional group to work a 60-hour week. Add family life and other responsibilities, and pretty soon you can feel like you have a lifestyle but no life. A life run by schedules, nurses, family obligations, children's school schedules, and board meetings is stressful enough—throw in a spouse who would like to see you once in a while, aging parents, disagreeable siblings, and a partner who is burned out, and it is easy to see why many physicians are fed up with the way they practice medicine and manage their career and skills, and they say "I want to retire."

A physician who works 60 hours *chooses* to work 60 hours. A physician who works in an environment in which partner, staff, and colleagues are simply no fun to work with chooses to do so. The physician who says he or she is trapped because of big mortgage payments, high malpractice insurance, or expensive payments for children's college or his or her own student loans needs to take responsibility for these choices.

CHAPTER 1 Financial Stewardship

"'I swear by Apollo Physician, by Asclepius, by Health, by Panacea, and by all the gods and goddesses, making them my witnesses, that I will carry out, according to my ability and judgment, this oath and this indenture. To hold my teacher in this art equal to my own parents; to make him partner in my livelihood; when he is in need of money to share mine with him; to consider his family as my own brothers, and to teach them this art, if they want to learn it, without fee or indenture. I will use treatment to help the sick according to my ability and judgment, but never with a view to injury and wrongdoing. I will keep pure and holy both my life and my art. In whatsoever houses I enter, I will enter to help the sick, and I will abstain from all intentional wrongdoing and harm. And whatsoever I shall see or hear in the course of my profession in my intercourse with men, if it be what should not be published abroad, I will never divulge, holding such things to be holy secrets. Now if I carry out this oath, and break it not, may I gain forever reputation among all men for my life and for my art; but if I transgress it and forswear myself, may the opposite befall me.' <u>Now</u> may I examine you?"

© The New Yorker Collection 1962 Richard Decker from cartoonbank.com. All Rights Reserved.

As stated previously, we trade time for money. My goal in this chapter is to help physicians understand how burnout happens. With understanding often comes finding a way to a happier, more enjoyable career path. The physician who has a balanced life chooses that life.

Early Enthusiasm

Being fresh out of medical school with student loans, a spouse, and the pressures of buying a first home and living with an old TV, crummy furniture, and secondhand silverware is par for the course. Then the smaller house becomes bigger. The couch that, although comfortable, is too tattered for another cleaning gets replaced. Throw children into the picture and it is easy to see why physicians early in their career are simply broke. Every extra dollar has multiple places it could go, from paying off student loans to being accumulated for a house to the first piece of nice furniture. This could go on for many years, depending on the choices made earlier in the career, the amount of time and financial sacrifice that was made to get through medical school, and so on.

A practical solution to always feeling broke is to work hard, put your head down, and maximize the opportunity for a high income. Often, the first decision on how to practice medicine is decided based on optimizing income and little more. If you have to drive an extra 10 to 20 miles to work but have more income—that is fine. If you have to practice with partners who are not ideal partners, you accept it. If you have to be on a schedule that limits lunch to slamming a bagel as you walk between blue and red flags, you do it. However, the effect of such compromises on psychological health is cumulative. After a while, young doctors can find themselves with lifestyle habits that are not what they signed up to be a doctor for, causing them to flirt with situational depression and feel trapped, overburdened, burned out, and unhappy.

We can choose to use reactive dysfunctional behavior such as blaming our spouse, our partner, our children, our parents, the healthcare system, and maybe even Medicare, the drug companies, and American society. However, burnout comes from failing to look in the mirror and ask, "How do I want to practice? What do I want my life to look like? What should my life look like? Am I happy? How do I balance my personal needs and my family needs? Can I believe that practicing medicine in the twenty-first century in the United States is a wonderful, happy, joy-filled, and fulfilling career?" With regard to the last question, yes, I think you can believe it!

The Happy Doctor

The key to an enjoyable career is realizing that you have choices and options. Some of the happiest physicians I know have been the ones whose home was more modest than their colleagues', whose car was smaller and older than the other cars in the hospital parking lot, who thought Disneyland was just as much fun as the beaches of Maui. They chose balance. They made a choice regarding the question, "What kind of lifestyle do I want to have?" and balanced it with how much and how they wanted to work. They made the conscious choice to work in environments that were fun, and they had the flexibility to try things out and to find out what worked or did not, and then they modified their financial practice and personal situation to accommodate their newfound knowledge.

For example, many physicians who move to a rural area choose to live far away from the hospital or their office because they want to live "in the country." Often, after a few years of driving for the third or fourth time in a day to the hospital, they realize it is probably smarter to live closer to the hospital and their office. Perhaps they compromise and have a second home in the country and the primary home near work, school, and office. For physicians who are driving instead of seeing one to five more patients a day, the cost of that extra commute can be somewhere between $100 and $1,000 a day. Not having to commute as far could save time for activities such as vacations, a shorter work week, volunteer activities, children, spouse, and so on.

There are few people in any field who do not at times challenge the career decision they made as an 18- or 25-year-old. It is healthy to challenge our beliefs and our daily situation. Doing so may cause us to realize that we are just about where we wanted to be. Often, with a few minor changes, we can get back on a path that allows us to feel happy and fulfilled. For example, selling the horses, changing our call schedule, hiring a cleaning person or cook—all add hours for relaxing and enjoying life. Most important is to realize that we have made the choice to be in the situation we are in. Often by just not feeling trapped in an unfulfilling career, the light switch can go on so that we are able to realize, "I do have choices and I do really enjoy working these 70- to 80-hour weeks, because I am just built that way."

After going through a period of mid-career burnout or the contemplation of burnout, most physicians end up being in what I call "mellow maturity," in which they accept the reality of their lives. Often, they take on staff or partners to create more personal time and to allow their life to be more manageable. They may add an extra nurse even though it is an added expense and puts their financial ratios out of whack. Staffing up to give you more time may upset your accountant, but realize it is more important to have a fulfilling and fun work environment than to have the best financial ratios in your advisor's group. In fact, my anecdotal evidence shows that often the happiest physicians have the highest staff-to-revenue cost of any group because they have learned the wonderful art of hiring well and delegating. They are able to delegate so they can concentrate on being a physician and doing what they like and nothing else. They do not need to worry about billing, risk management, keeping charts in order, calling in prescriptions, calling in medical supplies, and so on.

At the other end of the spectrum is the solo practitioner who has her or his spouse at the front desk working three days per week or who works in a rural environment in which only two or three patients are seen per hour. Such physicians are often happy with their situation, too. They enjoy the significant downtime but still enjoy the periods when they are needed to work 14-hour days because half of the local schoolchildren are sick.

Years ago, I attended a seminar given by a man who helped turn around one of the major motor companies in Michigan. He said that the key in our careers is finding out whether we are a camel or a polar bear. He explained that camels are ideally suited for the desert. They can go miles without water. Their eyes are suited for the hot sun and the harsh wind blowing sand in their face. Their feet are made to handle the rocky, sandy soil. At the other extreme, the polar bears ideal is 50 degrees below zero and windy. They can thrive in such an environment. They are excellent at catching fish and surviving in the Arctic; they are perfectly suited for that environment. But take the camel and throw it in the Arctic, and it dies. Take the polar bear and put it in the desert, and it dies. This man stated that the key to life is figuring out whether we are a polar bear or a camel, and then being in the environment that allows us to thrive.

That environment is often not the environment that our father, mother, trusted financial advisor, college professor, or mentor thinks or thought ideal for us, yet it is the environment that we are in. We may have to try on different environments until we find one that works well. Fear, inertia, complacency, or apathy can hold us back. However, once we find out whether we are a camel, a polar bear, or whatever, we can be at ease and enjoy life. Being at ease and enjoying life is something we all need to strive for if we want to avoid burnout and find career enjoyment as physicians.

Medicine for Medical Burnout

Feeling stale in your job? Not excited about driving to the hospital? Tired of dealing with your partners? Can't decide whether you should fire that staff member or put up with his or her rude behavior? If you chat with one sales person, do you think you'll scream? Need a change of scenery? Wondering why you became a doctor? There is a useful answer to all of these questions. However, the solution can have significant side effects: Take time off and volunteer!

Many physicians have joined volunteer organizations for a period in their career to help them get back on track and remember why they became a doctor. One of the primary organizations that can make this possible is Doctors Without Borders (www.doctorswithoutborders.com), founded in 1971 by a small group of doctors who believed that all people have the right to medical care regardless of race, religion, creed, or political affiliation. Doctors Without Borders has grown to an international network with sections in 18 countries with more than 2,500 volunteer doctors, nurses, and other medical professionals, logistics experts, water sanitation engineers, and administrators who join approximately 15,000 locally hired staff to provide medical care in more than 80 countries.

This organization, based on volunteers, is primarily involved in four situations: First, when conflicts erupt, Doctors Without Borders immediately sends teams of surgeons, anesthesiologists, and operating room logisticians into the field with the necessary equipment to establish operating rooms and clinics.

Second, refugees and displaced persons are served by Doctors Without Borders. Over the last 30 years, the world's refugee population has exploded to over 39 million. These people usually have to flee their homes because of armed conflict or food emergencies. Doctors Without Borders works with other nongovernmental organizations, local healthcare organizations, and other groups to help these refugee populations. This organization is especially well-suited to what it does because among the requirements of its volunteers is that they be neutral, nonpolitical, and non-evangelizing and that they abide by a strict code of responsible ethics. These requirements allow Doctors Without Borders to go where many may not be able to go. Natural or human-caused disasters and long-term assistance in countries with collapsed or insufficient healthcare systems are two other areas in which Doctors Without Borders works.

"Doctors Without Borders Description and Criteria" is on page 10. Also listed are other international volunteer organizations ("International Volunteer Opportunities for Physicians," on page 202).

Doctors Without Borders Description and Criteria

Doctors Without Borders/Médecins Sans Frontieres (MSF) is a private international association made up of doctors and health sector workers and is also open to other professions that might help in achieving its aims. All of its members agree to honor the following principles:

- Assistance is provided to populations in distress, to victims of natural and man-made disasters, and to victims of armed conflict irrespective of race, religion, creed, and political convictions.

- Neutrality and impartiality are observed in the name of universal medicine and the right to humanitarian assistance. Full and unhindered freedom is claimed in the exercise of its functions.

- Their professional code of ethics is respected, and complete independence is maintained from all political, economic, and religious powers.

- As volunteers, members understand the risks and dangers of the missions they carry out and claim for themselves or their assignees no form of compensation other than that which the association may afford them.

Frequently Asked Questions

What are MSF's requirement criteria? The general criteria for volunteering are at least 2 years of professional experience in relevant fields, availability for at least 6 months, and current professional credentials. Assets that benefit applicants are flexibility, experience working in developing countries, experience with community service projects, adaptability to basic living conditions, and foreign language skills.

What is the recruitment process?

- The candidate completes an application form (online or downloaded and mailed to the office), a motivation letter, and a current CV (curriculum vitae; résumé).

- A human resources officer (HRO) screens the application and responds within 2 weeks of receipt of application.

- Positively screened applicants are invited to interview with an HRO, either in the New York office during business hours or during recruitment visits to the Los Angeles office every other month. (The organization does not cover expenses associated with the recruitment process.)

- Following interview and reference check, successful applicants are accepted to the pool of active volunteers.

- Placement is entirely dependent on field needs and may take from 2 weeks to months.

- HRD suggests first mission training where applicable.

What expenses are volunteers expected to pay? Once a mission is confirmed, MSF will be responsible for all travel, visas, and relevant vaccinations. Volunteers should assume responsibility for routine health maintenance vaccinations.

The organization will provide volunteers with

- Round-trip air tickets from home to mission
- Accommodation in New York City or Europe during briefing and debriefing
- Monthly stipend of approximately $900 (US)
- Full medical insurance
- Accommodation in the field (shared housing, mostly with private rooms)
- Per diem while on mission, in local currency

How long are missions? The organization requires a minimum commitment of 6 continuous months. Many specific vacancies have 9- to 12-month durations; thus, a volunteer with more flexibility can be considered for more vacancies. Specifically, the minimum commitment for administrators is 1 year; surgeons and anesthesiologists may be accepted for a minimum of 6 weeks in the field.

How does MSF manage safety and security in the field? Working with MSF is not reckless. It maintains extensive risk management procedures and security guidelines for every mission. Volunteers are briefed on the country's security situation before going to the field and upon arriving at the project site are given specific security protocols. Adherence to MSF's field guidelines for personal and team conduct and safety is not negotiable.

Source: Doctors Without Borders Web site (www.doctorswithoutborders.com)

Getting Specific: Commitments, Goals, Priorities, and Values

The most important thing is to know what you want going into the financial planning process. Usually our commitments, goals, and values will guide us to our "wants." I remember being in a seminar in which the main takeaway message was that we should judge ourselves and other people based on our ability to make and keep commitments. The presenter said we should make verbal or written commitments to those we love and care about and expect the same from them. He went on to explain that it is the same in business.

For the 15 years since that seminar, I have very specifically said to employees or prospective employees, "What can I depend on you for?" When they make a commitment, they know they are going to be reviewed on their ability to fulfill that commitment. Thus, when an employee promises to review trusts or wills or portfolios by Friday afternoon, they had better have done it—barring an earthquake or family disaster! And, of course, if there was a disaster, because they are committed to having a harmonious business environment in keeping commitments to the firm, then they would call another colleague so that the task was taken care of properly.

Some people live their lives looking for reasons or excuses as to why they were not able to fulfill a commitment. I want people in my life who are able to keep their commitments and that I know I can depend on. In this chapter, we need to write down what we are committed to and take a look at it.

For example, if you have a family, what are you committed to with regard to that family? Financial security for them? Expressing love to them and giving them time? Providing school and education for the children? Being honest, expressing your needs, and so on? On the blank lines, finish the statement:

I am committed to

_____

_____

_____

_____

In order to determine what you are committed to, it is helpful to know what you want from life and what you have. Are there people in your life you can depend on? Do you have financial resources? Do you have a good career? What is the commitment of your partners? If employed, what is the commitment of your employer? What are your commitments to them?

A good way to see what your commitments are or whether your values are consistent with your commitments is to look at your schedule book or calendar and how you spend your time. If you say, "I am committed to spending time with my family" and, in actuality, rare is the time spent with them, then you need to get that into harmony or admit that your family is not such a big priority after all.

Priorities are an offspring of our commitments and values. For example, a priority might be to have a healthy life, which means getting 8 hours of sleep, eating healthy foods, and having time at the gym. The priority of having a healthy relationship with your spouse means spending time together, having holidays together, and so on. Everybody is different, so where that "rubber hits the road" on your love expression and day-to-day relationship with your life's partner would be dependent on your mutual values, expectations, agreements, and life circumstances all rooted of course in optimism, love, and reality.

If you are committed to providing excellent healthcare for your patients, you need to write out what that means. Should you be accessible to your patients? If you cannot be accessible, should you allow them to contact other physicians on call to make sure that they are taken care of or allow them to go to the emergency room?

Knowing your commitments allows you to budget time around those commitments and priorities. You only have 24 hours in a day, so you need to ask yourself, "What is my ideal day? What is my ideal week? What is my ideal year?" and stick with these priorities. As illustrated on page 14, getting to certainty regarding your goals, commitments, and priorities is the bedrock of a sound, sustainable financial plan.

The Role of Money in Your Life

Money is merely to support you in your commitments and goals. The reason we work is so that we can meet our commitments and goals and have a lifestyle consistent with what allows us to be happy and fulfilled and expresses our creative selves. We trade time for money; thus, if you had all the money in the world and did not need to work, how would you spend your money? How would you spend your time? That is a good starting point for how money intersects with your goals, commitments, and values. Imagine yourself with all the money you would want to support the lifestyle you desire. How would you spend your time? Would you spend 2 hours a day playing tennis? Would you have a 1-hour lunch with your spouse every day? Would you be at every one of your children's events after school? Would you have all day Saturday and Sunday off? What else would you do? If the values and goals are strong enough, then it is helpful to say, "I want to create my work schedule around those commitments." And then do something to make that statement a reality.

This process of visualizing what you want your life to look like is important for making appropriate career goals; having a comfortable, enjoyable life; and creating a financial plan. There are tradeoffs when you have partners. There are trade-offs when you have employees. It may require more management time. It may cause you to hire employees who perhaps are not as productive as you are. It may be that you have more conflicts or issues to deal with.

14 The AMA Physicians' Guide to Financial Planning

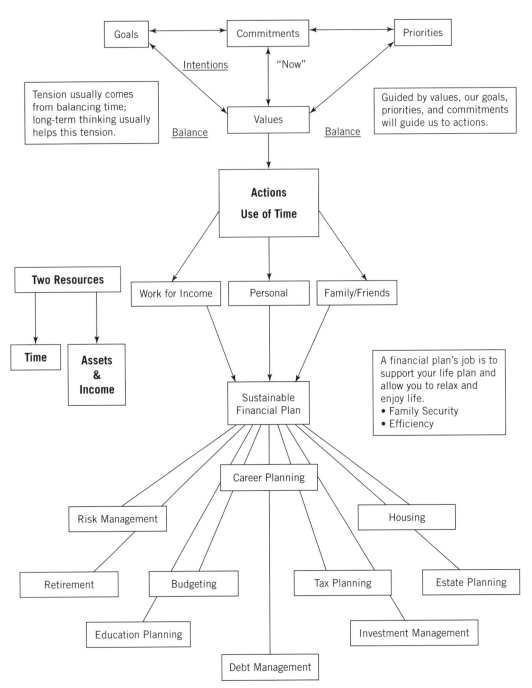

Source: Paul Sutherland, Financial and Investment Management Group (www.fimg.net). A printable copy is available at www.fimg.net.

Often, you can find other professionals who have values similar to yours, and that is the key to harmony. Your employees and coworkers' values need to be consistent with yours. If your colleagues have a family-first value system that balances family, personal life, and finances, there should be less conflict if you are clear with them about your values. If you have two high-achieving partners and one who wants to work a few days per week, often conflicts can arise primarily from the high-achieving partners who, when they start feeling stressed, realize that the partner who chose to have more of a balanced lifestyle seems to have more fun. This can create conflict and blow up a partnership or practice. Thus, when hiring or interviewing, the discussions with each employee must also be about the values and commitments of the partners so that there is consistency. It takes leadership and self-knowledge to communicate these principles. It is OK to have the 80-hour superachiever and the 40-hour family-first doctor in the same practice and it can work *if* there is acceptance of each other and no judgment about "whose path is better—best—worst."

As a senior person in my firm, I consider myself the keeper of the culture. My main job is to manage and arrange the resources of the firm, both human and financial resources, to ensure that we take incredibly good care of our clients. Everyone in the firm knows that they should enjoy taking care of clients and love people. If you love and enjoy people, then you need to make sure you are working with people who feel the same way.

"Everyone is different" is not a value statement. It is simply a principle to help physicians understand and imagine life at their practice consistent with what they truly want. Some of my happiest clients have very efficient practices and long workdays, but they also have robust personal lives. They have created the balance consistent with what they want. Balancing time and money is difficult. Once you have figured out how you want to budget your time, then the money can follow. If you are married or in a committed, loving relationship, it is important to discuss the how's and why's of balancing both time and money values and commitments with your life partner.

Planning Finances with the Family

In a committed relationship there are trade-offs regarding whether both spouses work, whether you work until you have children, and so on. There is a delicate play in this. A lot has to do with what is consistent with values. I saw an estimate that over 90% of female physicians are married to male physicians. It is also interesting that the average female doctor works fewer than 2 days per week. As more and more female physicians join the workforce, I think these statistics will change dramatically.

The following excerpt from *White Coat: Becoming a Doctor at Harvard Medical School* (Rothman EL. New York: William Morrow & Co., 1999. p. 79) discusses marriage relationships:

> That evening we heard the testimony of four couples at different stages of their careers who had managed to preserve their relationships despite the stresses of dual medical careers. They were honest about the challenges to their careers and their families. They wrestled with issues of child care. They fought over whose career should determine where to live and when, or whether, to have children. They struggled to find time to spend together. They battled chronic exhaustion. They were the successful ones. The divorce rate among physicians was rumored to be well over 100 percent when failed second marriages were taken into account.

Regardless of whom "works" (earns money) and the choices made regarding careers, everyone should have at least an informal budget to guide their spending. The key to family budgeting is communication. Everything is a trade-off,

---

US Cash, Euros, Liquidity

September 11, 2001, did not change anything. The risks had always existed. What would you do if your bank closed, your phones quit working, the Internet went down, and your area was experiencing an electrical blackout? How would you buy groceries, gas, or fuel for your car? How would you heat or cool your home? I have traveled to dozens of countries, and the one thing I know is that cash works. Cash does not bounce, it is confidential, and it is universally accepted. Cash is not affected by floods, monsoons, or viruses, and it always has value. I think it is rational for everyone to have some cash on hand in a secure fireproof safe. How much? It depends on what makes you feel secure. I think somewhere between $10,000 and 1 month's income is a good amount to go by. Everybody is different, but I have always been the one giving friends cash advances when the credit card or the automated teller machine does not work. Whether in Bangor, Boston, Bali, or the Bahamas, cash is always accepted; plastic and checks, well, who knows.... I keep Euros, Yen, plus, a handful of other currencies on hand, often from past trips, plus, of course, good old US $100s, $50s, and $20s. I travel a lot internationally; I am a global investment manager, after all. When traveling, I like dealing in the local currency as much as possible, and find it embarrassing to pull out US dollars in

> Singapore or anywhere in Europe to pay for taxis and the like. Cash on hand, to me, is for those "what if's," that I hope will never happen. Cash provides security. The security is worth the loss of a few hundred dollars in interest. Well, actually, Euros are up 50% or so over the past few years, so I guess I am ahead of the game, but that is not the point, security is!
>
> During my marriage, I was responsible for the entire family budget. My ex-wife, Kim, used her income for extras such as vacations, savings, taking care of the horses and farm animals, and gifts. When we had our second child, she quit her job and we continued with our routine, so Kim had $2,000 cash that I deposited into her checking account every month so that she had control and the freedom to do what she wanted. The main expenses that came out of that account were her car payment and personal bills. Depending on the needs, the budget worked well, but the key issue was communication. Everyone's system is different, but in any relationship, communication works wonders.
>
> If you have not yet bought a home, the "Size of Home Worksheet" (page 72) should help you figure out what you can afford to borrow. However, truly, I am anti-budget. In my experience, most people live well within their budget. Physicians who do even rudimentary budgeting and planning will find that they have significant surpluses that they can use for savings, vacations, or whatever. Often, I think this comes from the years of voluntary poverty that they lived with during residency and medical school, and the fear of being broke again motivates them to make sure they do not get into financial dysfunction.
>
> Often, people go overboard with the budgeting process. Budgeting needs to stay fun and enjoyable. One way to keep it this way is to realize that you and your spouse will each have a certain amount of money each month that should be spent or saved to spend on anything you darn well please that the other might have zero ability to relate to. For the husband, it could be a weekend in Detroit with buddies watching the Tigers play baseball, which puts $1,000 on the credit card when you include hotel, restaurants, and travel. For the wife, it might be a spa visit, clothing, visiting friends, or something else. The best gift that we can give our spouses is to accept them as they are.

and you cannot consistently spend $11,000 per month when only $10,000 a month comes into the checking account. This is a dysfunction that can grow and cause economic, financial, and emotional havoc in a family system. Budgets need to be kept. Usually there is a keeper of the budget, whether it is the husband or the wife. Someone has to do it, and the designated person has to work within a system that is consistent with the individuals values.

In the case of older couples, one spouse may feel compelled to help children and grandchildren by buying presents or doing special things for them. If this

Budget Worksheet*

	Month 1	Month 2	Month 3	Monthly Average
Total income after taxes	————	————	————	————
Payments	————	————	————	————
House payment (see Home & Real Estate section)	————	————	————	————

House insurance
Utilities
House maintenance
My "spend any way I want" money
My spouse's "spend any way I want" money
Food and restaurants/eating out
Phones, Internet, cable, BlackBerry™
Auto payments or lease
Auto insurance, gas, maintenance
Travel, vacations, seminars, family visits
Entertainment, gifts, recreation, health club
Clothing, makeup, hair stylist
Life, disability, hospital/medical insurance
Retirement plans; 401(k), IRA, 403B
  (10% minimum)
Childcare, school expenses, children's misc.
Food, toiletries, household expenses
  (cleaning service, supplies, etc)
Loan payments (spread out—see Debt
  Management)
Credit card "expenses" not listed above
Charities
Other (list) _____

Savings surplus for liquidity, children's
  education, retirement, second home, etc;
  10% to 30%, or whatever makes you
  comfortable not less than 10%

Payments Total/Month	————	————	————	————
Income − Payment = Net	————	————	————	————

*Budgeting is a fun process and should not be considered a chore. Most people live within their budget. Money is to support your life, life goals, commitments, and responsibilities. We trade time for money.
IRA indicates individual retirement account.

Source: © Paul Sutherland, Financial and Investment Management Group (www.fimg.net), All Rights Reserved. A printable copy of this worksheet is available at www.FIMG.net.

is difficult for the other spouse to relate to, the best gift you can give each other is to allow him or her to do it. Naturally, such expenses should be consistent with the budget. If you each have $500 per month to spend wherever you want without any value statement from the other partner, it can be very helpful.

I am a big believer in separate checking accounts. It is hard to manage a budget with two people drawing out of the same checking account. From my experience, it is best for each spouse to also have his or her own credit card. If you love to travel, you can get a frequent-flyer credit card so that you can get airline miles or a card that allows you to buy a car or accumulate points for other purchases.

Excess cash, of course, should be put into a money market fund at a discount brokerage firm such as Charles Schwab (www.schwab.com) or Fidelity (www.fidelity.com) or into a bank's product. Such cash management accounts are often available from brokers, and banks usually have checking accounts or privileges by which you can merely call to move the money from your brokerage account into your regular day-to-day checking account. This allows you to make sure that most of your money is earning at least money market interest rates to grow a few extra dollars.

Physicians should not have a lot of anxiety about finances. It is not worth it. Often, physicians develop bad habits during their broke period of medical school and residency when they are chronically concerned or worried about money. This should end after getting into a career in which the income starts. Often, people's emotions do not catch up with rational thinking even after they have a significant income. Life is long; relax and enjoy it. In the first few years out of medical school, often you are buying your first "this," taking your first decent vacation, and buying your first good-quality car and furniture, and debt can run up. If something fits into your budget, do not worry about it. You will settle into a budget that is appropriate and consistent with your values and is reasonable. If the first years are a little bit out of whack, do not assume that things will stay that way. No one got through medical school without discipline, basic common sense, and understanding.

However, if you or your spouse's spending is out of control, then it is good to sit down with an experienced financial advisor and get into a budgeting mode. Often, people can be irrational about spending and lack understanding about tax and budget issues. Use the budgeting process or some of the techniques discussed previously, for example, the $500- to $1,000-per-month allowance.

Consistent overspending is considered a condition similar to alcoholism or drug addiction. The American Psychiatric Association calls it accumulation disorder or spending disorder. If this is happening with you or your spouse, cognitive behavior modification techniques can be used. One solution is to not use credit, only cash, and to talk with a therapist to get the disorder under control. If you have a spouse or a situation in which this is a chronic issue, do not try to handle it only by yourself. Talk with a therapist and/or hire a sensitive financial planner who has budgeting experience, they will be able to help. NAPFA.org will list fee-only financial advisors you can call or visit.

Therapist and author Harville Hendricks has an interesting theory called *imago therapy*. It deals with people's natural desire for self-completion, especially as it relates to unsettled childhood issues. The theory suggests that in adulthood, we often are attracted to partners who are the least able to meet our needs and who allow us to experience the same dilemmas that we faced as children in relationship to our parents. Therefore, we often end up with a person who is least able to meet our needs. For example, if you are bad at budgeting, your spouse may be great at budgeting, or vice versa. This is where understanding, acceptance, and communication come in handy. If we choose the person least likely to meet our needs, then we need to work that out through mindful conversation so we can see the strengths in ourselves. Perhaps your spouse is more spontaneous or you are more methodical, and so on. This can be wonderful or disastrous.

Dance of Anger: A Woman's Guide to Changing the Patterns of Intimate Relationships, by Harriet Lerner (New York: Harper Paperbacks, 2005), describes how, for example, if one spouse is better at budgeting and at all the other rational parts of the relationship, the other spouse never gets to develop those aspects. In fact, the person might revert to the opposite behavior just to get to a balance. For example, if one partner is better at expressing anger and the less-vocal spouse comes home from work and gets out a sentence like, "Oh, I had a rough day today," the other spouse might spend a half hour yelling about his or her staff and why everything was so awful at work. Lerner explains that it is important to say, "I will express my own anger, thank you, because I want to be a complete person." Family finances can bring a family together and be fun and pleasant if built on a foundation of appreciation, communication, respect, acceptance, and agreement about values, goals, priorities, and commitments. Or if not, the dance is up to you.

One-Page Financial Plan, Stage 1

- Bisra, age 35; in second year of practice; salary, $15,000 monthly.
- Mayet, age 32; pregnant in first year of practice; salary, $20,000 monthly.
- Baby due in 4 months.
- Home value, $700,000.
- Owe $500,000 on first mortgage at $3,000 monthly for 30 years at 6%; plus second mortgage used for down payment at $200,000, with payments of $1,000 monthly, interest only.
- Vehicles: two cars, owe $38,000 with payments of $1,000 monthly for 42 months.
- Student Loans: $100,000; payments of $900 for 81 months.
- Bisra and Mayet each have hospital medical coverage, 60% of income disability that pays to age 65, and $100,000 life insurance provided through work, also malpractice insurance and matching 401(k) retirement plan.
- $10,000 each in 401(k) accounts totaling $20,000 in retirement plan assets.

Goals
- Financial security for family.
- Educate children.
- Retire someday. Once child is born, Mayet would like to stop working for an indefinite period so she can raise family; Bisra likes his 50-hour per week job but does not want to miss out on parenting children; both would like four children.
- Mayet would like to be able to go back to work when youngest is 5 "or maybe when they are 18," joked Bisra. "I can retire then and Mayet will support the family."

Recommendations
- Draft wills with testamentary trusts for children.
- Secure $1,800,000 life insurance on each spouse to pay off all debts and provide $5,500 monthly income to surviving spouse.
- Fund 401(k) accounts with the Utopia Growth Fund or another good absolute return globally oriented fund (www.utopiafunds.com) to maximum of $15,000 before arrival of baby to build a nest egg.
- Review everything (budget, debts, investment plans) with fee-only financial advisor a few months after baby is born and settled as parents and Mayet has an idea of career goals.
- Read the AMA's *Physician's Guide to Financial Planning* by Paul Sutherland.

CHAPTER 2
Risk Management

Prudence, Intention, and Fiduciary Obligations

Doctors Without Borders physicians serve mothers in sub-Saharan Africa who think that it is logical to stop feeding children plagued by diarrhea. After all, water or milk at one end would only seem to prolong the problem at the other end. However, these well-intentioned mothers are killing their babies because they lack knowledge.

How is it then that smart physicians take on roles that can sink them financially? Physicians driven by good intentions are employers, trustees, board members, and partners and serve in management or advisory positions. They often advise or sit on advisory panels for drug studies or review and render opinions on IPO (initial public offering) prospectuses relating to medicine or health.

If you said "yes" to the chief of staff position or the seat on the school board, did you talk with your lawyer first? Did you get a letter explaining your liability and describing insurance provided by the hospital or school protecting you and your estate from financial harm?

If you are an employer and you just set up a pension plan through your yoga pals' or golf buddies' company, did you have your Employee Retirement Security Act and Department of Labor obligations and your fiduciary responsibilities spelled out to you? If your plan is already set up, do you monitor the investment performance of all of the participants? Did you assume you were okay because you went with a giant firm?

The point is, we all have fiduciary obligations, and passively delegating these responsibilities to your golf buddy's company may not hold up if someone affected by your role feels disadvantaged by something you were involved in.

Doctor as Employer

As president of Financial and Investment Management (FIM) Group (www.fimg.net) for the past 21 years, I have called my lawyer many times before I dismissed someone, just to make sure I did it right. Other times I have consulted colleagues. It is interesting that statistically, 80% of those dismissed by US companies were considered competent in their job. They were dismissed for communication or cooperation problems, dishonesty, lack of follow-through, gossiping, not taking responsibility, and so on.

Employees can sink your practice. You do not need to give reasons for dismissing someone, but it is important to express expectations to those in your employ. See "Termination of Employment Definitions" below.

Each practice is unique, and its personnel must be consistent with the character of the culture and management. I learned quickly to hire great people!

You want great, responsible team members to protect your financial life. A fun, fulfilling workplace can only be that way with happy, emotionally mature, competent people.

Termination of Employment Definitions

Involuntary Termination	Voluntary Termination
All employees at Financial and Investment Management (FIM) Group are employed on an at-will basis. The employment of any individual is subject to termination, at any time for any reason, by FIM Group's management.	When an employee terminates employment, the company expects 2 weeks notice, and possibly more, depending on the employee's level of responsibility.

From Financial and Investment Management Group's Personnel Reference Guide.

I once met a man who lost the sight in one eye in a sports accident. He said his doctor was great and did what he could to save the man's sight. Then out of the blue, he said, "You know what bugs me though, is that the receptionist told me she thought he had used the wrong procedure!" She did not understand how much trouble she could have caused. No contract, employee agreement, or verbal promise will get a gossipy person to keep things confidential, and if loose lips sink your ship, what can you do? You can try to hire happy, good, responsible people with common sense.

Simple questions like, "Did you enjoy working for Dr. Karuna? Did you think the way they practice is good? What did you like and not like about your former employer?" will tell you about the candidate's ability to be confidential and if he or she is a team player.

An employee manual is useful, especially one with Health Insurance Portability and Accountability Act information. The Financial and Investment Management Group's Personnel Reference Guide table of contents on page 32 shows areas that should be covered in an employee manual. Another aid for your "gut checks" is annually asking team members to fill out a form that certifies, first, that they have not done something to sink your ship and, second, that they are still competent to practice.

This form can be e-mailed or put in a partner's box. Statements on the form could include checklist items such as, "I have no pending lawsuits, nor do I have knowledge that any are under consideration. I am licensed to practice as I am practicing. No changes have taken place since I was last reviewed that would hinder my ability to practice consistently, competently, and responsibly." Handling things before they become acute is a key to good medicine; it is also a key to good management.

Keeping Promises

When you write your employee handbook, be sure to keep the promises made in it. In a malpractice situation, you will be held against a standard-of-care benchmark similar to that which other physicians would consider reasonable. An employee manual could hurt your case in a trial if it is proven that you or your staff did not follow the standards of care in your written guidelines.

Financial and Investment Management Group's Personnel Reference Guide Table of Contents

Mission Statement
Statement of Equal Employment Policy
Harassment Policy
Drug/Alcohol Policy
Disability Policy
Compensation
    Pay Period
    Full Time/Part Time
    Exempt/Non-Exempt
    Overtime
    Lunch Break
    Vacation Days
    Holidays
    Personal Time
    Leave of Absence
    Community Volunteer Service
    Jury Duty Fringe Benefits
    Health Insurance
    Dental Insurance
    Life and Disability Insurance
    Sec 125 Plan
    401(k) Plan

Education and Professional Dues
Charitable Contribution Matching
Portfolio Management
Office Policy
Business Hours
Client Contact
Confidentiality/Solicitations
Employee Expense Reimbursement
Other Employment
Supervisory Procedures
Use of Company Credit Card
Evaluations
Telephone Calls
Home Computer
Mobile Phones
Worker's Compensation
Use of Stationery
Termination of Employment
FIM Group Property
Confidentiality
Receipt for Personnel Reference Guide

For issues regarding care, it is best to have staff meetings and provide instructions about them. The bottom line is, if you put it in your manual, know it is there and know you can abide by it 100%; not 99%, but 100%. It is wise to have systems for monitoring your employee handbook guidelines. Some lawyers suggest that if you are not sure you can deliver on it, don't have a written guideline for that issue—discuss it in staff meetings.

One-Page Financial Plan, Stage 2

- Bisra, age 43; in 10th year of practice; salary, $15,500 monthly; enjoys work.
- Mayet, age 40; stay-at-home mom and loving it; practiced as obstetrics-gynecologic physician 1 year until Masha was born.
- Four children ages 1, 3, 5, and 7.
- Home worth $700,000.
- First mortgage, $438,000 at 6%; payments $3,000 monthly; 22 years left on mortgage.
- Second mortgage, $218,000; pay interest only, $1,100 monthly.
- Vehicles: Bisra's 10-year-old Audi is paid off. Runs well. Mayet has a Honda van worth $15,000. Paid for with second mortgage draw.
- 401(k)s worth $80,000, both invested in Utopia Growth Funds (www.utopiafunds.com). Bisra contributes $100 monthly, which is matched at $100 monthly.
- Each has three $600,000 10-year term life insurance policies with 2 years left until renewal for total insurance on each other of $1,800,000.
- Hospital medical insurance and disability at 60% to age 65 for Bisra.
- Have wills and trusts.
- Mayet's mother has moved in with them. Lives in basement apartment; helps with childcare and goes bowling every day.
- Goals: financial security and financial efficiency; new car for Bisra at $25,000.

Recommendations
- Refinance home to new $560,000 first mortgage (80% loan to value) at 6%, for payment of $3,358 monthly. Pay down second mortgage and new $120,000 fixed second mortgage (15 years; $25,000 for car, plus mortgage at $96,000 for total of $120,000) with payment of $1,022 monthly.
- For retirement, raise 401(k) deposits to $500 monthly, so with match, $1,000 monthly is deposited.
- Discussed paying for children's college by having Mayet work when oldest is eligible for college. She said, "Sounds fine with me. So, we're okay if I don't work until then?"

Discussion Notes
Discussed wills and trusts. Mayet does not like the way the couple they have chosen as guardians interact with their own children, "They are too lax, they let the kids watch television, drink soda, and eat meat." Discussed other options; Mayet will "loosen up" because current guardians are better than the other options. Mayet said she would write a letter to the couple explaining their values, but so they will not feel she is imposing values on them. The letter will describe their desire to keep the children in their existing schools, for them to be vegetarian, and for them to go to private high schools and good colleges, no matter how expensive. Bisra and Mayet added incentive provisions to trusts (to have children finish college) and added contingent guardians to wills. Mayet realized that if Bisra becomes disabled, she will need to go back to work.

CHAPTER 2 Risk Management

"The doctor's lawyer will see you now."
© The New Yorker Collection 1992 Dean Vietor from cartoonbank.com. All Rights Reserved.

Trustees

Trustees encompass a broad category and cover everything from being named a trustee in your mother's trust to serving on the board of trustees of your local hospital. Trustees are held to very high standards. As a trustee, you first need to be aware of your responsibilities and what is expected of you. Second, you must act in the best interest of those for whom you have a trustee role, so you must not engage in self-dealing (loaning yourself money that is entrusted to you to manage). You must monitor and review the beneficiary's needs and the service providers under your control; for example, if money is involved, you need to know who the investment manager and the custodian of the funds are and why they are right for the situation.

If you are a trustee of a private school or your church, are those for whom you have an obligation (students or parishioners) being well taken care of by the administration and clergy? The way in which you find this out, of course, is a question that you will need to answer. Our lives are very busy, especially when children are thrown into the mix. Trustee jobs take time, and that is why so often you see a lot of gray-haired heads on boards. Older people often serve on boards, first, because of their wisdom and, second, because they have the time.

Before you take on a trustee's or director's position, be sure to get a handbook or letter outlining your responsibilities and liability and describing any problems, potential problems, lawsuits, or pending suits. Often a trustee does not find out "the rest of the story" until he or she has been on the board for a time. Organizations need trustees, they need volunteers, and being on a board can be fulfilling and fun. However, it is not an undertaking to be approached casually. Be sure that you are willing to commit a certain amount of time and even risk additional time if those you were monitoring were engaged in disagreeable behavior.

Boards

Usually, people are asked to be on a board for one of three reasons. First, to add credibility (through stature, name recognition, education). Second, to add skills to the board. Such skills might include management, specialized knowledge, judgment, time to do the "heavy lifting," vision, writing, verbal abilities, and the like. Third, money. The first thing I ask when I am approached about being on a board is, "Why?" Is it because of credibility, skills, or money? In other words: *Time, Talent, or Money*. Of course, the usual answer is all three. I would love for certain celebrities to be on my board, but I would not care if they ever made it to a meeting. On the other hand, I would love to have financial or leadership experts such as Marcus Buckingham, Martin Seligman, Dominique Purcell, or Warren Buffett on my board and I *would* want them to show up. So bottom line, find out why they want you.

Regardless of why or when you serve on a board, you have liability and fiduciary obligations. A fiduciary's job is to use common sense, judgment, and prudence to ensure that the tasks with which he or she is entrusted are carried out well. Just as it is with your role as a physician, as a trustee you need to follow certain protocols based on your knowledge and understanding to ensure success.

Do the Right Thing

If you hire giant firm X to manage funds for which you are trustee and the new young broker for an incompetent private banker suggests a speculative asset allocation plan favoring overvalued assets and it fails, you share in the responsibility. Fancy theories, charts, graphs, and size of the firm aside, make sure you know enough to delegate responsibility. When hiring advisors, employees, or consultants, did you check three to five real references? Did you do a background check on the employees or new headmaster? Keep in mind, it is not "whether you did well or poorly," it is "whether you used common sense and acted prudently, thoughtfully, and appropriately."

The Employee Retirement Security Act and Fiduciary Obligations

If you are an employer, a director, or an officer in a company that has a pension plan, 401(k) profit sharing plan, 403(b), deferred compensation plan, or other retirement or employee benefit plan, most likely you have a significant fiduciary obligation.

If you have a retirement plan and are a sponsor, you should have the required information.

A fiduciary involved with a retirement plan should know standards and laws and make sure plan assets are managed consistent with appropriate risk and risk tolerance of each participant.

Have information available, be able to prove you monitor the other fiduciaries involved with the plan (administrator, custodian, investment advisor), and use common sense to do the right thing for all plan participants. Keep in mind that because you have 50 investment options for your employees to choose from (such as mutual funds and independent accounts), your employees might not be able to assess or understand the risk of their portfolios or mutual funds. This is especially true if your plan is full of indexed, benchmark-oriented funds or mutual funds designed as tools for an asset allocation strategy. Remember index funds become speculative at a certain "price"—if you use indexing in your plan—who monitors when your investing becomes speculating on the index? Your plan investment advisor or the group helping you with the investments should be able to say to your employer, "Based on your mix, your portfolio could drop a certain percent, such as 20%, 50%, to 75% if we had a 1930s- or 1987-style crash" and should be able to give it to you in writing through an investment policy statement of review.

The information in the following list should be readily available:

1. Plan document trust
2. Thorough understanding of plan mechanics
3. Summary plan description
4. Copy of investment manager's form ADV (Registered Investment Advisors form filed with the SEC)
5. Investment policies
6. Investment advisory agreement
7. If using mutual funds, prospectus for all funds
8. Board minutes hiring the manager and establishing the plan
9. Documents pertaining to any conflicts of interest or transactions that were potentially self-dealing
10. Proof that statements and performance were reviewed for all portfolios, mutual funds (if used), and all participants
11. Custodian information and trusts/brokerage account information showing safety and security
12. Values statement or value-neutral statement (optional; a value-neutral statement says values do not matter) regarding ethical, sustainable, environmental, spiritual, moral, or religious criteria used in the management of portfolios
13. Periodic reports reviewing all aspects of the plan against best practices and other relevant performance objectives
14. If plan sponsor is a broker, commission-receiving financial planner, insurance agent, bank, etc., statement of 12b-1, fees paid, commission paid, referral fees, finders fees, etc., paid for investing with that firm and/or individual investment management fees paid, brokerage commissions paid, and assessment as to whether those fees are reasonable and that layered-fee systems are not excessive. (*Layered fees* refers to a trustee consultant or plan administrator "layering" a fee on top of the other fees, such as the money manager's or mutual fund's expense that can in some cases grossly increase the costs over a direct system.)

Debt Management for Risk Reduction

Physicians are generally huge consumers of debt. They have high incomes and stable careers and a skill set that allows them to earn a significant income. In every physician's back pocket is an option to take the job that he or she may not prefer. For some it might be practicing in a rural area that needs a physician badly or with an inner-city hospital working extra on-call duties on weekends, working two jobs, serving in the emergency room, or having a 7-day-a-week practice. Physicians can always make more money. Banks and financial institutions know this, and thus know that physicians are fine candidates to loan money to because they have a high ability to pay back the loans. This is very good for you if you are disciplined and manage debt appropriately.

Major corporations and institutions have finance officers to manage the capital needs of their organizations. These needs are often financed with debt. Households also have used debt for their capital needs such as homes, office purchases, cars, vacation homes, and other large, expensive items. The goal is to build your net worth so that eventually you can pay cash for items such as cars and second homes. This will happen sooner than most people expect if they manage their affairs appropriately at the beginning. You can do this by concentrating on managing debt efficiently and appropriately, building net worth consistent with tax laws, and using this cash to fund retirement plans and the like. You can be your own finance officer.

The goal is to manage your debt consistent with what your life is all about. To do this there are three things you need to understand.

Number one, debts are not a problem, they are a responsibility and, if used appropriately, are wonderful financial and family-lifestyle planning tools.

Number two, if you have had problems with debt or debt management, seek counseling with a financial planner who understands working with physicians and high-income professionals. This person can help you work out a plan to make sure your debt is supporting you in your life's mission rather than dragging you down.

Number three, make sure that you take all of your debts seriously; in addition, these responsibilities should fit into your life plan.

Ten Debt Rules

It is reported that during the depression, Walt Disney was asked if he was successful. He replied, "I must be successful if I'm a million dollars in debt." Disney survived the depression largely because he had liquidity and cash flow to support his debts. Likewise, the key to using debt is to make sure you have liquidity and income to pay the debts on time. Debt has never gotten anyone in trouble. What has gotten people in trouble is debt used inappropriately, managed inappropriately, or imposed as a financial constraint or discipline.

When managing your debt, use the following 10 rules to guide you. Never sign up for a debt that puts you in an uncomfortable situation if you lose your job or that prevents you from maintaining a 20% to 30% margin in your budget (see Rule #2).

Rule #1: Think liquidity. Have 6 months to 1 year of liquid savings on hand, large available retirement plan assets, or a line of credit equal to 6 to 12 months' budget. Always have at least 1 month's budget in liquid assets; the rest can be a line of credit or accessible retirement assets. Have some cash on hand.

Rule #2: Have a budget with a margin of safety of 10% to 40%. Usually when people are younger, which is when they need a lot of debt to purchase their first house or other major item, the margin of safety may be only 10%. If part of that margin of safety is being invested into your 401(k), you can always reduce your contribution. Also, the margin should be consistent with the lifestyle you want. If you are planning to have children and either you or your spouse will stay home with them, then you need to adjust your budget to make sure the margin is consistent with only one family income, even if it is only for a few years.

Rule #3: Your total debt payments should not exceed one third of your income, and as discussed in "Homes and Real Estate" (page 68), it is best that your home mortgage or rent be no more than 25%. There will be times when these ratios are exceeded, and that is okay. If you exceed the ratios, it is best to do so under the advice of a fee-only financial advisor, who can guide you in your budgeting needs, make sure your liquidity is appropriate, and help you structure your debts to minimize discomfort if something bad happens.

Rule #4: Think balance. Life is long and debt does not cause financial ruin. It is best to consolidate loans for your home, investment property, home improvements, and other investments into one large tax-deductible loan that requires minimal payments. As in Rule #5, debts can be appropriately structured to accomplish life goals (see also "Debt Management Illustration I" on page 34 and "Debt Management Illustration II" on page 36).

Rule #5: Take advantage of tax-deductible debt. Home loans and investment interest tend to be completely deductible, so try to have all if not nearly all of your debt in your home or financing deductible investments. You may want to have the deductible loan be against your commercial or rental property, with the nondeductible loan against your home. Your accountant and advisors can guide you in appropriate structuring of your debts.

Rule #6: Never pay down your interest rate by paying points. If you expect to be in a home for only a few years, always go for a mortgage (see the "Size of Home Worksheet" on page 72), which will tend to have a 30-year amortization, perhaps ballooning in 5 or 10 years. Points are just prepaid interest; they do not lower overall cost. You do not want to prepay interest only to have interest rates fall. If interest rates fall, you can always refinance.

Rule #7: Set a goal of being your own banker so that if you want something like a car, boat, or second home, you can pay cash for it. Anticipate large purchases by saving money in your liquid investment account, paying down the line of credit on your home, or drawing on other assets.

Rule #8: Maintain control over your credit cards. Like any other debt vehicle, credit cards offer wonderful benefits and convenience. However, they should be looked at as a convenience tool and not a finance tool. Regardless of what the interest rate is (0%, 5%, or 30%), they should be paid off at the end of every month to avoid interest charges. I am a big believer in credit cards and have accumulated hundreds of thousands of frequent-flyer miles by using them as a main source for purchases. But if you or your spouse cannot use credit cards appropriately, then cut them up, cancel them, or have only one that you use for special situations.

Rule #9: Do what you say you are going to do. Keep promises, protect your credit even when it is difficult, and make payments on time. If you commit to a large purchase using debt, make sure that it fits comfortably into your budget. If you do get into trouble, call your banker and discuss it when you are in good shape, not when your situation is out of control.

Debt Management Illustration I (Before)

Dr and Dr Stretched

Stats:

3+ years in practice

Income, $145,000

Two children (1 and 3 years old)

Wife works 2 days per week; income, $42,000

Savings, $0

Retirement accounts, $0

Have adequate life, disability, and medical insurance and wills

Current Situation

Asset	Value	Loan	Payment
Home (existing), 6% (original cost, $450,000)	$385,000	$359,000	$2,158 (left as is)
Auto #1 (existing), 4.8%	$10,000	0	
Auto #2 (existing), 4.8%	$22,000	0	
School loan (existing), 7%	n/a	0	
Credit cards, 8%		0	
Loan from parents (for home), 0%		$90,000	

(continued)

Debt Management Illustration I (After)

Dr and Dr Stretched
Stats:
3+ years in practice
Income, $145,000
Two children (1 and 3 years old)

Wife works 2 days per week; income, $42,000
Savings, $0
Retirement accounts, $0
Have adequate life, disability, and medical insurance and wills

Current Situation

Asset	Value	Loan	Payment
Home (existing), 6% (original cost, $450,000)	$385,000	$359,000	$2,158 (left as is)
Auto #1 (existing), 4.8%	$10,000	0	
Auto #2 (existing), 4.8%	$22,000	0	
School loan (existing), 7%	n/a	0	
Credit cards, 8%		0	
Loan from parents (for home), 0%		$90,000	
Bank line of credit, co-signed by parents		$105,000	$500 (interest only)

Summary

Dr and Dr Stretched were stressed, just out of school, and 3 years in practice with two kids, a house bought at the top of the market, student loans, busy practices, and a value system of family and kids first. They wisely had wills, good term insurance, disability insurance, and other insurance policies set up by Dr Stretched's fee-only financial advisor and their attorney

(continued)

when they were expecting a baby 4 years ago. But since then the debts have piled up, and they would like some real furniture someday and maybe a vacation somewhere other than at his parents' Lake Michigan cottage or her parents' Florida home. They realized they needed help and called a certified financial planner who said he could help them with budgeting and debt management. He said, "Cut up your credit cards, sell your cars and lease, and turn your term insurance into universal variable life." They thought his advice sounded fishy and overly simple and called Dr Stretched's doctor-dad who set up a conference call with a fee-only firm he knew could help them. That firm helped them set up and walk through a solid budget, talked with them about the importance of staying on a budget, and suggested they ask their parents about co-signing on a loan. Dr Stretched's dad said he would co-sign a line of credit for them if they would set up a budget and work with his fee-only advisor to help keep them on track. They set up a budget that allowed them to save 10% of their income into 401(k)s and set aside another $1,000 or so monthly to pay extra on the line of credit. The bank that they set up the co-signed line of credit with said they would look at releasing the dad's signature in a year if they were timely on their payments and did not take on fresh debt. The couple was excited to know they would eventually be able to pay off dad, educate their children, retire, and enjoy time with family.

Source: Paul Sutherland, Financial and Investment Management Group

Debt Management Illustration II

Charlie and Ellie

Asset	Value	Loan	Payment
Home (existing), 6% (cost, $650,000 w/improvements)	$785,000	$325,000	$2,637 (16 years left)
Auto #1 (existing), 5%	$45,000	$12,000	$553 (57 months left)
Auto #2 (existing), 4%	$32,000	$18,000	$505 (38 months left)
Total payments (w/o second home)			$3,367

Goal:

Buy second home for family's use at $350,000 and manage new debt from second home

Debt Restructure II

Asset	Value	Loan	Payment
Home (existing), new first mortgage	$785,000	$628,000	$3,816 (30-year fixed jumbo loan)
New second line of credit loan		$93,000	$1,500* (line of credit loan on first and second home at prime rate)
Auto #1 (existing)†	$45,000	0	Paid off
Auto #2 (existing)	$32,000	0	Paid off
Second home	$350,000	0	Paid with first and second line of credit on main home
Total needed to consolidate debts		$721,000	$5,316

To replace car in future, use line of credit and second mortgage on home to try to keep interest deductible. Goal is eventually to pay cash for cars.

*New second line of credit loan balloon is 15 years; must pay at least interest only at prime rate, each month; can raise amount to $160,000 or lower to 0. Goal is to pay off loan with $1,500 monthly so that loan can be used for new cars and to buy furniture for new place if need be. Charlie and Ellie have consistently saved 10% of their income minimum in their retirement plans and will buy new term insurance on each other at $350,000 through a low load term policy. Disability insurance, wills, trusts, budgets, and financing of the new second home were reviewed by phone with their fee-only advisor as part of the process of buying the second home. Their lawyer is reviewing the best way to title the asset—most likely, Ellie's trust.

Source: Paul Sutherland, Financial and Investment Management Group

Rule #10: Do not wait for a crisis to get your debt liquidity life in order; do it now. Difficulties could be losing a partner in your practice, medical disability, going through a divorce, losing your job, or a malpractice claim. The Debt Management Illustrations (page 34 and 36) show how you can add efficiency to a financial plan through appropriate debt management and restructuring. Use the illustrations as a guide

> ### Budgeting Advice from Judy
>
> Put your money where your values are. If the education of your children is a priority for you, you may have to delay the purchase of a new automobile for a time. If you value your freedom, you may not want to have a mortgage that keeps you working two jobs. If you value your health, you may want to quit smoking (these days a very expensive habit). There are really only two ways to deal with a budget deficit—spend less or earn more. Credit will not solve the problem.
>
> Whenever you try to spend less by giving up an expensive habit, it is important to replace it with an activity that means more to you than the one you are giving up. When I quit smoking, I was in Micronesia. I used the times when I had most enjoyed smoking to go diving. It opened a new world for me and cost virtually nothing (outside of the one-time cost of the mask and fins), and I never missed the habit.
>
> Shopping, also potentially expensive, is one way I decompress after a long day. As a lover of shopping, I have often gone through a store picking up things that catch my eye, but before checking out, I evaluate critically whether the items really are needed. Often, I return everything. This allows the satisfaction of the activity without the cost. Another diversion is going to the local gym.
>
> I don't really like the word *budgeting*. It is very much like dieting—it implies giving up something. I would rather look at it as allocating my resources to that which is important to me.

By Judy McCorkle, Financial and Investment Management Group; Trust, Estate Planning and Advising

in your own financial planning, and when in doubt, hire someone who is familiar with budgeting, financial planning, and debt management for high-net-worth and high-income professions.

Risk Management Strategies

As mentioned previously, the proper management of risk is an important cornerstone to any financial plan. It is also the most misunderstood, which I discovered when I taught classes in financial planning. The definition the class and I used was that risk management encompasses, first, acknowledgment that various risks exist; second, the need to evaluate the magnitude and effect of those risks; and, third, strategies that can be undertaken to minimize or accept the risks. Some risks in life can be accepted; for example, the risk that your ice cream will melt or that your fruit will go bad in your refrigerator. These simple risks are unnecessary to insure. Other risk management is just a hassle, such as low deductibles on your car, health, or homeowner's insurance. Often, for $50 to replace the broken window, it is simpler to pay it than to file a claim.

There are four basic risk management techniques. First, avoid the risk. For example, avoiding driving on icy or snowy roads or prohibiting children from swimming in a swimming pool unsupervised are ways of avoiding risk.

A second method is risk minimization or reduction. Most physicians use this in their daily practice by telling their patients to slow down, avoid smoking, avoid certain types of food, or take a certain drug. Putting a sprinkler system in your office does not reduce the risk of fire; however, it does reduce the risk of a fire destroying records and equipment. Putting a snow shovel, a bag of sand, mittens, and boots in your car before driving during a snowstorm reduces the potential of spending the night in a snowdrift.

Accepting the risk is a third method used by risk managers. Many simple daily risks are easy to accept. Nonetheless, other risks such as lightning strikes or riots—you are stuck with.

When most people think of risk management, they think of insurance. Insurance is a fourth method of risk management. Insurance transfers the risk. Financial risk is reduced or limited by transferring the risk to the insurance company. That risk is then transferred to a regulated and supervised pool under actuarial assumptions to assure the claim will be paid if an event occurs.

You should transfer only those risks that you cannot handle to an insurance company. Insurance agents may want to insure everyone and everything. But, you should insure against large losses, not small ones. For example, a $500 deductible on your car or homeowner's insurance is appropriate. Deductibles on your health care coverage, especially for a physician, are appropriate. For many of us, filing a claim to get $100 or $200 is not worth it. Not that we do not file those claims, but raising the deductible is the best way to save time and avoid the inconvenience, and save on premiums.

Every physician should have adequate car, health, and homeowner's insurance. All policies that you have should be overlaid with an umbrella insurance policy. Auto, health, and homeowner's insurance are significantly regulated by state insurance bureaus, and a quality insurance agent who gives you good references representing top-quality, well-respected companies is best. After you get an insurance quote or join, for example, Charles Schwab's insurance program (www.schwab.com), it is good to have a fee-only advisor or another insurance agent review the coverage.

In addition to good homeowner's and auto insurance, you should have comprehensive personal liability insurance that covers risk in excess of the liability covered by your homeowner's and auto insurance. This coverage is called an *umbrella policy* and comes in handy if your dog bites a neighbor or the mailman, a visitor slips on your front walk, or your neighbor's child falls into your swimming pool.

Such losses can run into millions of dollars, and you need a good, comprehensive personal policy to cover the risks. Personal liability coverage is especially important to physicians, because they are prime targets for lawsuits.

Computer Security Checklist

1. Backups should be done on computers to protect against lost data. This must be done for all computers on which you keep important data.
2. Every computer should be running updated virus software.
3. All computers need to be updated with your current program's security patches. Microsoft® (www.microsoft.com) releases updates and patches almost daily to its Windows® line of operating systems. These updates and patches should be installed as soon as they are released.
4. If you are connected to the Internet, you need to have a firewall. There are two kinds: A hardware firewall is a small device that goes between your connection to the Internet and the computers on your network or even your home computer. A software firewall is a program running on your computer that stops outside computers (computers from the Internet or on your own network) from making connections to your computer.
5. Do not open Internet e-mail attachments unless you know that the sender has security similar to yours. In fact, it is best to never open e-mail attachments unless you trust the source.

6. Consider using a program other than Microsoft's Internet Explorer® for Web browsing. For example, Mozilla's® (www.mozilla.com) Firefox® has not had the security problems that Internet Explorer has.

7. Never give out a password. If someone tells you they need your password, something is not right.

8. Never make a purchase online unless you see that the page you are using is encrypted. Most web browsers will let you know when a page is secure by putting a small lock symbol on the page or on the frame around the page.

9. Lock or log out of your computer anytime you are not working on it.

10. If you are using a wireless access point or wireless router, make sure you have turned on the security features of your wireless device. This is commonly called *wired equivalent privacy* (WEP) encryption.

11. Do not allow other people to use your business computer, especially children, without your permission or supervision.

12. Have confidentiality wording similar to the following on all e-mails:

*************************** CONFIDENTIALITY NOTICE ***************************

This e-mail message and any files transmitted with it are legally privileged and contain confidential information intended only for the person(s) to whom this e-mail message is addressed. If you are not the intended recipient, you are hereby notified that any disclosure, copying, distribution, or taking of any action in reliance on the contents of this e-mail is strictly prohibited. If you have received this e-mail message in error, please notify the sender immediately by telephone or e-mail and destroy the original message without making a copy. Thank you.

****

Source: Russ Riker, Financial and Information Management Group

Attorneys go after physicians because physicians have higher-than-average incomes and usually have adequate assets to pay clients. Often, physicians settle out of court to have the potential claim go away.

Over the years, insurance especially homeowner's, auto, and health insurance, has become so regulated that, except in a very few states, most people are well protected against, for example, their house being uninsured if lightning strikes from the north. When working with your insurance agent, ask him or her to put in writing what is not covered. Most quality insurance agencies providing casualty, homeowner's, and business insurance do not want to risk their reputation by recommending insurance that does not cover your needs adequately. From my experience, insurers are reluctant to review your coverage to reduce premiums without your asking. So every year or so, have your insurance reviewed and re-quoted by another quality agency. The quality casualty insurance agent will review your risks and give you written proposals on how to cover them.

Prenuptial Agreements

Marriage is wonderful and beautiful. It is about keeping a commitment. But as we all know, people and circumstances change, and about half of all marriages end in divorce. Divorce can be trying and traumatic. Even the most loving and reasonable people can end up with disastrous divorces. During a divorce, significant wealth can go to lawyers, and careers and reputations can be destroyed. However, these are unnecessary and happen because problems were not handled in the beginning or they got so bad that they could not be repaired.

Prenuptial agreements can help prevent problems during a divorce. A prenuptial agreement is made before the marriage and sets out how the marriage would end. Generally, in a prenuptial agreement, financial matters are spelled out in the event of either death or divorce. Sometimes, non-financial topics such as lifestyle may be included. The prenuptial contract may be written to preempt any state, federal, or other laws that might apply. Any such agreement needs to be made with the help of a lawyer in the state in which you have your primary residence to make sure that it is consistent with state laws.

There are two keys to prenuptial agreements ("pre-nups"). One is that each spouse should have separate and independent legal counseling and, two, full disclosure needs to take place about assets or any other encumbrances that are being brought into the relationship. It is important to approach the idea of a pre-nup in such a way that each spouse realizes that he or she has a lot to gain from the agreement. It is not planning for things to end badly; it is an agreement between reasonable people who want protection if something does happen, for example, in the case of death. Prenups are necessary in second marriages, especially when there are children or significant assets involved or if there are calls on those assets because a spouse has commitments to support charities, family members, or practice partners.

Prenuptial agreements should include the following:

1. A list of assets, income, liabilities, and any expected inheritances.
2. An explanation of how these assets would be distributed in the event of death or divorce.
3. What happens to the debts in the event of a divorce?
4. An explanation of how the house or homes are distributed.
5. An explanation of how assets that are inherited will be handled.
6. If alimony is to be paid, how much alimony will be and how it will be figured. Will it be a flat amount or based on a percentage of income? Some agreements, for example, might say that for every year of marriage, the less financially well-off spouse gets a flat $50,000 in cash plus the home in Florida.
7. An explanation of how medical, health, and disability income insurance should be handled.
8. An explanation of how legal fees for the dissolution would be handled and how any disputes would be handled in a divorce situation, such as mediation, a named lawyer, appraisals, and so on.

Premarital agreements allow you to discuss with your spouse what is important to you and what your values are. If a prenuptial agreement discussion would ruin a relationship, then probably it is best not to enter into that relationship. Communication is the key, and prospective spouses should be able to talk about anything.

When I give seminars, I talk about friendship being the ability to ask that friend to do anything for you and the ability of that friend to ask anything of you. Either should be able to say to the other simply "no" without explanation or guilt if he or she does not wish to do something that is asked. Thus, if a friend asks me to help him move from his home to an apartment on a Friday afternoon, I should simply be able to say "no" without having to explain myself. Whether I want to sit and watch the football game or serve in a soup kitchen, it is my prerogative. A friend should not ask me for an explanation. He or she should trust that I know well enough whether or not I can help.

Relationships are about getting to what is real and important in our lives. A concrete relationship in which both spouses know each other intimately is stronger than one built on fantasy or romantic illusions. In a healthy relationship, both parties need to be able to recognize and embrace the beauty as well as the ugliness within themselves and others. It is necessary to know what is real in that person's life, what strengths are there, what weaknesses are there, what idiosyncrasies are there, and be able to celebrate the differences. A prenuptial agreement should be an easy document to discuss, set up, and solidify. Communication between the prospective spouses about the agreement is the key to a successful prenuptial document.

Marriage Decisions

How will you split the duties? Will you look at your marriage as a partnership? Will you look at your marriage as "he keeps his and I keep mine"? Will your marriage be about sharing, in which his assets are my assets and vice versa? These are all important to discuss. Who will stay home with the children? How will you handle parenting? Is one spouse assuming that the other will stay home and that the one working will work less? All of this needs to be woven into the financial plan. Naturally, we need to allow ourselves to change our minds, but all this is helpful if discussed before marriage with good humor and acceptance.

As someone who found himself suddenly single 10 years ago, I discovered that discussing prenuptial agreements at the beginning of a romantic relationship was appropriate. Women were for the most part receptive to this discussion, especially because I had two children, significant assets, and was a big charitable giver. I wanted them to understand the importance of my children's security should I remarry. The first few times I brought this up, it was awkward, but the women also thought about such subjects and understood that it was better to get them out in the open.

The best analogy I have found for prenuptial agreements is that they are like insurance policies. You buy insurance and hope you will never need it. If you choose to have a prenuptial agreement, make sure you work with a family and marriage lawyer who has experience and sensitivity to avoid creating conflict in the relationship. When you celebrate your 50th wedding anniversary, you can both laugh about how you wasted money on legal fees to have that pre-nup drawn up and wink at each other knowing that nothing is ever certain in life.

Income Protection Insurance

The most important insurance for someone who is dependent on his or her own personal income is income protection or disability income insurance. As a physician, you are a money machine, and your main asset is your ability to produce income through your craft. If you become disabled, all the years of medical school and study will be for naught. If you had a factory that was going to produce $100,000 to $1 million a year in income, you would insure it without looking twice at the premium. When you are young and have not yet built up a net worth through your skills, you need disability income insurance to make certain you have financial security. The "Disability Insurance Income Worksheet" on page 46 can help you determine how much disability insurance you need.

Generally, you should have disability insurance with at least two companies. If, for example, you need $5,000 worth of insurance, perhaps you would have $2,500 of insurance through a group policy and another $2,500 through a low-load insurance provider or on the advice of your fee-only insurance advisor.

Most policies for physicians are written in such a way that you are well protected should you become disabled. The American Medical Association's (AMA's) contract provisions are adequate for most physicians. Also, the policies that you can purchase through a company such as Low Load Insurance Services (www.llis.com) or other commercial carriers have excellent provisions for physicians. You should have a policy that pays you at least to age 65 and ideally for life and that does not have unnecessary riders.

Generally, policies that cover extended periods of your occupation or specialty are expensive. Insurance coverage of your specialty is often unnecessary. In fact, many companies have stopped issuing them. That is okay—you need to insure your income, not your specialty. If your income drops in half, your insurance policy should keep paying you a residual or part-time benefit until it goes back up, if ever, to what it was before you were disabled. Most policies have residual benefits for working part-time. Residual provisions allow you to receive disability income from the policy until your income comes back to what it was before the disability.

Disability Income Insurance Worksheet*

A. Monthly income you need to support your lifestyle (debt payments, utilities, food, entertainment, education, etc)
$_____

B. Current investments that could be quickly converted to cash $_____

Divided by monthly income needed
$_____

Equals number of months personal funds will support you: _____

C. Income expected from noninvestment sources, such as receivables, should you become disabled:

1st month $_____ 2nd month $_____ 3rd month $_____

Elimination Period Calculation

Number of months receivables will support you: _____

Number of months liquid investments will support you (B): _____

Equals the elimination period in months: _____

Income needed to support your lifestyle (A): $_____

Subtract income from assets not figured in liquidity analysis such as pension plan assets, individual retirement accounts, income partnerships, etc (in excess of $500,000), multiply value of these assets by 0.005 =
$_____

(For example, $1,000,000 × 0.005 = $5,000 monthly.)

Amount of income needed from disability income insurance: $_____

_____
*Benefit period should always be at least to age 65 for sickness or accident and usually lifetime for both sickness and accident. Social Security disability benefits are not figured in because they cannot be depended upon; they are a margin-of-error benefit.

Source: © Sutherland, PH. *Zenvesting, The Art of Abundance and Managing Money.* Suttons Bar, MI: Financial Sourcebook, 1998, All Rights Reserved. A printable copy of this work sheet is available at www.fimg.net.

Typically, it is unnecessary and a waste of money to buy policies that have provisions whereby the amount of disability payment goes up with inflation. It is better to take that premium and buy all the disability income insurance you possibly can. For example, rather than buying a $7,000 policy that has a benefit that will increase over time, it is smarter to have a $10,000 monthly benefit that is leveled. The extra $3,000 that you do not need initially can be reinvested to help offset future inflation, saved, used for additional medical expenses, or used to keep your practice open.

Disability Letter

Dear Disability Carrier:

I have the following questions regarding my policy:

1. What is your definition of disability?
2. If I were unable to perform my job, would I be disabled?
3. If I am only partially disabled (at work one quarter time), does my policy give me a benefit?
4. If I am partially disabled and *working* half-time, do I get a benefit? If so, how much and for how long?
5. If I am partially disabled and *earn* one-half of what I earned prior to disability, what would my benefit be?
6. If I had a heart attack and was out of work for 1 year and started working again but only worked half days, would you pay me? If so, how much and for how long?
7. If I were disabled by a heart attack for a period of 3 years, then went back to work full-time, most of my clients would have found other professionals to handle their needs. Would you pay me (while I was working full time) a benefit while rebuilding my practice? If you would pay me a benefit, what would that benefit be and for how long?
8. Is this policy cancelable by you?
9. Are my premium rates guaranteed never to go up?
10. Does this policy pay a dividend?
11. Does this policy cover conditions existing prior to my taking out the policy?
12. Does my policy have any waivers on it? If so, why?
13. What is my current elimination period, and can I change it?
14. Is there a waiver of premium benefit on my policy?
15. If I were disabled and collected benefits for 6 months and then went back to work for 6 months before becoming disabled again, would I have to satisfy a new elimination period?
16. Does this policy have a presumptive disability benefit that pays me if I lose my sight, hearing, etc, even if I continue to work?
17. What is my policy's benefit period?
18. Can my policy's benefit period be changed to a lifetime sickness/lifetime accident benefit? If so, at what cost?
19. Does my policy have a cost-of-living benefit that raises my benefit as the Consumer Price Index rises? What does it cost? Can I add this benefit? Can I drop it? At what cost?

(continued)

20. I have lost my policy. Please send me forms to request a duplicate policy.

21. When was the last premium paid on this policy? When is the next due, and how much?

22. Does your policy offer a nonsmoker discount?

23. Is my policy a participating dividend-paying policy? If so, what dividends do you project? (I understand that dividends are not guaranteed.)

24. I am now in a group practice. Does your company have a group billing discount?

25. Who is the owner on this policy?

26. Who is the beneficiary?

27. What is your company's rating for financial strength?

28. Please send me a copy of my policy's complete application.

Please send me the above information in writing, and thank you for your prompt attention.

Sincerely,

Source: © Sutherland, Paul H. *Zenvesting, The Art of Abundance and Managing Money.* Suttons Bar, MI: Financial Sourcebook, 1998, All Rights Reserved. A printable copy of this letter is available at www.fimg.net.

Insurance agents make significant money on the bells and whistles (riders on policies) and add-on sales. A simple disability policy is best, one that gives you a benefit you know will pay should you become disabled. If you have a current policy, the "Disability and Income Letter" on page 47 can be written to your insurance company. The answers will give you a good understanding of what your policy would pay under various circumstances.

Overhead Expense Insurance

Overhead expense insurance pays the costs of keeping your office open if you are disabled. Often, receivables, liquid assets, and your partners cover for you if you are disabled. If you are a solo practitioner or partners could suffer financially if you were disabled for a year or two, consider having office overhead insurance to keep your practice open. In deciding what amount of office overhead expense is appropriate, use similar criteria to

> ### Disability Insurance: Where to Buy It
>
> Following are some good sources of disability insurance:
>
> - Low Load Insurance Services at www.llis.com, (877) 254-4429, represents three fine companies. (If you use the Web site, type "AMA Guide" in the Advisor blank. If you have an existing policy, it can be modified to be consistent with the guidelines in this book.)
> - Northwestern Mutual Life (www.nmfn.com) has a very good disability policy called Annual Renewable Disability Insurance (ARDI). The policy is especially good for younger physicians, because the premiums are low based on the fact that people are less likely to become disabled when they are young. The premiums rise with age, but as net-worth grows and needs change, you can increase the elimination period and lower your benefits to keep from wasting premiums or unnecessary coverage. If you have a policy from this company, usually it can be modified so that it is a good fit. Your fee-only advisor or Low Load Insurance Services can guide you to rewrite your existing policy to fit your needs. My advice is to avoid buying anything except the ARDI disability policy from Northwestern Mutual Life or other commission-driven companies for that matter.
>
> Note that underwriters need (usually both medical and financial) to know why you need the insurance and will ask questions about hazardous avocations. This is normal to the underwriting process.

that for purchasing a personal disability policy. You should always buy enough coverage to pay only the expenses of maintaining your office should you become disabled. If you have four or five employees, you may be able to cut down to one or two just to keep the office open, collect payments, do billings, and take care of monthly expenses while disabled. Some office overhead policies even help pay debt services in addition to the normal expenses such as utilities, taxes, insurance payments, staff costs, telephone, answering services, legal services, stationery, postage, laundry, and car services.

Office overhead insurance should be purchased after you have the maximum amount of personal disability income insurance. Office overhead insurance pays only office expenses. If you have a $10,000 office overhead insurance policy and are permanently disabled and need to close up your office, you will get no or very little benefit from that policy. If you qualify for $10,000 to $15,000 per month personal disability income insurance, it is better to have that amount to use as you wish rather than owning a smaller disability insurance and an office overhead expense policy. For example, if you feel that you need an extra $5,000 per month for a few years, add an extra $5,000 benefit to your personal policy for 1 to 2 years and have the option of keeping your office open or using the money for personal expenses. Your fee-only advisor should be familiar with this technique in determining whether office overhead insurance is appropriate for you.

Professional Liability Insurance

Being a physician has many associated risks. The primary risk is being sued in the line of providing professional services to your patients. There are two primary kinds of malpractice insurance: occurrence and claims-made policies.

The terms of an occurrence policy carry a perpetual liability under negligence that may have occurred while the policy was enforced.

Under a claims-made policy, the insurance company assumes liability only if a claim is made or the potential for a claim is filed before the policy is terminated. Some claims-made policies will, however, cover claims that are made after the policy has run out. Regardless of the event and type of policy, your coverage should handle attorney fees as well as expert witnesses, court costs, costs of gathering evidence, and any settlement. These costs should be covered even if the loss is fraudulent. The average award has been going up substantially every year. Choose the best, most up-to-date professional liability insurance that you can buy, and make sure your policy will cover you adequately. In addition, it is important that any of your associates who work for you or fill in for you during vacations have good malpractice insurance policies. You should also minimize the risk of malpractice, encourage proper communication with your patients, and prudently run your practice.

Finally, it cannot be overemphasized that your policy should pay legal costs incurred in defending yourself in a liability case. You could win the case and lose the war by having thousands of dollars in attorney fees that are not covered by the policy. Read your policy carefully and make sure you understand it. High deductibles on malpractice insurance can keep premiums to a minimum. As your net worth increases, your deductible and amount of insurance should increase.

Life or Death Insurance

This section helps you assess whether you have a need for life insurance and, if so, how to cover that need in an efficient manner. Although many physicians let commission-driven insurance agents assess their life insurance needs and buy their insurance, it is better to do your own insurance

Life Insurance: Where to Buy It

With life insurance, it is important to diversify your coverage. If your coverage need is under $300,000, then coverage from one company is fine. However, if your need is between $300,000 and $1,000,000, then have your coverage split between two companies; for any amount over $1,000,000, go with three companies. The following are a few good companies:

- USAA Life, (800) 531-8000
- Schwab direct, (800) 838-0650
- Ameritas, (800) 745-6665
- TIAA-CREF, (866) 966-5623
- Low Load Insurance Services (www.llis.com), (877) 254-4429. Low Load has access to many companies and will place your whole insurance portfolio of multiple policies or coordinate with any other group policy.

Low Load will review your current policies without charge, if you mention this book, to see which of your current policies you should keep. If you go to their Web site to get quotes, enter "AMA Guide" in the Advisor field. If you want a quote for more than one policy, type, for example, "three policies totaling $2,200,000" in the Amount of Insurance field.

Note that underwriters need (usually both medical and financial) to know why you need the insurance and will ask questions about hazardous avocations. This is normal to the underwriting process.

planning or get objective help. It may seem complicated, but it is not that difficult. In a half hour to an hour or so you should be able to assess your needs and make the phone calls to collect the insurance quotes. From there, usually the companies from whom you have collected the quotes will take the ball and run with it and help you set up medical exams and do the underwriting. Some firms, such as Low Load Insurance Services, will efficiently do personal interviews over the phone. I have known the founders of Low Load for a number of years, and they do a fine job.

Assessing your need for life insurance is simple. If you were to die, who would suffer financially? Would your current financial resources comfortably take care of them, and for how long? For example, if you were to die and you have young children, a mortgage, and few assets and the income that you are earning from your practice is spent at the end of each month, then you probably need life insurance, depending on how much is in your individual retirement account or retirement plans.

The "Life Insurance Worksheet" on page 54 helps you assess your insurance needs. First, you list who would suffer financially if you should die, then the type of loss. For example, if you are a two-income household and you each earn $15,000 per month, then you write down that the household would lose $15,000 per month in income. If you have a partner depending on you, write down the partner's name, the type of loss, then calculate the specific amount of financial loss. Often, it is harder to assess the loss of our partners, but it is a good conversation to have because recruiting physicians can be expensive and time-consuming. You may want to have a life insurance policy on him or her that can help you hire someone temporarily into your practice while you are looking for a full-time associate. After this is done, you need to quantify the need. Generally, with young families a significant income replacement is needed because most of a young physician's income is being spent.

In Step II on the worksheet, you can write down, for example, monthly income to spouse of $5,000, monthly income to mother-in-law of $1,000, pay off debts of $500,000 for home and cottage, cash resources of $20,000 to go to charity, cash for children's college of $50,000 each at $100,000, and so on.

Step III simply is taking those needs and doing the math to end up with a total insurance death benefit that you would need.

After you calculate the total need, your insurance should be diversified. No one would be foolish enough to have 100% of their money invested in one bond, even if it is issued by a triple-A company such as General Electric (www.ge.com). You should not assume that insurance companies will be around and able to meet their obligations indefinitely. Insurance companies go bankrupt or go under, and often there is no safety net to protect the insured at the end of the line.

Challenge the Research

1. Were the researchers specifically trained to do research?
2. Who funded the research? Could the research have been affected by the point of view of the funder?
3. Was the research published in a professional scientific journal?
4. Did the researchers clearly define what they studied?
5. Exactly what population was researched?
6. Did the sample represent the population?
7. Was the sample large enough?
8. Was a control group used?
9. Did study conditions affect the outcomes?
10. Did the researchers have opportunities to influence the results?
11. Were research questions carefully worded?
12. Were the questions pre-tested?
13. Were the data complete?
14. Were the data considered fairly?

Analyze the Analysis

1. Were all the averages reported?
2. Were results hidden in percentiles?
3. Were the data as precise as the calculations?
4. Was cause confused with correlation?

Question the Conclusions

1. Were the results abused to force a conclusion?
2. Did the conclusions overstep?
3. Did graphs summarize the research findings clearly and fairly?

Source: Swanson, D. *Nibbling on Einstein's Brain: The Good the Bad and the Bogus in Science.* Toronto, CANADA: Annick Press, 2001.

If you have a need for less than $1 million in life insurance, you should have two policies. If you have a need for over $1 million, you should have at least three policies. Although this sounds complicated, it is not that difficult; for example, you can make a quick phone call to one of the companies listed. If you need $2 million in life insurance, type in, "I want $700,000 of 5-year term." Each company will send you the forms and walk you through the medical underwriting process. For the balance of your insurance needs, or for simplicity, simply fill out the Low Load Insurance quote. Asking for three policies of $650,000 each will get you a response quickly, and they also will walk you through the underwriting. You may want to fill all of your insurance needs through Low Load. A number of providers are listed in the box, "Life Insurance: Where to Buy It," on page 51.

Life Insurance Worksheet

Step 1

List below who would suffer financially if you died. (Example: spouse, children, parents, business partners, charity, friends, and siblings.)

Name   List type of loss (i.e., income, debt payoff, family care, etc)

_____

_____

_____

_____

Step 2

List a specific amount of economic support for the above-listed people.

Monthly income to _____ of $_____

Monthly income to _____ of $_____

Pay off debts for _____ of $_____

Cash resource for _____ of $_____

*Special cash to _____ of $_____ (lump sum)

Step 3

A. Total monthly income desired at $_____ divided by 0.005 =   +$_____

B. Total cash needed to pay off debts, mortgages, for cash reserves, and special cash   =   +$_____

C. Total assets needed to provide for above   TA = $_____

(A 6% interest rate is used so if there are any, excess earnings can go to help offset inflation.)

D. Total assets needed (from above, same as C)   TA $_____

E. Less liquid assets you own and assets that could produce income   −$_____

F. Total insurance death benefit you need $_____

Life insurance needs should be reviewed as circumstances change; for example, when you stop birth control, take on debts, become a partner, or adopt.

Note that Social Security benefits add "margin-of-error" to your insurance planning so it is not figured into this calculation.

---

*Special cash could be for purchase of a home if renting, lump sums for college for children, liquid fund for charity, etc.

Source: © Sutherland, PH. *Zenvesting, The Art of Abundance and Managing Money.* Suttons Bar, MI: Financial Sourcebook, 1998, All Rights Reserved. A printable version of this sheet is available at www.fimg.net.

Death Benefit Insurance Checklist

Check your insurance coverage amount:

- The day you or your spouse decide to try to become pregnant
- If your debt structure changes— you take on a new debt or pay off an old one
- If you become engaged to be married
- If someone becomes dependent on you (parent, child, sibling)
- If your net-worth changes by $100,000 or more
- If you change jobs, take on a partner, change business form (incorporate)
- If you have not reviewed your insurance within a few years

Source: Sutherland, PH. *Zenvesting, The Art of Abundance and Managing Money.* Suttons Bar, MI: Financial Sourcebook, 1998.

One-Page Financial Plan, Stage 3

- Bisra, age 53; 20 years in practice; salary, $16,000 monthly
- Mayet, age 50; practiced 1 year, then children came; not working outside of home.
- Four children ages 11, 13, 15, and 17 (nearly 18; junior in high school)
- Home is worth $750,000
- First mortgage at $468,000; 20 years left at 6% interest rate
- Second mortgage at $100,000 used to buy new cars; turned it into interest-only second mortgage payment at $600 monthly
- 401(k)s now worth $310,000, invested in Utopia Global Funds. Funding at $500 plus $500 match, total $1,000 monthly to 401(k).
- Cars both good for another 2 or 3 years
- Bisra has hospital and medical insurance plus $100,000 group life insurance and 60% disability after 90 days until age 65
- Have will and trusts
- Have $1,800,000 10-year term on each with 2 years left until new 10-year renewal
- Local obstetrics-gynecology offered Mayet 3-day per week job, office schedule 8:30 a.m. to 4 p.m. and one Saturday evening and Sunday "day call" schedule each month with $10,000 monthly salary, 100% matching 401(k), 4-weeks off in summer, with alternating off-days for Christmas and spring holidays. Goal: decide if she should take it. Her mom, who bowls till 4 p.m. each day, said she could come home by 3 p.m. on days when Mayet works to watch the children

Goals
- Financial security and financial efficiency.
- Mayet wants his children to go to the local private day-school and high school at a cost of $12,000 each
- Take one month and travel each summer (Bisra's partners agreed to this)
- Decide if Mayet should take the job

Discussion Notes
- Discussed Mayet's goal of private school and need for her to work to pay for it—Bisra offered to work more, but Mayet said that's not fair and she liked the women in the practice that offered her a job, so she wants to take it. Discussed how it is hard to go from private school to public school because children have friends, and a private school can "grow on you." So, to displace children if Mayet changes her mind might be uncomfortable. She is "fine" with working three days, realizes the commitment, and is excited to go back to work.
- Discussed costs of 1-month holiday in the summer, went through budget and will budget $12,000 for summer vacation.

Recommendations and Actions
- Refinance home and pay off all debts and get an extra $32,000 for cars or help in replacing cars, $600,000 first at 7%; $3,990 monthly payment for 30-year mortgage.
- Max out on both 401(k)s at $700 monthly from pocket and $700 matching, each total $2,800 monthly toward retirement, which will grow the $310,000 currently in retirement plans to $1,570,000 at 6% return by the time Mayet is age 65 and youngest is out of college. The $1,570,000 retirement plans along with Social Security will give them an approximate income of $7,500 from investments and another $2,500 to $3,000 from Social Security, or about $10,000 total monthly retirement income.
- Bisra and Mayet said they like the idea of being able to retire around 65, but said they will probably work until age 80 or so because they like to be busy and they enjoy their patients.

More money is wasted on life insurance than probably any other insurance product. I cannot emphasize enough the importance of sticking to simple, unencumbered term life insurance—it fits 99% of insurance needs. The reason there is so much cash value, variable, and so-called permanent insurance out there is because it is sold by insurance agents who use fancy charts, tax tables with unscientific science (see Challenge the Research on page 53), statistics, and math to manipulate consumers into buying the expensive unnecessary product. In a financial plan one goal is to build your net worth so that you have no need for life insurance. The idea that you have a permanent need for life insurance is as ridiculous as thinking you will have a permanent need for birth control.

The goal of financial planning is to build enough net worth so that your financial security is not dependent on an insurance company to take care of your family. It is better to depend on the assets that you have accumulated, which can provide income. Ideally, by the time you retire, your net worth and income-producing assets will be sufficient so that if you were to die, your spouse and other loved ones would have adequate income to provide for them for the rest of their lives, from the assets you have built up.

The Permanent Insurance Sales Pitch Looks Inviting

Many insurance agents say, "Gosh, at your death, you're going to have to pay a million dollars in taxes. So, instead of your family getting $4 million, they will only be getting $3 million. So buy this expensive million-dollar estate tax–paying policy! You love your family, don't you?!" This sounds compelling, doesn't it? But if your family only needs $3 million and you think that will adequately provide for them for lifetime income security or give them adequate assets, then life insurance is unnecessary. If you want to leave your family $4 million worth of assets and your net worth is $2 million, it would not be smart to buy $3 million more worth of insurance just so your children will have "more money" to pay the taxes.

All of your assets can be left to your spouse estate- and income-tax-free. The insurance you would buy to pay estate taxes is only to benefit your children. Often through trusts, ownership, and the appropriate use of beneficiary designations you can significantly minimize the income and estate taxes to your family. My advice is, do not buy life insurance just so your children will have more money to pay taxes.

Insurance agents want to sell policies and will give many reasons to buy cash-value whole life, second-to-die, first-to-die, universal, or variable life insurance products for estate planning. These products should not be purchased unless you get a letter from fee-only advisors, who say that the use of these policies is absolutely the appropriate strategy, based on their understanding of the facts and constraints of *your* financial situation.

The "Life Insurance Worksheet" on page 54 should be used for both you and your spouse or business partner. Anyone who may be dependent on you financially should be included on the worksheet. Often, we are dependent on our business partners, and it is important to evaluate those needs. Generally, that need should be fixed with the cheapest (term) insurance you can find, because partners in business tend to change.

You will notice in the life insurance worksheet that the monthly income continues forever to your spouse or the loved ones who need it. When you or your spouse die, the surviving spouse's best gift to their children is time—perhaps accomplished by significantly reducing work schedule or not working at all until the children are older or go to college. During that period, no money is accumulated toward retirement, and therefore the life insurance income should continue for life. It is very hard for a 50- or 55-year-old widow or widower to suddenly enter the workforce and try to accumulate enough money for retirement. Life insurance, especially term insurance, is inexpensive. It is reasonable to have adequate death insurance to make sure that your family and loved ones have lifetime income security.

Beneficiaries

Naturally, any beneficiaries on your insurance policies, investment accounts, or retirement plans should be coordinated with your lawyer and estate planner. As a general rule, if you are married and do not have a trust set up, you would typically have your spouse as primary beneficiary and your children as secondary beneficiaries. For individual retirement accounts and pensions, most planners will advise that you name your spouse as a primary beneficiary and often the children as secondary beneficiaries. If you have beneficiaries other than your spouse for qualified plans, there are significant tax issues, and you should have a letter from whoever recommended the beneficiary. The letter should state why a different beneficiary was recommended, or it should be under the recommendation of your lawyer.

Life Insurance Trust

If you have young children who are unmarried, because of estate taxes and efficiency, a life insurance trust can be an ideal financial tool to make sure that your children have available income for college education expenses, perhaps a nest egg to get their career started, and income for their caregiver until they reach an age of maturity. A life insurance trust, if used properly, can help minimize or eliminate estate taxes while assuring that your children have financial security. Life insurance trusts are especially useful for divorced

---

Summary of Insurance Rules

1. Buy only as much life insurance as you really need and only if you need it. Assume that your insurance needs will decrease as the children get older and as your net-worth increases.

2. Make sure each policy's ownership and present beneficiary designation is consistent with your estate and financial plan. If you purchase insurance through insurance agents, be aware that they are often sloppy about beneficiary designations and ownership. An "improperly owned" policy or a policy that has an improper beneficiary can wreak havoc with an estate and cause unnecessary tax consequences.

3. Use only companies that have the highest Moody's ratings (www.moodys.com), Standard and Poor's (www.standardandpoors.com), or other rated agencies. As explained in **Life Insurance: Where to Buy It** (page 51), it is prudent to diversify your risks against any defaults on your policy. Therefore, if you need more than $300,000, but less than $1 million in life insurance, use two policies from different insurance companies. If you need more than $1 million, have three separate policies with different insurance companies.

4. Get your life insurance advice from an objective, fee-only advisor or a low-load insurance company. It is worth paying a few hundred dollars an hour for good, objective advice. A good financial advisor should require no more than a few hours to help you with your "insurance prescription." If he or she suggests that you buy cash-value life insurance, seek out another advisor for a second opinion.

5. Use low-load policies with low-load agencies where marketing and commission costs are minimized. Use term rates on page 66 and 67 to compare premiums.

(continued)

6. Have your estate planning attorney review your policy beneficiaries.

7. Review your insurance at least every couple of years.

8. Make sure your term insurance is tiered to benefit your pocketbook by realizing that your needs and net worth will change. For example, if you assume that your net-worth will increase by $500,000 over the next 5 years, you might purchase a $500,000 5-year term insurance policy that would lapse after five years. Following the 5 years, you might purchase a 10-year term policy that would be dropped after 10 years as your net worth increases. Assume that you will decrease or drop insurance policies over the years. This is one advantage of having multiple policies; you can layer them or allow them to lapse as your insurance needs change.

9. If you are one of those rare people who wants a cash-value policy such as a universal, adjustable, or variable life insurance policy, then carefully review the cash-surrender value in years 1 to 5 and buy only low-load or no-load policies (unless, of course, your spouse is a commissioned life insurance agent). If you buy an adjustable life, universal life, or other cash-value policy, your cash-surrender value should exceed the amount of premiums paid, less pure term costs, plus interest, *in the first year* if you were to cash in the policy. If your policy has characteristics other than this, you are probably not buying a true low-load policy or the policy is misrepresented. A good source of information or for second opinions with integrity regarding cash-value policies is Low Load Insurance Services.

10. A list of the insurance policies and their beneficiary designations and ownership should be with your financial advisor, in the file of your lawyer, and with your estate planning documents.

11. If you have old policies that have significant cash value, have significant loans, or are very old, do not assume that it is rational to just cash these policies in, because they could have embedded tax consequences and be good to keep. Seek out a good insurance counselor to look at these policies.

12. Generally, do not purchase life policy-riders like accidental death insurance or waiver of premium during disability. Dollar for dollar, it is a high cost to protect your policy if you become disabled. It is better to have enough disability insurance to pay for the insurance premium than to have policy-riders.

> ### Bottom Line
>
> Most young physicians, although they may be earning significant income, have not yet acquired significant net worth. Often, money is tight, and each dollar has a number of places it could go. Unfortunately, you most need life insurance when you have a young family with children. That is when your family is most vulnerable, and your priorities should include adequate life insurance. As you get older, your insurance needs change and diminish, and then you can reduce those policies. Nothing is more important than adequate life and disability insurance to young families without significant assets living on every dollar that they earn. Never purchase decreasing term insurance, and never buy insurance through your mortgage insurance provider, your car loan company, your home loan company, or your leasing company. Those policies usually are two to three times more expensive than you would pay through insurance outlets such as those mentioned in this chapter. It is also best to separate your insurance from your credit union account or other loans.

Source: Sutherland, PH. *Zenvesting, The Art of Abundance and Managing Money.* Suttons Bay, MI: Financial Sourcebook, 1998.

parents with children, second marriages in which there are children, or when children are involved with life partners.

Through a life insurance trust, you can have event-driven dispositions so the children get the money when they graduate from college, marry, join the Peace Corps, and so on, as described in the estate-planning event-driven disposition part of this book (page 97). Because children eventually become independent and do not need life insurance, it is best to have term insurance—depending on how long you perceive the need to be, which is often based on the age of the children—that funds life insurance trusts. Usually a 5- to 15-year term policy should be purchased within the life insurance trust. Your lawyer working with your fee-only financial advisor can guide you in this regard.

Insurance on Children

Do not waste insurance premiums on significant amounts of life insurance on children. The main reason to purchase insurance on children is to provide them with a guaranteed right to buy more insurance as they get older when they will need more insurance. Otherwise, it is possible that they could become uninsurable. Some companies sell policies that have, perhaps, an initial $10,000 death benefit, and the policies can then be changed up to $250,000 worth of insurance when the child reaches a certain age, buys a home, gets married, and so on.

Financial Privacy

Often when you are shopping for insurance, you are asked to give out significant amounts of medical, personal, and financial information. The companies you provide this information to should have a strict policy of financial privacy. Although the companies we recommend have privacy policies, the strictest I have seen is through Low Load Insurance Services. Your information should not be used except to issue policies or for the purpose for which it was intended. Maintaining privacy is not about hiding anything from anyone but about controlling the information about you and your family.

Confidentiality

A banker once said to me, "Sutherland, I don't think it's appropriate to look at your client's financial situation, because I heard through the rumor mill that his partner is going through a protracted divorce, and it could affect the value of the practice." Such "soft" information can influence ability to borrow or have the most favorable rates in relationships with various service providers. It is best to keep confidential as much financial and personal information about yourself as possible. In our practice, we simply do not disclose who our clients are. Once when I was in the hospital, two clients happened to introduce themselves to each other. They walked away not knowing they were both my clients.

Confidentiality starts in the office. Explain to your staff that anything about your personal situation and the practice is not public knowledge: a new home, a second home on Maui, the trip to Bali; all is private information that is unnecessary for your staff, friends, or business associates to give out. The bottom line is that, within reason, everything they know about your situation, patients, partners, family, marriage, and friends should be kept confidential. As a condition of employment, there should be agreements they sign to keep this information private.

Phone Calls

The most irritating and common methods of invading privacy are phone calls and solicitations on your home phone.

Following are some tips to keep solicitations and calls to a minimum:

1. Use your business address or post office box for newsletters, magazines, and subscriptions

2. Do not put Doctor, MD, DO, and PhD as part of your name in subscriptions. Often, first initial and last name is best.

3. Use your first initial rather than your first name.

4. Have subscriptions to personal periodicals addressed to your spouse, or use your children's names. Use first initial and last name for spouse and children, too.

5. Use your initials and your last name with credit cards, if they will allow this. Have credit card statements, even the personal ones, sent to your post office box or office address.

6. Leave MD or DO off your checks, credit cards, and signature.

7. Instruct your family, friends, and acquaintances to call or write to you by just your first name. Tell them you are not offended if they write Sam Jones instead of Dr Jones.

8. When you meet with your banker, attorney, certified public accountant, insurance agent, or financial planners, always begin and end the conversation by talking about and stressing the importance of confidentiality. If incorrect information gets out about you, set the record straight. If an unreasonable or incorrect story circulates about an event that happened in your life, sit down with a public relations person or your lawyer to discuss options for minimizing any damage. If you know someone who is spreading rumors that could be harmful, meet with that person and say, "I just want you to know that what you have been saying about me (my family, my partner) is not true. If you repeat it, you will know you are being untruthful."

Additional Steps for Financial Confidentiality

- Use an assumed name when filing "doing business as" (DBA) names, trusts, or limited liability corporations, as advised by your lawyer for larger transactions to keep information confidential.
- Put only your initials on your mailbox. Paint the box red so friends can find it.
- Use a safety deposit box for your possessions. Photocopy the contents of the box and keep a list of the box's contents in your home's fireproof safe.
- Conduct your business only with companies that have a reputation for a high degree of honesty and sustainability and that have an impeccable reputation.
- Check references, financial stability, and the principals of the companies and their representatives, and in general the people that you do business with.
- Check your credit records at local credit bureaus periodically to assure that the information is accurate and up-to-date.
- Be honest in all of your business dealings and in all aspects of your life.
- Pay your bills on time.
- Always maintain the highest level of integrity in all your relationships, both business and personal.
- On a lighter note, here are some "sample" phone messages for security-conscious people:

    "We are either out walking the Doberman or cleaning the rifles and unable to get to the phone. Please leave a message."

    "We are gone for the week. Uncle George, could you please call our neighbor Bob and ask for the home security system code so when you feed the pit bulls, you don't set the security system off?"

Jokes aside, if you have children at home alone, instruct them to take a message and to tell strangers that you are not available at the moment. For most of us, use of high-tech gadgetry (phone recorders, beepers, high-tech fences, scanners) is going way too far. But, what offers peace of mind will be different for everybody. There are many resources on the Internet that can meet your security needs.

Passports

Everyone should have a passport. You never know when you will need to take an emergency trip to another country, and waiting for a passport could be frustrating. A US passport is the highest form of personal identification that can be obtained. If you are traveling anywhere in the United States or abroad, a passport will not be questioned, unlike a birth certificate, photo identification card, or state driver's license. A passport is worth the money. One can be obtained by checking out the Web site, www.travel.state.gov. In addition, contact the National Passport Information Center (NPIC) toll-free at (877) 487-2778.

When should you get a passport for children? When you know their names!

Frequently Asked Questions About Passports and Citizenship Documents

Where do I get a passport application?
You may download forms from the Web site, www.travel.state.gov.
Forms are also available at public offices like post offices, courthouses, and municipal offices where passport applications are accepted.

What are the passport fees?
Age 16 and older: The passport application fee is $67. The execution fee is $30. The total is **$97**.
Under Age 16: The passport application fee is $52. The execution fee is $30. The total is **$82**.

The passport application fee includes the $12 Security Surcharge, which became effective March 8, 2005.

My child who is under 18 needs a passport. How do I get it?
If your child is under 14, he or she must appear in person. Parents or legal guardians may apply on behalf of their child.
Either parents' or legal guardians' consent is required for minors under age 14.
Either parents or legal guardians must show current, valid identification.

If your child is aged 14 to 17, your child must appear in person. Your parental consent may be requested.

Low-Load Insurance Term Rates 1

Term Life Quote from *Low Load Insurance*

    Advisor Name: Advisor   *Date: 0/0/00*

Proposed Insured Name: Mr. Client   *State:* **TBD**

DOB: 0/0/00   Non-Smoker   **Insurance Age: 45**

Face Amount $300,000

Term: 10-Year Guaranteed Rates

	Preferred Plus	Preferred
Company A	$233	$290
Company B	$233	$290
Company C	$236	$293

Term: 15-Year Guaranteed Rates

	Preferred Plus	Preferred
Company A	$314	$404
Company B	$317	$362
Company C	$320	$365

Term: 20-Year Guaranteed Rates

	Preferred Plus	Preferred
Company A	$401	$473
Company B	$401	$473
Company C	$407	$476

Rates quoted on an Annual Mode (monthly bank drafts available for an extra charge)

Ratings: Insurance companies have an A+ or higher rating by A.M. Best and an 85 or higher Comdex rating by Vital Signs. Exceptions will be identified and explained.

Optional Benefits:
  Children's Protection Rider (Rates & Features Vary Among Companies)
  Waiver of Premium Rider
  Accelerated Benefit Rider (Most States)

Low-Load Insurance Term Rates 2

Term Life Quote from Low Load Insurance

Advisor Name: Advisor *Date: 0/0/00*

Proposed Insured Name: Mr. Client *State: **TBD***

DOB: 0/0/00   Non-Smoker   Insurance Age: 41

Face Amount $250,000

Term: 10-Year Guaranteed Rates

	Preferred Plus	**Preferred**
Company A	$130	$160
Company B	$130	$160
Company C	$132	$162

Term: 15-Year Guaranteed Rates

	Preferred Plus	**Preferred**
Company A	$160	$202
Company B	$160	$198
Company C	$162	$210

Term: 20-Year Guaranteed Rates

	Preferred Plus	**Preferred**
Company A	$192	$240
Company B	$192	$240
Company C	$195	$245

Rates quoted on an Annual Mode (monthly bank drafts available for an extra charge)

Ratings: Insurance companies have an A+ or higher rating by A.M. Best and an 85 or higher Comdex rating by Vital Signs. Exceptions will be identified and explained.

Optional Benefits:
  Children's Protection Rider (Rates & Features Vary Among Companies)
  Waiver of Premium Rider
  Accelerated Benefit Rider (Most States)

CHAPTER 3
Homes and Real Estate

Houses versus Homes

Your home should not be considered an investment; it is a lifestyle asset. You should buy the house that gets you to "wow" and that keeps you in "wow, gotta own it" mode after you have reviewed this chapter, especially the "Size of Home" worksheets (page 72 and 73) and the "Pay Up/Don't Pay Up" box (page 69). General rules about houses are area-specific. In some areas, it is difficult to spend more than 15% of your income to support a 30-year fixed rate mortgage. In others, like Los Angeles, San Francisco, Hawaii, Boston, New York, and West Palm Beach, it is difficult to spend less than 25%. Usually, incomes are higher in high housing cost areas, but often not high enough for a primary care physician to buy all the house he or she wants or needs. Balance and knowledge of your needs and wants are key. I have met and worked with physicians who have happily raised families of four in a 1,400-square-foot home, and others who need 6,000 square feet for just the two of them. Both would say they love their home. Regardless of the house you buy, if it meets many of your "pay up" criteria, it will grow to be your dream home. When children go off to college, the house might be sold or the child's bedroom might become a library, exercise room, or walk-in closet and bath. Kitchens become like the ones featured on the cooking channel, and yards become gardens. Regardless of your lifestyle, your house is a place of security, comfort, and utility as well as a place to sleep, eat, work on hobbies, socialize, and relax.

The worksheets in this chapter are designed to guide you in making good choices regarding your home. For most physicians, housing is usually the largest expense after taxes, and for young physicians, it usually exceeds savings by a wide margin.

Trading at Home: Time for Money

Nowhere in my experience do values intersect with money more than in the home decision and the lifestyle it reflects. We trade time for money, and each of us must balance how much we will work to afford the home we want. It is okay to forego the retirement contributions or savings for our children's college to buy "more home" if we realize the consequences of paying up, such as working longer into retirement age.

Young families are going to be broke, so "don't sweat it" as I say in the debt management chapter. Life is long; relax and strive for balance.

Pay Up/Don't Pay Up

Pay Up to Be. . . .
- Close to work
  - Saves time
- Close to schools
  - Saves time, easier on children
- Close to family and friends
  - Great for children to be near them
- Where you like to play
  - Parks, rails-to-trails, water, health club, golf course
- A homebody
  - Want home to be a castle; for entertaining, ease of living, prestige
- Near airport, bus route, trails, if you spend weekends flying to your second home
- Add your own "pay ups":
  - _____
  - _____

Home: You can build a house anyplace, but a home is where the kitchen table is—where the family eats.

Don't Pay Up . . .

For more house than you will need, unless it meets a lot of your "pay up" criteria

Because all the docs live there! (Often, however, there is a reason all the doctors live in a certain area: good schools, close to hospital, close to recreation, etc)

For temporary needs
- To be near best schools for 2 or fewer years; in that case, rent or commute
- To be near ailing parents (It is great to be near them; however, rent if you cannot find that perfect or sort-of-perfect "wow" house.)

Double Your Pleasure, Triple Your Pain, With Debt

We all know, especially from recent experience, that significant wealth can be generated through ownership of real estate. But, what many do not understand is that the bulk of such gains often is the result of leverage rather than pure appreciation. What many people also do not realize, especially those who have not yet had the privilege of experiencing a real estate decline, is that this same leverage can be devastating when it works against you if you buy in a real estate market bubble. For example, if you purchase a property at a price of $1 million with 30% down, the down payment would be $300,000. If the property appreciates 30% in market value, the investor's equity appreciates by 100%, from $300,000 to $600,000. However, if that property declines in value by only 15%, the investor loses half of the equity, with the $300,000 of equity falling to $150,000. The following table summarizes some hypothetical situations:

Percentage of Gain or Loss on Net Investments

Equity Amount	Debt Amount	25% Decline	50% Decline	25% Increase	25% Increase
90%	10%	−28%	−56%	28%	56%
70%	30%	−36%	−71%	36%	71%
50%	50%	−50%	Total loss	50%	100%
25%	75%	Total loss	Total loss	100%	200%

Borrowing for investment has a place, for your home or office building, for example, or for the lot next to your home that gives you enjoyment. Borrowing to invest in stocks, raw land, art, commodities, private investments, or bonds carries special risks and, of course, heightened rewards. Before you borrow for stocks, to buy that oil deal or to leverage your balance sheet and risk your neck in some real estate deal, know the special risks. The first question to ask is, "Would I be bothered, lose sleep, or feel wiped out if the investment lost value?" The second is, "Does this purchase fit into my life plan?" The third is, "What would my level-headed advisor say?" Finally, the fourth question is, "If the investment doubles would it make a difference in my lifestyle if it dropped by half?"

Disaster Relief

Hurricane Katrina happens. Fires happen. Volcanoes and earthquakes happen. Simple electrical outages sometimes happen, and go on for many days. Common sense would direct having a backpack filled with supplies in case you had to leave your home in a hurry. Flashlights, safety matches, water purifying tablets, prescription medications, flares, survival ponchos, a space blanket, a medical kit, duct tape, a compass, a shortwave radio, and other supplies specific to your needs should be in the backpack. If the electricity or gas went out for a week, would you freeze to death or burn the furniture to keep warm? A simpler plan might be to have firewood for your fireplace or a portable gas heater. Of course, water and food would be logical, too—your grocery store might not open. Maybe you would allow yourself to be a victim and say, "Where is the government? I have no heat! I have little food!" My suggestion is to think, "What if a hurricane, a forest fire, or an earthquake hits my home? What would I have wished I had done beforehand?" For example, is your car full of gas or at least half full at all times?

Selling Your Home

The sale of your primary home is generally unreported on your tax returns unless the gain exceeds an exclusion amount. The Internal Revenue Service (IRS) has provided the ability to exclude from income up to $250,000 (if single) and $500,000 (if married and filing jointly) on the gain from the sale of your home, if certain requirements are met. First, the residence needs to meet the ownership test and the use test: **both spouses must have** owned and used the residence as their principal residence for at least 2 out of the 5 years prior to the sale. In addition, each spouse is limited to selling a home no more than once every 2 years. A single person must also meet the same time frame for ownership, use, and frequency. Even though the exclusion rules have removed a lot of the complexity from the calculation and reporting requirements from home sales, it is still important to track improvements to your home. Home improvements become part of your investment or cost-basis, and may potentially aid you in staying under the gain-exclusion limits.

A common question is, "How do the exclusion rules apply to the sale of my second home?" Unfortunately, the gain exclusion only applies to your primary residence. The IRS has issued final regulations regarding taxpayers who alternate between two homes, whereby the home that is used for the majority of the time during the year is considered the principal residence.

Size of Home Worksheet #1

This worksheet can be used to help you assess how much home you can afford. Your estimated monthly income coming into budget is your income to budget (ITB): $_____.
After taxes and employment deduction:

Where you chose to spend your income; estimate monthly:

- A. Food and restaurants — $_____
- B. Phones, Internet, cable, BlackBerry™ — $_____
- C. Auto payments or lease — $_____
- D. Auto insurance, gas, maintenance — $_____
- E. Travel, vacations, seminars, family visits — $_____
- F. Entertainment, gifts, recreation, health club — $_____
- G. Clothing, makeup, hair stylist — $_____
- H. Life, disability, hospital/medical insurance — $_____
- I. To retirement plans through 401(k), IRA, 403(b) (10%) — $_____
- J. Childcare, school expenses, children's miscellaneous — $_____
- K. Food, toiletries, household expenses (cleaning service, supplies, etc) — $_____
- L. Loan payments (spread out*) — $_____
- M. Credit card expenses not listed above — $_____
- N. Savings surplus for liquidity, children's education, retirement, second home, etc, at 10% to 20% or whatever makes you comfortable — $_____

Non-housing spending (NHS):

Total all spending before housing A through N: $_____ (NHS)

    ITB: $_____ (Income to budget, from above line)

    NHS $_____ Non-housing spending, subtract from above ITB

    AFH $_____ (Available for housing) first home, second home, etc

---

*See "Debt Management" illustrations on page 34 and 36.
IRA indicates individual retirement account.

Source: © Paul Sutherland, Financial and Investment Management Group (www.fimg.net). A printable version of this work sheet is available at www.fimg.net, All Rights Reserved.

CHAPTER 3 Homes and Real Estate

If there is any question about which home is your primary residence, the IRS will use relevant factors such as your place of employment; the principal place of abode of your family; the address listed on federal and state tax returns, driver's license, automobile registration, and voter registration card; mailing address for bills and correspondence; and the location of banks, religious organizations, and recreational clubs. Go to www.IRS.gov for more details. Of course, your certified public accountant can guide you in the specifics of how these rules apply to you.

Size of Home Worksheet #2

Amount available for housing, $_____ monthly*
(from "Size of Home Worksheet #1" on page 72)

Estimated monthly cost of owning a home without debt (payment included)

- Approximate utilities*: electric, heat, gas, condo fees, etc $ +_____
- Approximate property taxes† ÷ 12 $ +_____
- Approximate maintenance: 1% of home value ÷ 12 $ +_____
                                                         Total $ =_____

Amount available for housing $ _____
Estimated cost of owning home without debt $ −_____
Available for debt service $ =_____

Now that you have the amount available for debt service, you can do "upside-down math" to figure out how much home you can afford, or ask a mortgage broker. A mortgage broker can guide you to the right mortgage, which usually is a fixed rate, no points, fully amortized over 30 years mortgage or one that balloons in 4 to 10 years (if you do not think you will be in the home for over 10 years). To check the broker's numbers, enter www.netbank.com, or type "home mortgage/your town & state" in your browser's search engine.

Payment $_____ ÷ factor from below = amount of house payment will support $_____

Example: Payment of $3,000 ÷ $665 = $451,000. Mortgage amount supported by a 7%, 30-year loan. (See "Interest Rate/Mortgage Payment Table" on page 74.)

---

*If you rent or lease, this is what you can afford including utilities.
†Your Realtor® can provide this information to you in writing.

> ### Interest Rate/Mortgage Payment Table
>
> Payment at various maturities and interest rates for $100,000 mortgage:
>
> 30 year at 5% = $536; 6% = $600; 7% = $665; 8% = $734; 10% = $878
>
> 15 year at 5% = $791; 6% = $843; 7% = $899; 8% = $956; 10% = $1,075
>
> Interest-only at 5% = $417; 6% = $500; 7% = $583; 8% = $667; 10% = $833
>
> If current rates are 7% on a 30-year mortgage and your home costs $600,000 with $100,000 down, your mortgage would be $500,000 and your payment $3,325 (665 × 5).

Buy or Rent?

Whether you buy or rent a home depends on how long you plan to be there. It usually makes sense to purchase outright if you plan to stay 4 years or longer. Owning your home will increase your feeling of well-being and stability. If you plan to live in an area for a short period, for example, during residency, renting is a better choice. This allows you to save the difference toward a down payment on a future home. There are many methods of figuring the economic sense of buying or renting. Most people like the stability of ownership. It truly should not be a financial decision. Rather, home-ownership should be an attitudinal or emotional decision. Naturally, if you do not like the idea of being tied down, renting or leasing is probably your best bet.

Whether to purchase or rent real estate to live in is a unique decision based primarily on comfort, personal preference, and lifestyle. Although you should be aware of financial limitations, remember that your home is the cornerstone of a balanced life. If you start looking at a home as an investment, it will drive you and your family crazy.

Resalability

Always buy the house you want and need, which meets your pay-up criteria and budget. Do not assume your house will be worth more in the future because you paid up. The housing market can be a fickle story: one day big houses on big lots are in; the next day, downtown condos or townhouses are hot.

Selling a Home

If you are considering using a Realtor® when selling your home or property, the "Selling Your Home" checklist on page 76 will help you appraise your needs, find a Realtor, and analyze whether he or she can help you sell your home. Using an experienced, successful, full-time Realtor as the marketing professional for your home can greatly benefit the sale. A poor one, on the other hand, can do more harm than good. If you decide to use a Realtor, make it a point to choose the best. The checklist should assist you in making this decision.

Statistics show that the average person moves every 5 to 7 years. Each of the houses you own during your lifetime will be a major financial transaction at the time of sale. Obviously, it is important that you get top-dollar while minimizing costs associated with the sale. Depending on the location and market, it may be possible to sell your home yourself. This saves you Realtor fees of between 3% and 10%. Remember, choosing to do so takes time and knowledge (your lawyer can help), but may be worth trying, even for a few months. A Realtor, of course, can also help when purchasing a home. His or her experience may enable you to choose between two seemingly equal homes in separate subdivisions based on sales history or news of future industrial developments, which could lower the joy of owning the home and lower the surrounding property values. A savvy Realtor can also help you with financing decisions (whether to buy or rent) and refer you to a competent lawyer to help you review legal documents. Often Realtors work exclusively for their clients on a fee-only basis—this is often the best arrangement.

Your Office

The choice of location of your office should be based on the convenience of your patients and your proximity to the hospital. Ideally, it should also be easy to find and have adequate parking. For primary care, often it is best to have your office stand alone so that the building can serve as an advertisement for your practice. Keep the purchase cost as reasonable as possible, and consider spending an extra dollar or two per square foot for a great location. In my experience, one of the best investments a physician can make is buying his or her office. By doing so you avoid the potential misfortunes of landlord and tenant relationships, including property misuse. As an owner, you will be able to build to suit your specific needs. Make sure, however, that you are satisfied and comfortable with the area you are practicing in, as

Selling Your Home

What to look for in your Realtor®:

1. Experience and honesty
2. Full-time and career-oriented
3. Successful and competent
4. Professional in attitude and appearance
5. Aggressive
6. Up-to-date on new marketing methods and the real estate business
7. Willing to work on a fixed commission or fee-only basis

Your Realtor should

1. Give you a written market value appraisal listing the specifics of how he or she came to the asking price for your home
2. Give you a written marketing plan of action on how he or she will market your home (open houses, newspaper ads, brochures, etc)
3. Give you a list of references that you can call
4. Assist you with a home appearance checklist to help make your home more marketable

Your real estate agent's firm should:

1. Be a member of a multiple-listing service
2. Be reputable and serve your local area
3. Be career-oriented; hire only full-time career professionals
4. Have a local and national network referral service if you are in major metropolitan areas such as New York, Chicago, or Detroit.

For more information, contact the National Association of Realtors
430 N. Michigan Ave.
Chicago, IL 60611-4087
Web site: www.realtor.com.

You should:

1. Consider selling your house on your own before listing it if you and your spouse have the time and temperament. You can hire a competent real estate appraiser and lawyer to help.
2. Make sure you feel completely comfortable with your Realtor and his or her firm, if you choose to work with a Realtor.
3. Complete the tasks highlighted in your home appearance checklist (keep lawn mowed, fresh cut-flowers, fix watermarks, etc).
4. Read over a listing agreement carefully before signing; make sure you write in exceptions, such as listing fixtures or built-in items (bar, chandelier, bookshelves, desk, light fixtures, etc) that are not included in the sale of the property, to the listing.
5. Be away from the house during showings and open houses.
6. Have a lawyer review all closing documents regarding your real estate transactions prior to closing.

well as with the type of practice you have (associate or sole practitioner) before you purchase an office building.

Advantages to owning an office building:
1. Tax benefit
2. Inflation hedge
3. Build equity
4. Building improvement benefit
5. Tenant control

Disadvantages to owning an office building:
1. Lack of liquidity
2. Inability to pay the mortgage
3. Lack of mobility
4. Possibility property value could go down
5. Tax laws could change

Real Estate as an Investment

If you are considering a real estate purchase for investment reasons, analyze the property as you would any other investment. Real estate tends to be clouded by tax benefits. One of the best ways to break down any real estate investment is to disregard the tax benefits completely. Imagine you are buying the property with cash. If the deal looks good without the tax and leverage benefits (debt) to finance the property, you probably have a project that merits further consideration.

Real estate should never be purchased as a tax shelter. Buy only if you feel it will make money in excess of the rates of return that you could receive on other investments. Although many people have become wealthy through real estate investments, many others have been ruined. As with any investment, diversify your real estate holdings, and make sure that you do not purchase any single investment that could harm you financially if it failed completely.

Real estate partnerships offer a piece of the action if you do not have a lot of cash. Many partnerships tend to be formed casually, so proceed slowly into deals with friends, family, or anyone else. Again, there is no reason to jeopardize your financial health with a get-rich-quick (or slow) scheme; any deal that sounds too good to be true probably is.

When considering a real estate investment, make a point to have a fee-only real estate professional, financial planner, accountant, or attorney familiar with real estate review the transaction. Contingencies like balloon payments on debt, lack of total occupancy, and zoning problems can usually be spotted by a financial service professional, further protecting you from unpleasant surprises. The professional's advice will be cold and objective, but the decision will still be yours.

If you are considering purchasing real estate as an investment, educate yourself by reading up on the subject, or make use of the many fine professionals who can help you. Hire them just as you would other professionals. You or your spouse should consider getting a real estate license if you plan on investing heavily in real estate.

CHAPTER 4
Children and Education

Saving for College

The College Board (www.collegeboard.com) reported that average college cost for 2004 to 2005 at a 4-year private college was $20,082 (up 6% from the previous year) and at a 4-year public college was $5,132 (up 10.5% from the previous year). Medical school's average cost is $14,577 for public medical schools and $30,960 for private schools according to the AMSA (American Medical Student Association). This is up 528% and 345%, respectively, from 1981.

Understanding available options and carefully mapping out a long-term strategy are key to successfully funding a child's college education. Several steps can help you meet this goal: start early, estimate projected needs, select appropriate investments, take advantage of available tax deductions and savings incentives, and, if necessary, borrow wisely. In general, physicians who have an adjusted gross income of $130,000 or more are unlikely to qualify for government grants, subsidized loans, or other types of education tax incentives (eg, Hope Credit, Lifetime Learning Credit, or Tuition Deductions). Therefore, one of the keys to successfully investing in your child's education is to start saving early. Saving early will produce the benefit of compounding of investment return over the long investment horizon, which will have a great impact on funds available for college. Although there are many ways to pay for college (eg, personal savings, current income, financial

> ### Education Advice from Judy
>
> While we used to think of education as "college," it seems that more and more we are funding education from preschool through college, and the costs are rising. In some areas, public education is no longer a viable choice for many. However, private school costs are rising at more than double the cost of inflation. Preschool costs can run from $4,000 to $10,000 per year, elementary education ranges from $4,000 to $20,000 depending on the area, and high school costs range from $6,000 to $50,000. Add to this the cost of a university education at $25,000 to $60,000 per year, and you begin to talk about real money.
>
> Some people attempt to pay for elementary and high school through cash flow and save for college through longer-term accounts. My own children relocated from Pasadena, California, to Richardson, Texas, largely for our grandson to be able to attend a quality public school and thereby avoid the cost of private education at the elementary and high school levels.

By Judy McCorkle, Financial and Investment Management Group Trust, Estate Planning and Advising

loans), the more net worth personal savings (even if in retirement plans) you accumulate, the more options you will have and the less you will have to rely upon borrowing, student loans, and other means of funding college costs. Always fund your tax-qualified retirement plan at 100% of what you can deposit in it before setting aside any funds specifically earmarked for your child's college expenses.

529 College Savings Plan

The 529 College Savings Plan is a great option that allows you to make contributions on a tax-efficient basis to your child's future tuition needs. One of the major benefits of the 529 plan is the power of compounded investment returns realized because the assets grow tax-free until the funds are needed for college. In addition to being able to make tax-free withdrawals from the 529 plans to meet qualified higher education expenses, some states offer an immediate state tax deduction for contributions made to an in-state 529 plan. (Note that as currently legislated, the tax-free withdrawals are set to expire after 2010.) Some states even offer matching contributions as an effort to stimulate participation. Each state has adopted at least one 529 plan. Investors have flexibility in investing in either their own state 529 plan or an out-of-state plan. Caution should be given to investing in an out-of-state plan, because investors sometimes miss out on important in-state tax advantages, and several states impose taxes on qualified withdrawals from out-of-state plans. However, it should be noted that several states have been singled out as having plans with excessive fees and poor choices of investments. (Excessive plans are considered those with annual fees of 2.5% or more, sales fees, high fund expenses, and, often, low performance.) Morningstar (www.morningstar.com) has noted the following states as major offenders: Maine, Arizona, Pennsylvania, Nebraska, and Ohio. Listed among the best programs were Michigan's Education Savings Program, Virginia's College America, and Minnesota's College Savings Plan. (Information reported in Kristin

---

The Education Culture Concept

Do you want your children to go to college? Want them to excel in school? Would you like them to get a good job that they enjoy? This all starts with creating an education and "work is fun" culture in your home. Children learn from observation and tend to be guided by our actions more than our words as parents.

Simple phrases like, "When you go to college . . ." not, "*If* you go to college . . ." and, "Gosh, I loved learning about the human body, DNA, or history while I was at Michigan State University . . ." are going to be the "honey" that draws them to college.

Studies have concluded that how much children enjoy their work is reflective of how much their parents enjoyed work as well as the first-job experiences the children had (*I Love This Job! The Ms. Foundation for Women Makes It Easier for Working Parents to Connect with Their Kids.* New York, Wednesday, April 20, 2005). Work is fun, it is enjoyable, it is work, but personally, I would rather work than read a romance novel, watch golf, or ice fish. As parents, we need to make sure our children's first jobs are fun, enjoyable, and meaningful. An education culture nourishes curiosity, discipline, excellence, optimism, ideas, discussion, trying, and trying again.

Family travel, books, discussions, plays, movies, sports, school events, and the like are all part of creating an educational, "work is fulfilling" culture. Video games, television, drugs, alcohol, and being alone in their room all the time or at the mall with friends also create culture.

Source: The Education Culture concept comes from many sources, including the books *Children Are from Heaven* (New York, NY: Harper Collins 1999) and *The Optimistic Child* (New York, NY: Houghton Mifflin, 1995). Both are great reads.

Davis. "College Bound–State College Savings Plans." Kiplinger's Personal Finance Magazine (Aug. 2000): 59[5]; 110–117.

Compared with a Uniform Gifts to Minors Act (UGMA) custodial account (http://en.wikipedia.org/wiki/Uniform_Gifts_to_Minors_Act), the 529 plan (http://www.sec.gov/investor/pubs/intro529.htm) offers more control over the assets, because unlike UGMA accounts, your child does not have legal title at the age of majority (18 or 21 in most states). As the account holder of the 529 plan, you can change the beneficiary of the plan to another child, your spouse, or even yourself if issues arise and the original beneficiary does not elect to further his or her education. Even though you maintain control over the use of the funds in the plan, these assets are out of your taxable estate if you were to die.

For each beneficiary, you are able to contribute, without affecting your taxes, up to $11,000 per year to the 529 plan. In 2005, the government gave the ability to "front-end load" the investment plan with $55,000 per beneficiary in 1 year. However, you will not be able to make any additional contributions or other gifts for the same beneficiary for 5 years unless you use some of your unified estate tax credit. The maximum contribution that can be made for one beneficiary over his or her lifetime can range from $100,000 to $235,000,

---

"Problem Kids" Advice from Judy

When a child is a "problem kid," what is the nature of the problem? Is he or she doing something really destructive—using drugs or alcohol, showing aggressive behavior, or not performing up to your expectations? It is important to separate real problems from differences. Obviously, if the behavior is such that it will harm the child or others, intervention is in order. And as a parent, you need to be aware that your control only goes so far. Sometimes in spite of your best efforts, you may become powerless over your own children. Drugs and alcohol are strong forces, and you have about a 50-50 chance when dealing with these challenges at later ages. The best prevention is to develop your relationship with your child very early and provide a firm foundation for self-worth and security. A rich intellectual and personal life and a strong sense of self are the best antidote to drugs. Whatever the challenge, my personal rule is that the children only get to blame their parents for their messed-up lives until they are age 40. After that, they are responsible.

By Judy McCorkle, Financial and Investment Management Group Trust, Estate Planning and Advising depending upon your individual state's plan. You should consult with your fee-only financial planner or certified public accountant (CPA) to determine if you wish to exceed the $11,000 or $55,000 one-time limit.

Depending on the individual plan offerings, you typically will have three investment options: an equity option, a guaranteed fixed-income type option, and an age-based or managed allocation. Extreme caution needs to be taken in this selection, because most plans only allow for a reallocation of investments once a year. The portfolio management chapter can help guide your allocations. My advice is, when in doubt, choose the fixed or bond option.

For an up-to-date list of 529 plans and a state-by-state comparison tool, go to www.savingforcollege.com, or visit www.irs.gov for the detailed description in Internal Revenue Service Publication 970.

Education Individual Retirement Accounts for Private High School

Depending on your income, you might be able to also fund a Coverdell Education Savings Account (ESA), formerly known as an Education Independent Retirement Account (IRA). For joint filers, the phase-out range for contributors is $190,000 to $220,000 of modified adjusted gross income. ESAs enable parents to contribute up to $2,000 per year per child. Contributions to an ESA are nondeductible. Earnings in the account are tax deferred, and subsequent distributions are tax-free if used for qualified educational expenses. One of the major differences between an ESA and the 529 plan is that distributions from an ESA for elementary and secondary education are also considered qualified tax-free withdrawals. This might be beneficial if your children or grandchildren attend private elementary or high school. For individuals who exceed the income limits, a planning opportunity allows for the grandparents to make the contribution to your child's ESA, assuming they fall under the income limits.

For the physician who comes up short on savings at college time, funding your child's education out of pocket or with other financial assistance are two options. The chances are good that a physician with high income will be disqualified from financial assistance. There is no set amount for what is considered as high income because the expected family contribution calculation takes into account both income and assets owned in both the parents and child's name. The calculation also takes into account size of household, other family members attending college, and mortgage amounts. Do not automatically assume you do not qualify for tuition assistance. At a minimum, you should go through the motions of completing a financial aid application to verify if you have any eligibility. A financial aid calculator is available at www.finaid.org. This Web site also has a special section devoted to financing medical school.

Scholarships

Scholarships are also an excellent source of funds for your child's college. Scholarships come in many different sizes and shapes and are largely dependent upon your child's academic, extracurricular, or career plans. Your child's high school counselor's office and the college aid section of your local public library or bookstore are starting points in researching scholarships. Counselors will know about scholarships for students graduating from their high school. They may also be aware of scholarships for residents of your town, county, and state. The large national scholarship programs include the Reserve Officer Training Corps (ROTC), National Merit, and larger corporation sponsors. Because a great deal of scholarship money is disbursed directly by colleges, it makes sense to also research what kinds of scholarships are available at your child's favorite colleges. There is a considerable amount of latitude in this area. Your child's ability to secure scholarship money is largely dependent on how attractive he or she is as a total candidate package to the institution.

Loans

Finally, there are a variety of financing options available for families concerned about their ability to meet their share of costs. These alternative sources of aid, most often in the form of loans, can help to cover financial aid gaps or unmet needs in a financial aid package. There are two primary types of education loans to parents of children attending college. The Federal PLUS loan is the most popular for the parents of dependent undergraduate students. You can borrow up to the full cost of education minus any financial aid. The loan interest rate is variable, with the cap on the interest being 9%. Repayment of the loan can be deferred until the entire loan is fully disbursed to the college. Qualification for the loan is dependent upon a good credit standing. Private banks also offer direct education loans for parents to help pay educational costs with applicable interest rates that are typically higher than PLUS loans.

Another college financing avenue for children of high-income earners is the Unsubsidized Federal Stafford Loan Program. The program is available to all students regardless of need and offers the deferral of interest until the end of college. This should not be confused with the Subsidized Stafford Loan that offers the additional benefit of the government picking up the tab for the interest while your child is in college. Unfortunately, the Subsidized Stafford Loan, as well as the Federal Pell Grant program that offers free money for college and the favorable Perkins Loan program, are awarded to students with exceptional financial need. It is unlikely that children of physicians will qualify for any of these programs based on income and net worth. More information is available about these loans at www.staffordloan.com.

Today, a child's ability to go to the college of his or her choice involves more than just getting good grades or writing the perfect application essay. The upward spiral of tuition and room and board means cost is more a factor than ever before. Although most parents want their children to attend the school of their choice, many either fail to plan in advance for the expense or are unable to cope with costs that are rising faster than the inflation rate. Planning early for your children's college education can help you determine how best to use your resources to help them to go to college.

Cows Plus Ice Cream Equal College

When his oldest child turned 14, my uncle bought an ice cream store that was open only in the summer so that his children could have a summer job to accumulate money for college. All through school, my cousins worked long days at the store. They were able to earn a significant amount toward their college education through the store's revenues and learned a lot about business. Living in rural Michigan, I once interviewed some 4-H children who raised cows to earn money for college, for a local radio station. These children also worked on their mother and father's farm during the summers. A great way for children to accumulate money for college is through work, because the earnings accrue to the children who are in a low tax bracket. It is much easier for them to have the income coming to them, filing their own tax return, and paying the modest, if any, tax on that income. Usually, there are some well-paying jobs around, and in fact, sometimes the child could work for the parents. For this to work, first he or she has to actually work for you, and second, he or she has to be paid a reasonable compensation. For example, if everyone else doing light duty in your practice is earning $20 per hour and you pay your son $50 per hour, the $30 extra income would be considered nondeductible by you. However, the reasonable compensation is deductible, and this allows you to have a significant part in the children's college education paid for at low tax rates. Also, some schools look at an emancipated child who is filing his or her own tax return and considered independent of parents more favorably when it comes to financial aid than they would otherwise.

Another popular technique has worked, especially with larger families who have card-carrying members of the school (ie the parent who says, "All of my children will go to XYZ college."). I have found that such parents have bought college rental homes or apartments for their children to rent to fellow students, which manage to provide income for school.

Finding good renters and making sure that the children do not party too hard and destroy the place with raucous behavior are all great educational experiences for young adults. They learn to be assertive, strong, and good communicators. They also learn something that is discussed in other chapters: the importance of making sure the people they allow into their circles come with appropriate, clean, neat, and respectful habits. The education that they get from this experience is probably more valuable than the 4-years of college education at most colleges. Last year, one of my clients bought a home for his daughter to live in and rent to other students throughout college. For the first year, she had all college kids sharing the house. For the second year, she only rented to non-college kids. From chatting with her Dr Dad she had "quite a lot of learning about honesty, responsibility, and follow-through that first year," he explained proudly. He said she learned to be tough and straightforward—and was proud that she had the creativity to only rent to serious, responsible non-students. "It's been better than business school for her," he said.

With the high costs of college, you may need to use multiple strategies. One that was often used before the 529 plans was UGMA accounts, which become available when the child reaches age 18, or the age of majority. When the child reaches 18 and has access to the money, he or she can use it for anything, not necessarily college. One of my client's children found out at age 19 that she had a significant amount of UGMA money, and a week later the money was gone and the young woman was in Texas with her boyfriend. This is why I favor keeping the money in your name so that you have control over it and can say, "I can pay for college, and when you graduate, I will give you and your girlfriend a cruise in the Caribbean as a graduation present." Or, have the money put in a 529 plan where it is used to pay for an education or returned to you. You can use it to help another of your children, but it still gets significant tax benefits. Building efficient net worth is, however, most important to think about when financing future education for your children. First, it is important to fully fund your retirement plans. They are the best tax-deferring vehicle and also the ideal way of building net worth quickly. It is best to fund these as fully as possible and max out on their contributions before setting aside money for college. When your child is 18 or 19 years old, you can stop the contributions and use that income to pay for his or her college education if you so choose. The chart, "Qualified Retirement Cash-In Breakeven Period" (below) gives an illustration of cashing in your IRA or retirement plan to pay for college education or other needs. You would be further ahead to have accumulated the money in a retirement plan rather than outside of one.

Qualified Retirement Cash-In Breakeven Period

Tax Rate	Number of Years		
	6%	8%	10%
20	12	9	7
25	10	8	6
30	9	7	6
35	8	6	5
40	8	6	5
45	8	6	5
50	8	5	5

Constant marginal tax rate: average annual yield to withdraw is continuously compounded. Number of years to breakeven was rounded up. Bottom line is that the use of a tax-qualified plan can make sense even as an emergency fund.

Source: © Paul Sutherland, Financial and Investment Management Group, All Rights Reserved.

Education Funding Just Builds Net Worth

All money set aside for children's college should come after your tax-qualified 401(k), 403(b), or other retirement plan contributions. Even if you must partially cash in your retirement plan or borrow against it, you will

Preschool Advice from Judy

Avoid preschools that push children too hard too early or are overly rigid. Yet at the same time, avoid preschools that are just baby-sitting and playing with no structure or curriculum. Preschool can set the stage for lifelong learning and a child's attitude toward it. Ideally, at preschool children should develop a yearning for learning, an attitude of excitement that learning is fun. Also ideally, the foundation of reading, socializing, and achievement should be developed.

Visit several potential schools; become acquainted with their philosophies, curricula, and instructors. Start your search early so you have time to be diligent in your choice. Compare and contrast the schools, and discuss them with your spouse before choosing one. Forget about which school has the best reputation or the best socioeconomic class of students. Instead, focus on what is important to you, and let your research and your instincts tell you which one will best prepare you child for lifelong learning. If you have to drive farther, if it is not in the nicest part of town, or if the children of your contemporaries turn their nose up at the preschool you choose, ignore all of that.

Then, after you child begins attending a preschool, visit the classroom frequently. Get involved with the school as well as with your child and what he or she is learning. This stage of life truly sets the path for the rest of your child's life. It is very important and should not be considered just a replacement for a babysitter.

By Judy McCorkle, Financial and Investment Management Group Trust, Estate Planning and Advising

---

most likely be ahead compared with funding a 529 or other plan. For example, say you only have $10,000; that means before taxes, you could put $15,000 into a 401(k)- or 403(b)-qualified plan that, after tax, would cost around $10,000. A total of $15,000 annually for 10 years will grow (at 6%) to $204,849 from those $15,000 annual deposits. At college time, you will have the option of stopping all or part of your deposits to the retirement plan to fund college, freeing about $10,000 toward college or borrowing on or cashing in the plan. Any of these options place you ahead of having funded a 529 plan or other non-tax–deductible options to fund college. The 529 plan comes after you fully fund your retirement plan; $10,000 annually to a 529 plan would yield $136,500 in 10 years. Even if you cashed in 100% of your retirement plan, you would be near breakeven with your 529 plan options. (See "Qualified Retirement Cash-In Breakeven Period" chart on page 87.)

Teaching Children about Money

Children need to learn how to manage money and time. Most of what they learn comes from the way their parents and the significant people in their life manage time and money. Before I had children of my own, I felt I had more insight and understanding about the ideal way to teach children about money; in fact, after I wrote *Financial Strategies for Physicians* (Orlando, Florida: Harcourt Brace; 1986), the publishers asked me if I would write a book on financial planning for children. We discussed the project at length, and I decided that because of time and family constraints I would not write the book. I still have not written a kids financial book, but I do have some ideas that I think work in helping to teach children how to handle money.

First, children need to learn that we trade time for money, and that the reason Dad and Mom go to work is for enjoyment, fulfillment, and to earn income to support their lifestyle. Second, if you want your children to enjoy work, to get a job, and to get excited about going to college to get a good job, then you should reflect joy and happiness in your own work. If you come home and complain about how awful work is and about the terrible people at work and how awful it is that you work your tail off and they do not appreciate it and all the things that you do for them, your children will reflect those same values, and they will find work to be drudgery and no fun.

I was raised by parents who found their work fulfilling and enjoyable. I never heard them complain about going off to work. As a son of an elementary school principal, I was able to see my father at work, because his school was right next to my high school. I have many physician clients whose children have gone on to be physicians, and in some cases are third- and fourth-generation physicians. Their family culture is balanced about this, and they enjoy their practice. The one key seems to be that they have been able to achieve a good balance between work and family life while placing a high value on education as a norm and part of the family culture. If you want your children to be educated, then you need to raise them in a culture that emphasizes education as fun and enjoyable and curiosity as a thing to be cultivated. So reflecting curiosity about science, math, what is going on in the world, and politics and having vibrant discussions at meals will help build these attributes in your child. Time together at the dinner table or breakfast table will help provide the cues for your children as to how they look at their own careers.

Likewise, how you discuss money at the dinner table, reflect on vacations, and shop at the mall is going to influence how your children think about money. They need to learn about the value of money and that Mom and Dad trade time for money. For example, recently my daughter, because she would rather go to the public school than the private school, said, "Daddy, think about all the money that you'll save." I said, "Honey, if Daddy has to work an extra year before retiring, that's fine with me. Nothing is more important to me than you having the best education possible, and so it would be a joy for me to work an extra year so that you can go to school. The cost of your school has zero value on the decision as to where you should go."

My children have been raised in a family in which there are significant assets and resources and with a father who works voluntarily because he enjoys it. My children have been taught that just because we have the resources to purchase a boat, an extra-fancy car, or snowmobiles, it does not mean that we do. The children understand that. Often, we have discussions such as, "The reason that Daddy does not want a boat is that it takes a lot of time to worry about the boat, take care of it, have a boat slip, and so on, and I want to spend more time with you on the beach and doing other things. Besides, when we need a boat, we can always use Uncle Mike's or rent one." The children accept this as plausible and appropriate.

Before going to a movie, we may go to a local food court, because my daughter always wants to go to the sub shop or taco stand, whereas my son wants Chinese food. I usually give them their own cash and have been doing this since they were 4 or 5 years old. I give them the largest bills I have. Thus, my young daughter might come back with change from a $100 bill plus a bean burrito. She counts the money back to me exactly, and has from early childhood. My son just puts the money on the tray uncounted and in disarray. Children have differing behaviors in life and where life intersects with money. In addition, as soon as the children have been able to figure percentages, when I remember, I have them figure the tip on our bills for restaurants.

One aspect of our family's values is that we never look at the cost of the food in a restaurant. I want the best quality food and the best quality calories possible to go into my and my children's system, thus we neither look at the food budget nor do we have a clean-plate policy. We have a dirty-plate policy whereby I trust the children to know when they are full, and if that means that they ate three bites of the bean burrito, drank four sips of the juice, and left the rest on the tray, that is fine with me. There will be plenty of time when they are older to discuss the idea of ordering what they can eat. I find that when I am traveling with the children, I tend to not order anything for myself and often just order coffee. I remember doing this once at a restaurant where a mother with three children looked over at me and said, "You don't order anything for yourself because you end up eating everything off of their plates, don't you?" I just smiled at her and said, "Yes." She said, "I've been doing the same thing for years."

When I purchased houses, I had my children show up at the closings and have gone through the closing statement with them. They have little relationship to the big numbers, but I want them to feel comfortable in a board room or conference room. I want them to feel comfortable watching a live financial transaction. I have also had them sign the documents for our house purchases because the house will be their home. I have asked the Realtor® before the closing to please make special forms for the children to sign. When my children were very young, we bought a house for $295,000 (two ninety five, I told the kids). My two children each brought a dollar and a pen to the closing and said, "Daddy, we had to pay more for your house than you did—that doesn't seem fair." I just smiled and said, "Thank you very much, honey." They felt empowered that they had helped.

In airports, my children help find the terminal and gate, and they have their own carry-on luggage so that they can make their own decisions regarding their baggage. They travel extensively with me. They have passports and frequent-flyer mileage statements from three different airlines. Although I do not give them their tickets, they do have the gate information in their pockets.

When we stay at hotels, the children are allowed to order at poolside, but they understand the value of money and say, "Well Daddy, don't you think it's better if we go up to the snack bar and order the grilled cheese sandwich, because it's $5 up there, and here at poolside it's $8.95?" Sometimes they say, "Well, we think the extra $4 is worth it, Daddy, to just sit here and enjoy the pool." I like that they are learning about valuing the relationship of time and money.

I find it funny that my mother drives 30 miles from home on double-coupon days to save $10 on her groceries, not realizing that even when zero value is placed on time, the expense of gas and wear-and-tear on her car is more than the savings. When I talk to her about this, she says, "Well, it's fun for Aunt Tishy and me to go into town and get our groceries, so there is an additional economic benefit to this." My children hear these conversations and they learn about money. They also learn that the intersection of money with life is fun and enjoyable, and that money helps support the lifestyle we want.

When my children ask me why we don't live in a giant house, I tell them that it is because we have a nice adequate house, and that I like to travel with them and would prefer not to work more hours and to be able to spend more time with them. Often, the conversation lasts about 1 minute and then we are off playing Monopoly®, chatting about a book, or hitting a tennis or soccer ball.

As a financial advisor and someone who spends his life negotiating with companies, I find playing Monopoly with my children especially fascinating. The children understand the importance of developing a monopoly at a low cost quickly in the game. They understand the importance of getting four instead of two railroads. If they get the third railroad, they will pay even more for the fourth. It is all in fun and played with enjoyment, but it is fascinating to watch how my children have gained a good understanding of finance by playing this game. We play by the rules. They understand that fines go into the middle of the board, and if you land on free parking, you get the money. We would not put an additional $500 there, which my children will explain to you causes significant inflation and makes the game last forever. They also are not allowed to "take a dive" and give their properties to their best friend so the friend can win. In addition, all transactions have to be settled in cash, and the person has to take off houses at half their value and mortgage property to make their payments. No one gets free turns or free passes.

On a trip to Las Vegas, my children's mother and her husband and I made sure the children understood that casino gambling is purely for entertainment. We do not expect to get rich, and the children understand the math—which is that if Grandpa earned $200 in Las Vegas from gambling and we offset what he spent on the plane and hotel, the children will always answer, "It's just for fun, I understand, Daddy." It is fun whether you have a $50 limit, a $25 limit, or a $10,000 limit, but dysfunction is when people express their ego through large bets. My limit for craps is $50 per night. Any winnings I make, I leave at the table; I have left significant tips over the years because if it truly is for fun, then you give the money to the crew or the waitress and leave the table "even."

As for my children's allowance, I have found a system that seems to work for us. My children are expected to help with household chores including help keep the house clean; I do not believe it is appropriate to pay children to do household chores. Whether it is taking out the garbage, helping to clean up dishes, or something else, they do it because they are part of the family and not for economic benefit. To get paid for everything creates a transactional system in which the children think they need to get paid to do things. Creating a transaction relationship with young children teaches them to be transactional in adulthood. This can carry into unhealthy relationships with their partners, in their romantic relationships, and with their friends, in which they are always keeping score. Life is not about keeping score.

As part of the family system, the children tend to get what they need. Now that my daughter is in high school, we give her a set amount for school clothing at the beginning of the school year. She also gets cash each month to pay all her school, car, savings, charity, and other expenses. Now that she is 16 she will pay all of her own expenses and I will give her one lump sum of cash each month. We have just implemented this system and she has six boxes for each of her ongoing budget items. One is for long-term savings—it goes into the Utopia Core Fund (www.utopia.com), of course (managed by her father), some is for charity—she gives to the Sierra Club (www.sierraclub.org), animal organizations, and other causes she is excited to support. The other $50 is to spend any way she wishes; she tends to save most of this, too. My 13-year-old son gets three checks for $25 each—his checks seem to pile up until I say something. Then, the long-term goes into the Utopia Core Fund (it will take $25 monthly), and the $25 for charity goes to a Guatemalan charity through his school to buy soccer balls for children as well as other things. He tends to accumulate the last $25, his "spend anytime" money, or he may put it into the Utopia Fund. My daughter Akasha works now. I place 100% of what she earns from working at Cherry Republic, as a cashier, and re-stocker into a Roth IRA in the Utopia funds. We sat down with the prospectus and figured out what it could grow to if she lets it compound out. The money she earns is hers to do with as she wishes. She is saving up for a car, horse, or college depending on the day. I care little what it is saved for, but I am excited she gets the "save" part.

My children seem to enjoy movies, dinner, games, and traveling with their parents more than anything. We do not encourage video games or computer games. The children have computers, but they are not allowed to spend over, perhaps, half an hour to two hours a day on them. Our family system is consistent with spending time together as a family. As a therapist said in a

Inheriting Great Wealth: Two Cautions

It is a common notion that children who inherit great wealth rarely do as well as their parents. It is a popular suspicion that many of the inheritors actually do a good deal worse in life for having inherited such great wealth. The sample size is much too small, so there is of course no scientific study of how inheriting wealth affects the recipient. So whether inheriting wealth is damaging is not known, but for the sake of argument, we will assume there is a real danger of not living successfully as a result. And should this be true, every thinking family would want to guard against it.

There are two well-documented considerations that can help families guard against some of the negative consequences. The first is *learned helplessness*, and the second is what is now known about the building blocks of *life satisfaction*.

Learned Helplessness

When people and animals experience bad events that are not under their personal control, they collapse in certain predictable ways. In the laboratory (and in real life) electric shock, loud noise, and other traumatic events that happen regardless of what the victim does, cause

- Passivity (the victim gives in easily when later challenged)
- Cognitive difficulties (the victim sees himself a failure even when he actually is successful)
- Emotional difficulties: pessimism, depression, and anxiety

Surprisingly, the same things happen even when good things are showered on people and animals. Uncontrollable good events produce the passivity and the cognitive difficulties and perhaps the emotional difficulties, at least in the laboratory. Inheriting great wealth, which happens uncontrollably, fits the operational definition of a learned helplessness experiment. So simply bequeathing great wealth to your children may produce learned helplessness. Perhaps, therefore, we should not make such bequests. Period. But if we do, what is known about how you can prevent learned helplessness that may mitigate these effects on your children?

- A life history of mastery, in which one's own actions matter a great deal, immunizes against helplessness. So, for example, having chores in childhood is an excellent predictor of success later in life. Ask yourself, if it is not too late, how, in your particular circumstances, you can raise your children with much more mastery.

- Optimism (the belief that bad events are temporary, controllable, and limited, along with the belief that good events are permanent, controllable, and pervasive in their effects) mitigates helplessness. Optimistic people are at low risk for depression, they bounce back resiliently when they fail, they succeed better at work and sports, and they live longer and are healthier than pessimists. They do not easily become helpless, and there are known ways to instill more optimism in children and adults.

So teaching your children substantial mastery while they are young and instilling optimism at any age are both likely tactics for mitigating their becoming helpless upon inheriting. Further, making the inheritance contingent on what they do in life, stage by stage, will make the wealth earned and more under their control, and so be less helplessness-inducing. What would you like to see your children accomplish by themselves at different stages of life in order to come into what parts of the inheritance?

Life Satisfaction

What should your children do with great wealth once they inherit? Some uses of wealth do not bring much life satisfaction, while others bring enormous life satisfaction. In 15 replications, involving thousands of people from around the world, we measured the pursuit of pleasure, the pursuit of engagement, and the pursuit of meaning. We wanted to know how each of these contributed to total life satisfaction, and we were surprised by the answers:

- The pursuit of pleasure only slightly increases life satisfaction.
- The pursuit of engagement and meaning hugely increase life satisfaction.
- If you have both meaning and engagement in life, only then does pleasure add more life satisfaction. The life satisfaction of people who have all three pursuits totals to more than the sum of the parts.
- The life satisfaction of people who have none of the three is lower than the sum of the parts.

This suggests some intriguing provisos on how inherited wealth should be spent, as well as ways for you to spend—and not spend—your own great wealth. What provisions might you make to ensure that the funds are expended, not so much on pleasure, and more on engagement and meaning?

Written specifically for this guide by Martin E.P. Seligman; Director, Positive Psychology Center; Fox Leadership Professor of Psychology, University of Pennsylvania.

family seminar, "The family that plays together stays together. The family that fights together stays together." The children's mother and her husband and I spend a lot of time with the children, and they have grown up enjoying various activities such as horseback riding, tennis, playing Monopoly®, reading books, and just being together.

Death and Dying

Trusts, Wills, Gifting, and Event-Driven Dispositions

There are two certainties in life: one is that we will die; the second is that we do not know when. Death should not be a financial trauma to a family. Naturally, it is difficult psychologically and emotionally on those we leave behind. The goal of estate planning is financial ease after death. It is inconsiderate and inappropriate to leave your heirs with financial insecurity that only feeds the pain of loss. The first key to estate planning is to ask, "If I were to die, who would suffer financially?" If you are married with young children, you need to make sure that you have an estate that will support your spouse and perhaps educate and support your children until they are able to get through their education. (Chapter 2 discusses life insurance for family security.)

If you remember only one thing from reading this chapter, it should be that your death should cause no one financial harm or burden.

Intentional Estate Plan

Driving estate planning are your goals and desires being reflected in the responsibilities that you have taken on. These manifest in estate planning documents that direct your assets to *whom you want, how you want,* and *when you want*. Married people usually leave their spouse the assets and the income from them until the spouse's death. Then, if they have young children, the plan would usually provide for the children's care and the management of assets left behind for them. The person who serves as guardian of young children is not necessarily the one you would want to manage your assets.

After spouses and children are cared for, you may want to consider funding your favorite charitable causes. Trustees or foundations chosen to receive these assets should be those who care about your endeavors and are close to your heart.

In addition, it is appropriate to leave letters to loved ones that explain why you set up your estate plan as you did; these personal letters can also be a tool to deliver messages about your hopes and dreams for them as well as any information or legacy that you have hoped to leave them. A personal

One-Page Financial Plan: Estate Planning Consultation 1

- Nicholas, age 71; healthy; three children from previous marriage, ages 42, 44, and 47
- Kae, age 50; healthy; five children from previous marriage, ages 20, 23, 24, 24, and 27
- Married 5 years; postnuptial agreement leaves Kaye $500,000 cash, use of main home, and $10,000 monthly for life in divorce and/or death.
- Nicholas is on board of local private boys' school but rarely makes board meetings. Kae is on local church board and makes one out of two meetings. Spend summers at home in Traverse City, Michigan, winters in Maui home, and usually spend October, April, and May traveling. Children fly to see them in Traverse City or Maui.

Assets:
- Traverse City home, $1,750,000; bought for $300,000 in 1982.
- Maui home, $1,350,000; bought in 1996.
- Kae's divorced daughter's home in Chicago; bought for $200,000, charge no rent, and help daughter out at $1,500 monthly; plus Nick and Kae pay tuition to private school for three grandchildren at $1,200 monthly. This could go on for years.
- Old Traverse City office building that is rented to medical group worth $1,850,000 (cost basis due to depreciation at $250,000). Receives $10,000 monthly-rent net because the group pays taxes, insurance, and maintenance.
- Grandma's old 80-acre farm that was inherited from Nicholas's mother that has 20 acres of cherry trees leased out, rest is left natural; has home and old buildings that writer/teacher son lives in and pays $500 monthly rent. (Gets $10,000 or so annually from cherry harvest, worth $650,000; cost basis at $150,000.)
- Old rollover individual retirement account (IRA) from old profit sharing and pension plan, $3,800,000; drawing on it at $15,000 monthly (managed for income).
- Managed income portfolio, mostly Michigan municipal bonds at $1,400,000 worth, provides $6,000 monthly income.
- Other assets at $400,000 to $500,000 including furniture, rare coins, jewelry, cars, boat

Income Needs:
Figure they need $20,000 monthly for lifestyle; try to give $100,000 away annually to charities; get $1,800 monthly from Social Security.

Goals and Planning Discussion Notes:
1. Now that Nicholas feels Kae "thinks he is a keeper," he would like to make sure she has the ability to maintain her lifestyle for life. Wants her to have the use of both homes, and receive $15,000 monthly income.
2. Leave the Traverse City home to his children and the Maui home to Kae's children.
3. Let his son and Kae's daughter inherit the homes they live in but reduce their additional inheritance by the value of those properties.
4. After reading about them Nicholas wants to look at setting up a $1 million legacy trust at death that gives $50,000 in perpetuity to any offspring or grandchild or grandchildren's children of his or Kae's who gets a Bachelor of Science degree. Keep paying $50,000 per child until the money runs out, if ever. If the account goes 20 years without a claim, the trust is instructed to give it equally to 10 orphanages in the poorest countries.
5. Have chatted about drawing on IRAs aggressively and gift $22,000 to each grandchild's 529 plan until each has $100,000.
6. At Nick's death, leave all of IRA to charitable foundation that will be run by Kae and perhaps their children.
7. Not leave complicated mess for Kae or their children if something happens to him (eg, Alzheimer's or death).
8. Find out how they can help their children now when they need it without being nosy; "some children are fine; others are paycheck-dependent," Nicholas explained.

Because of the size of the estate and complex issues regarding its make-up and tax issues, on the advice of their fee-only advisor, Nick and Kae went to an all-day seminar to learn about family trusts, interfamily partnerships, wills, trusts, tax issues, and family legacy and charitable planning. They came back to see their fee-only financial advisor and attorney feeling like they knew "enough to be dangerous," but also understood the issues and complexities of their situation. Nick and Kae said about the seminar, "It was the best $1,500 we ever spent," but they also realized that the hard work would be done by them, making all the complex decisions, their fee-only planner, certified public accountant, and attorney to create a flexible, creative, personal, and whimsical (Nick's words) legacy, estate and financial plan.

memorandum outlining any specific bequests of personal property to children, a living will, and medical power of appointment are also helpful. A medical power of appointment allows your designee to advise your doctor of your desires regarding your care. In addition to the no life-support-type of wish, it allows for more comprehensive involvement regarding your care and comfort in addition to burial directives. Perhaps documents would be included that permit those who care about you to allow your life to terminate if that is your desire.

Old Age Reality

We grew up dependent on our parents. They provided for us through our years of education, and then we become dependent on our own skills. Over time, we accumulate wealth and become dependent on our investments and the income from them. Then once again, we return to being dependent on someone else to help with our basic needs. Nurses, cooks, maids, nursing homes, day nurses; all might be at our beck and call in old age because of our limitations. The reality is that one third of individuals over 75 live alone but has one or more limitations in use of the toilet, preparing meals, putting on shoes, and so on. For most physicians who have planned adequately for people to nurture and care for them when they need help, there is no need to worry about affording them. Part of a sound financial plan should include making sure there are adequate resources to provide for such care. You also need to have trust documents and friends or family involved to make sure that if you lose your ability to reason (become incapacitated) you do not do something stupid such as get into a scam, give the deed to the house to your dead brother's sister-in-law, or hire a broker who churns your account or sells you an insurance rip-off.

It is generally unnecessary to create special accounts for assisted living. If there are no living children, you must be more concerned about the ability to remain in the home and pay for help or have adequate resources to provide for the level of assisted living you prefer. The need for people to help you as your ability to take care of yourself diminishes is a natural, normal occurrence. It should be part of a retirement budget. Usually, what happens is that one spouse becomes unable to perform some of his or her daily functions and the other steps up and helps by dressing, helping to bathe, and so on. After a time, a nurse may come to help the spouse get out of bed, put him or her to bed at night, and help with daily care. This usually evolves until the nurse needs to stay 8 to 24 hours a day; then it is obvious that the

"You needn't feel guilty. You earned the fortune you inherited by giving her great happiness while she was alive."

© The New Yorker Collection 1992 Henry Martin from cartoonbank.com. All Rights Reserved.

spouse who is disabled would do better in an assisted living or nursing home situation.

During this period, the able spouse is charged with arranging for care, obtaining nursing, scheduling, finding qualified and trustworthy people, and, it is hoped as the care progresses, getting a case manager to oversee and control the care process. Enormous paperwork is involved if there is any need for in-home equipment via Medicaid (ie, hospital beds, oxygen, walkers, portable toilets, etc). If the caretaking spouse is not able to handle these details, it is necessary to hire a service, which increases costs. These are not easy financial decisions, but what is easy is that it is obvious when the spouse is going to be better cared for somewhere other than in his or her house.

Naturally, the advantage of being a physician is that you know what care is needed and also can be objective about that care. This is helpful in situations in which a physician is part of the family system. There are many nursing care options: 24-hour live-in care, assisted care, assisted living, apartments with staffing to allow the couple to have as much independence as they wish, knowing that a trained staff is always available. Keep in mind, however, that over the past few years, eight nursing home chains have declared bankruptcy and 15% of all nursing home beds in the United States are in bankrupt homes. (Source: The Center for Long-Term Care Financing [www.centerltc.com; visited on date and time]). This is taking place just prior to a huge onset of baby boomers and the aging 80s reaching the need for care. So check out the creditworthiness of any chain or home facility you look at. Statistically, of course, once one spouse dies, the other may have another 5 to 20 years of living alone. After all, there are over 70,000 Americans over the age of 100 today. When one spouse dies, things need to be reassessed. It is hoped that with the help of family and friends, the surviving spouse can decide what the rest of his or her life will look like—whether that means buying a new home, moving in with the children, or staying in an assisted living situation—all of which is dependent on the goals, desires, and personal circumstances of the widowed individual. The "My Way/Our Way" flow charts (page xviii and 109) can be used to help in this analysis.

Talk

What choices are best? It is best to have discussed care issues hypothetically with your spouse before they happen. Questions such as, "Honey, what should I do if you become disabled or if you died? I think I would like to move in with the children. If I died, what do you think you would want to do?" Questions like these can start some great discussions that lead to help with future decisions. It is good to have extended family and your financial advisors involved. To find out what commitment your children have to your situation, ask them with acceptance, love, and without judgment questions such as, "If I became disabled or I died and Mom became disabled, what can I depend on you to help her with?" If your child says, "Well, I will make sure that she is well-taken care of in the hospital or nursing care facility and visit every 3 months," accept that. Do not expect more out of a child than that. You cannot force someone to behave the way you want. You do want to know exactly how they will help, and then you can weave that into your estate plan or care plan for you and your spouse.

"Let's Talk" Checklist

Discuss these issues with your family, financial advisors, certified public accountant, lawyer, and other trust advisors.

Wills and Trusts: Where are they and what do they say?

Assets: What are your assets? Is there a list of who owns what and what each is worth?

Goals to Discuss

1. Should you die what special preparations have you made for your spouse and survivors, such as insurance, power of attorneys, special trust fund provisions, etc?
2. If you become sick and unable to take care of yourself or have dementia or some mentally disabling condition, what would you want to happen?
3. Are there daily living limitations that should be addressed, ie, toilet, showering, dressing, etc?
4. Are there special needs of any children because of mental or physical illness limitations, alcoholism, drug abuse, depression, etc?
5. Should you have someone monitor significant purchases? For example, should either or both spouses sign checks over $10,000?
6. Should a child sign checks with you on any check over $10,000?
7. Should the children or other trusted advisors have copies of all portfolio or investment information for monitoring purposes?
8. Whom do you trust?
9. Whom do you not trust?
10. What would be the nightmare scenario if you were to get Alzheimer's disease, and what would happen to your estate?
11. What would be the nightmare scenario, such as if you and your spouse were to die in a car accident together?
12. If you develop an incurable disease and become incoherent at the end of your life, who would make the end-of-life decisions? Who would be able to "pull your plug"?
13. Who should advise you on medical decisions, eg, artificial feeding tube insertion, extreme measures to keep you alert, etc?
14. What charities would you have a bias towards supporting?
15. Is there any charity or person who would make you roll over in your grave if they got 5 cents from your estate?
16. What goals do you have for your children?
17. What type of a funeral would you want? Do you prefer cremation or burial? Who would you want invited?
18. Where would you want to be buried? Where would you want your ashes scattered or kept?
19. What is important to you that we have not discussed?

Source: Paul Sutherland, Financial and Investment Management Group. A printable copy of this is available at www.fimg.net.

One-Page Financial Plan: Estate Planning Consultation 2

- Bisra, age 93, Mayet, age 90; two adult children; have 25-year-old wills and trusts
- Assets: individual retirement account (IRA) of $1,500,000; taking $7,500 monthly income from it; $500,000 first home
- $500,000 second home (cottage)
- $500,000 other assets; no debts, no life insurance

Goals:
1. Provide economic security to each other
2. Have flexibility if need assisted care or need to move into a nursing facility
3. "Don't leave a mess if one or both of us gets Alzheimer's"
4. Leave what's left to children not taxed, if possible
5. Keep cottage for children "if they want it"

Catalyst for meeting: an insurance agent told them they would have $500,000 in estate taxes and that they should buy life insurance to pay the taxes.

Recommendations and Actions
Living wills, power of attorney agreements, revocable living trusts for Bisra and Mayet were drafted along with changing title of home and vacation home so (new) trusts are funded under their attorney's guidance; documents signed.

Bisra and Mayet will also discuss issues on the "'Let's Talk' Checklist" (on page 000) with children; idea of having part of IRA ($250,000 or so) go to Doctors Without Borders, a local private school, a Third World entrepreneur education charity for homeless girls, and their church. Want children to feel okay about this, so will discuss it with them. Once implemented, these recommendations would save Bisra and Mayet $500,000 to $550,000 in estate taxes and allow their assets to help their children, grandchildren, and others.

Result
Lots of documents to sign at the lawyer's office; no need for life insurance or nursing home coverage the agent was trying to sell them and "no mess" for children when they die.

Additional Discussion Notes:
Chatted about setting up a family limited partnership for cottage and gifting interest in it to children to reduce size of estate. Will talk about it in the future; wanted to "think about it for a while."

Source: Paul Sutherland, Financial and Investment Management Group

Everyone's family situation is different. Our family cultures are different. Do not assume that your children will make it all okay unless they say that they will, and define what "okay" is.

There are strictly fee-only financial advisors who are able to walk through the "what-ifs" of elder planning and help with the financial aspects, budgeting, and sorting through the options. These will include age-related life events such as choosing a nursing home, buying a home, making the "who will help" list, moving in with the children, and so forth. Be prepared to be asked some hard questions such as, "Who can you depend on? If dementia sets in, what then? Do you trust your in-laws if your child is ill or cannot carry out these duties? It sounds like your daughter is ideal to care for you. Do you think we should chat with her about this and help her economically while she cares for you?"

Let's Talk

Discussing finances and personal issues with your loved ones can be difficult. The "'Let's Talk' Checklist" on page 101 helps to make sure that certain issues are covered regarding your elder care needs.

CHAPTER 5

Retirement: A Second Career Choice

To Work Or Not To Work

In 1987, when I wrote the book, *Financial Strategies for Physicians* (New York: Grune & Stratton; 1988), I described retirement as "working when you want, if you want, how you want and where you want" (p. 139). In 1999, when I wrote the book, *Twelve Steps to a Carefree Retirement: How to Avoid Pre-retirement Anxiety Syndrome* (Chicago: American Medical Association; 1999), I defined retirement as "the ability to live, relax, and enjoy life dependent on a well-constructed retirement plan" (p. v of Foreword). Now remarried, working voluntarily at age 52, I see retirement as simply another career choice. Retirement means having the ability to live life as you wish, unencumbered by economic constraints. A healthy retirement allows you the ability to make choices appropriate for you and to savor what is most important in your life. Retirement is a choice. It is a choice that we have control over. The economics of retirement are naturally constrained by what type of lifestyle and choices we make regarding the "My Way/Our Way Life Retirement Plan" flowchart (see page 109) and the cost of that lifestyle.

I have worked with people who live comfortably on $3,000 per month and with others who have lived uncomfortably on tens of thousands per month.

From experience I have found that if a client's resources are slightly higher than her or his wants, the result tends to be happiness and ease. We do not need a psychiatrist to tell us that if due to our desires we are constantly feeling constrained by our resources we will be unhappy. Thankfully age seems to wire us for retirements reality. No one wants to be "old" for 30 to 50 years! We want to live happy, fulfilling lives for our whole life.

We have choices, and we make them every day. Choices, of course, create conflict. If we choose one thing, it means that we are not choosing another. With maturity, we learn to make the choices that are best for us.

Most of us want three things: to be rich, to be happy, and to be healthy. Naturally, each person's definition of rich, happy, and healthy is different. When my children ask me, "Are we rich, dad?" I say, "Yes, we are rich, because Amy and I love you, your mom loves you, your aunts and uncles love you, we are healthy, and we have many people who love us, and who we love." When I answer this way, their follow-up question is always, "Yeah, but dad, are we rich?" To which I naturally answer, "Yes, because we have love." There is a Chinese saying, "Family, friends, fame, and fortune all have a value of zero unless you put a 1 in front of them: that 1 is health." The first step in retirement is to allow oneself to feel rich, to be happy, and to have a healthy lifestyle that is sustainable over many years.

First Step: Visualize

What is the ideal retirement lifestyle? With the help of your spouse or significant other, imagine the most outrageous retirement you can think of. You should already be used to this if you did the "My Way/Our Way" life planning in earlier chapters. On the "My Way/Our Way Retirement Plan Worksheet" on page 105, write down every ridiculous or wild idea, and let it sit there for a while. Think about and discuss your ideas until you have a more permanent image. I believe that you can "have it all" in retirement: the freedom to relax and enjoy life, the freedom to spend time with your children and those you love, the time to read that book you have been wanting to read forever, being able to watch a football game without the beeper going off. The problem is that when we visualize our ideal retirement lifestyle, we often do not have a clue about what retirement is going to feel like. We need to look at it as an adventure. Attitudes, values, and desires change over time, but we still need a target. See My Way/Our Way Life Retirement Plan Relaxing and Enjoying Life chart on page 109 for an example of how to chart your retirement plans.

Most of my retired clients have sat in my conference room and heard my retirement speech, which basically is, "Retire and spend the first one to two years looking at it as an adventure, seeing what works, seeing what is different, seeing what you like to do, doing those things that you have always wanted to do. Then, after a year or so you will settle into a lifestyle. Coming off of a demanding career and moving into retirement can be unnerving. There is plenty of literature regarding the depression, anxiety, and other mental woes that can befall us in retirement. Retirement is a big change and can be daunting even when you are prepared emotionally. Activity helps! My editor of *Twelve Steps to a Carefree Retirement* felt that a successful retirement requires a lengthy list of avocations and goals with plenty of opportunity to pursue them. The retirement adventure will change over time. Remember, you can always go back to work. Many do! The main goal of this book is to give you financial robustness so you can retire with many choices without worry about the economics of retirement. Retirement is for a long time. However, it does not feel that way, because as we age, time shrinks. When you were 20, a year was one twentieth of your life. When you are 70, that year is only one seventieth of your life. As Einstein said, "everything is relative." Time compresses as we get older. Understanding this helps when you are planning your retirement. When you think about travel, plan for longer, more leisurely, and less hectic trips. Ideally, with the help of this book's tips, in your retirement cycle you will not be merely old for 30 years.

Age is a state of mind. When I lived on Maui, I got up at 3:30 a.m. to get to the office. Once in a while I would cross paths with a certain retiree in his 80s. This man biked up Haleakala Crater all the way to the top just so he could watch the sunrise when he started his descent. If you believe you are going to be old and frail at age 70, chances are you will. The same holds true for being 90, or even 100. In your financial planning, you must plan on living forever. There are more than 70,000 Americans who are 100 years old. Actuarial tables now go to age 111. Retirement plans have to assume that your need for income will continue indefinitely. We do not know when we will die, so we cannot assume that it is okay for our portfolio to expire just because an actuarial table says that we were supposed to die at age 84. If you hire a financial advisor who shows you a retirement plan based on the assumption that you are going to die at a certain age, pick up your belongings and walk out of the room, or hang up the phone!

CHAPTER 5 Retirement: A Second Career Choice

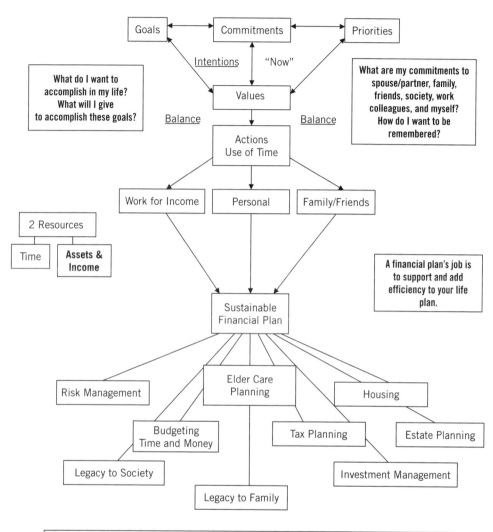

Source: Paul Sutherland, Financial and Investment Management Group. A printable copy of this chart is available at www.fimg.net.

To assume that your life expectancy is less than 120 years is, to me, financial malpractice. If you had a patient who was 70 and you were going to put in a device that would keep their heart ticking, would you choose to have it tick on for 20 years or 50? I am quite sure you would choose the

50-year device. To think that a person will die before age 100 is reasonable, but to make a retirement plan around that is irrational; just ask those 70,000 Americans who are over a century old. A retirement plan should be designed around the possibility that our lives are by some estimates extending by one half year to 2 years every year that we live because of medical discoveries, new drugs, new therapies, and smart lifestyles.

Second Step: Retirement Budget After You Have Visualized Your Lifestyle

The second step in retirement planning is to quantify your retirement lifestyle costs in today's dollars. Do not fret about inflation or deflation when completing the retirement plan worksheet. Do not make the assumption that gas will be $12 per gallon or that cars will cost $200,000. Use numbers as if you were retiring today. It is your portfolio's job to make sure you have enough at retirement. You just want to be as reasonable as you can in completing your retirement budget.

The "My Way/Our Way Retirement Plan Worksheet" (on page 105) will help you with your retirement fantasy. It will help you describe your ideal lifestyle now and in a few years. The second step is to quantify that financially. On page 111 is a retirement budget worksheet, "My Way/Our Way Retirement Costs," that you can use for this purpose.

Third Step: Estimating How Much You Will Need in Retirement Assets

After you have a budget, you will need to estimate your resources needed, which is shown in "Estimated Income Needed From Portfolio" on page 112. Thus, if you work for a hospital or corporation that has a fixed pension plan or have a long-term lease on a commercial real estate property, that income is put in the blank for *income from fixed pensions*. Estimate the pension income, assuming joint and 100% survivor benefit that continues for life. Do not assume anything other than 100% survivor life benefits, unless of course, you are working with a competent, fee-only planner

Step 2: My Way/Our Way Retirement Costs*

My Way/Our Way Retirement Budget	Annual Estimate		Monthly Estimate
Home maintenance (estimate 2% of value) (plus mortgage payment if any)	$_____	÷ 12 =	$_____
Second home maintenance (estimate 2% of value) (plus mortgage payment if any)	$_____	÷ 12 =	$_____
Travel/vacations	$_____	÷ 12 =	$_____
Home insurance	$_____	÷ 12 =	$_____
Property taxes	$_____	÷ 12 =	$_____
Car payments[†]	$_____	÷ 12 =	$_____
Auto expenses	$_____	÷ 12 =	$_____
Phone	$_____	÷ 12 =	$_____
Electricity/heating	$_____	÷ 12 =	$_____
Food/vitamins	$_____	÷ 12 =	$_____
Entertainment (movies, plays, eating out)	$_____	÷ 12 =	$_____
Education	$_____	÷ 12 =	$_____
Subscriptions/computer expenses	$_____	÷ 12 =	$_____
Sanity (yoga, counseling, sports, bridge)	$_____	÷ 12 =	$_____
Fun (wine, books, lattes)	$_____	÷ 12 =	$_____
Personal development	$_____	÷ 12 =	$_____
Tithing (religious, usually monthly)	$_____	÷ 12 =	$_____
Charitable contributions (budgeted amount)	$_____	÷ 12 =	$_____
Insurance/healthcare costs (usually $700 to $2,500 per person per month)	$_____	÷ 12 =	$_____
Helping children/grandchildren, gifts	$_____	÷ 12 =	$_____
Helping others (usually lump sum gifts)	$_____	÷ 12 =	$_____
Total annual/monthly expenses estimated at	$_____	÷ 12 =	$_____
Plus 65% of above to estimate expenses for taxes and "margin of error" surplus[‡]	$_____	÷ 12 =	$_____
Equals total annual/monthly income estimate	$_____	÷ 12 =	$_____
	$_____	÷ 12 =	$_____
	$_____	÷ 12 =	$_____

*This exercise should be done with your spouse.

[†]Most likely you will pay cash for cars in retirement but will need to budget for them based on your needs. For example, if you plan to replace your $36,000 car every 3 years, you will need to put $1,000 aside monthly as your car payment.

[‡]For example, if your monthly budget comes to $9,900, round it up to $10,000 and add $6,500 for taxes and margin-of-error surplus.

Source: © Paul Sutherland, Financial and Investment Management Group, All Rights Reserved. A printable copy of this worksheet is available at www.fimg.net.

Step 3: Estimated Income Needed From Portfolio

	Annual	Monthly
Estimate of total income needs from last line of Step 2	$_____	÷ 12 = $_____
Less estimated Social Security income*	— $_____	÷ 12 = $_____
Less income from fixed pension, etc	— $_____	÷ 12 = $_____
Equals total income needed from investment portfolio	$_____	÷ 12 = $_____

*If both you and your spouse or partner work and earn over $50,000 each, estimate Social Security annual income for each as follows:

Retired at 50 = $ 9,000
Retired at 55 = $10,000
Retired at 60 = $12,000
Retired at 65 = $18,000

If just one spouse or partner worked, estimate Social Security annual income for second spouse at ½ of working spouses income, for example, age 50 = $4,500.

Retired at 50 = $ 4,500
Retired at 55 = $ 5,000
Retired at 60 = $ 6,000
Retired at 65 = $ 9,000

who understands your needs. Some insurance agents recommend buying life insurance products designed to allow you to take a joint- and 0%-survivor benefit so that you allegedly end up with more income at retirement. I have seen these schemes, which are often called *benefit-guaranteed plans* or *retirement-enhancers*, but they are destined to fail. First, because people tend to live a long time. And second, because these insurance agents are using products designed by the same insurance companies that are guaranteeing you the lifetime income on the annuity. So they are working out of the same playbook. The insurance agent, however, is manipulating the information to make the assumption that perhaps you will die at age 83 or 88. If the insurance agent can give you a letter that guarantees the policy to age 110 and the letter comes from a representative of the insurance company, then perhaps you can consider a retirement-enhancer program. There are many widows in America who trusted their husbands to make the right choices and found that the retirement-enhancer policy passed away before their husbands did.

Once in a Lifetime

For many first-time retirees, an extravagant once-in-a-lifetime holiday, perhaps including children or grandchildren to celebrate retirement, is often an expense that comes in retirement's first year. If this expense will be substantially more than what you estimate you will spend on vacations on an ongoing basis, it is best to take that estimated cost and add it to the retirement lump sum. Usually, retirees settle into a lifestyle that is consistent. Whether that consistency is two months at home in Virginia, two months on Florida's coast, three months traveling through Europe, and the rest of the time bouncing among the children and grandchildren's homes, so be it. The cost of that plan can be estimated.

Fourth Step: How Much?!

How much do I need? Step 4 is to take the estimated total income that you will need from Step 3 and divide that by the factor in Step 4 ("Quantify Your Lump Sum Need" on page 114). You may not be able to complete Step 4 until you have an assessment of your risk tolerance, which is discussed in other chapters in this book. A good rule of thumb is to assume you can take roughly $48,000 from every million dollars of investment assets. As an example, if your estimated total income needs after subtracting Social Security (and any other fixed pensions) is $10,000 per month, you would need $2.5 million invested at retirement to meet this need. The goal of your retirement income portfolio, for example, might be to beat inflation by 4.8% consistently over time. This does not mean you will earn 4.8% plus inflation every year. It means that some years you will earn, perhaps 15%, other years your portfolio will lose, but over time, your portfolio should consistently make money based on historic correlations and prudent and appropriate investment management. You should not get into a situation in which, because your portfolio earned 20% one year, that you say, "Oh gosh, now I can really splurge." When your portfolio earns 20%, you should say, "This is wonderful. It gives me a significant margin of error so that when I have a bad year or two I will not feel like I am drawing down my principal." Retirement portfolios need to be managed with binoculars looking out 30 to 50 years. The goal of a retirement portfolio is to provide consistent compounding—real, positive income returns that can be depended on over time. In retirement, you want to live on the income and dividends from your portfolio and to have your portfolio constructed in such a way that at least 70% to 80% of what you are drawing comes from income and dividends.

One day my mom kissed me on the forehead and said, "I'm driving down to see your 76-year-old grandma. This will probably be the last time I see her." With that, she drove the eight hours from northern Michigan down to southern Ohio. When mom came home, she complained about Uncle Frank, who managed Grandma's money. She had said to him, "Gosh, Frank, don't you think you could let mom have more income? She's probably going to be dead next year anyway." My uncle replied, "Mary, when you're managing money for retired people, you only want them to live on the eggs, you never want to eat the chicken." At first my mom was resistant to this idea, but later after I had entered my financial planning career, she told me how Uncle Frank gave

---

Step 4: Quantify Your Lump Sum Need*

The percentage of income you can comfortably draw upon from your portfolio will depend on your risk tolerance and how your portfolio is managed as described below and in future chapters. Take your monthly income needs and divide the total sum by the following factors:

Aggressive investor—long-term global equity income–oriented	.005
Balanced investor—long-term total return–oriented	.0045
Yield income investor/bond/income stocks–oriented	.004
Capital preservation money market and bond investor	.003

Value at Risk: Volatility Constraint	Percentage to Draw Annually	Percentage to Draw Monthly	$1 Million = Income of Annually	Monthly
35% aggressive investor[†]	6.0[†]	.05*	$60,000	$5,000
25% balanced investor[†]	5.4[†]	.045*	54,000	4,500
15% yield income investor	4.8	.04	48,000	4,000
5% capital preservation	3.6	.03	36,000	3,000

*Portfolio income need equals balance from Step 3 divided by your annual percentage to withdraw from above, which will in turn equal the lump sum you need to retire. These steps help do this work for you.

[†]Use these strategies only under the advice of an experienced, fee-only advisor who feels that drawing at these rates is consistent with your needs and risk tolerance with a margin of error "baked" into your retirement plan.

Source: Build a "You'll Live Forever" Retirement Portfolio.

her this advice every year. Every year mom would call me and say, "I'm driving down to Ohio. This will probably be the last time I see your grandma." Grandma lived on those "eggs" until she was 96. She was full of health and vitality and had a rich life until she died. Uncle Frank constructed a strong portfolio for her that he managed with great forethought. It consisted of high-income stocks, bonds, and other preferred income-oriented stock investments that he managed with skill and expertise. The bottom line is to make sure your portfolio is managed in a way such that your retirement will be comfortable and long-term. It needs to be designed to provide you with a reliable lifetime income.

Putting it all together and quantifying your investment needs is the fifth step. You will want to have liquidity of approximately six months and a lump sum to pay off debts; a lump sum for a second home; a lump sum for any boats, dream vacations, or similar items; and a lump sum to provide for your lifetime income need. The total of Step 5 is the amount you will need to have saved

Step 5: Quantify Your Total Investment Needs

Generally, you will have paid off all debts before retirement. If not, you will need to anticipate the lump sum needed for these debts and add that to the lump sum you need to retire. It is okay to have debts at retirement; there can actually be advantages to it via tax savings, but to make your projections work, you must turn debts into lump sums or account for them as part of your budget in Step 1 as monthly payments.

Lump sum of 6 months' budget/liquidity needs (half of total annual need from Step 2)	$_____
Lump sum to pay off debts on home, car, etc	$_____
Lump sum for second home	$_____
Lump sum for boat, dream vacation, etc	$_____
Lump sum for retirement income needs*	$_____
Total liquid investment/income assets needed to retire	$_____

*Later chapters help you build a plan to achieve this lump sum need. Do not worry about this big number right now; savings, time, and compound returns will get you there.

Source: © Paul Sutherland, Financial and Investment Management Group, All Rights Reserved. A printable copy of this is available at www.fimg.net.

prior to retiring. Do not worry about how big that number is. That is what compounding and saving money is all about. Remember, when you are young and managing your retirement portfolios, over time you will progress from having these managed more for long-term growth to having these managed for long-term predictable income where safety, predictability, growth, and income are blended into a realistic retirement-portfolio strategy.

Retirement Chapter's "After Five" Stops

Whether you are 2 years or 30 years from retirement, the exercises in this book are designed to help you get your hands around values and the reasons you are working. There are many trade-offs in retirement planning, and one of the primary ones is time. We trade time for money, and we trade extra time to have extra money to fund our retirement plans. I heard on the radio about how lazy the Europeans are with their six-week vacations, long weekends, and other normal holidays. I have visited Europe many times and lived with the easy pace of their lives. Many Europeans are able to work into their 70s or 80s because of their balanced life. They enjoy the pace and are able to spend plenty of time with family and friends. Saying they are lazy is short-sighted. Americans "work their tails off" until they are 55 and then retire so they can be lazy for the next 45 years. It is ridiculous to judge either lifestyle as bad or good. We are all different.

Instead, each of us must determine what is right for us. Many people have to compartmentalize their lives into different phases, for example: (1) education, (2) marriage, (3) career-building, (4) parenting, (5) children out of nest, and, finally, (6) retirement. Each phase may be obsessed over. Other people try to have more of a balanced, cycled life and allow the phases to integrate with each other. This usually means balancing time with family, children, and loved ones. To make sure you do not get off track when planning for retirement, you can ask yourself, "What do I want from my life now? Do I want 3-day weekends? Do I want to take summers off? Do I want to have a balanced life now, or do I want to work very hard toward early retirement?" In my experience, the physician who is married with children and works 65- to 80-hour weeks with few vacations does not retire earlier than his more balanced brothers or sisters. This apparent paradox is usually for one of two reasons: one, there may be two to three divorces along the way, which can cause significant financial setbacks; or two, not being able to slow down and get off the treadmill.

Life should be fun, and work should be fun. An enjoyable lifestyle should support your work life. Notice in the Step 1 retirement exercise on page 105 that there is no mention of retirement age. Basically, you need to know what annual income you will need for retirement. When you are 30, you can say to your financial planner, "Somewhere between the ages of 55 and 70, I want to be able to retire as I wish." As you get closer to retirement, your target could narrow to 10 to 15 years or 2 to 5 years. Ideally you will be able to say "Somewhere between age 60 and 65, or in a specific number of years, I'll be able to retire as I wish." The closer you get, the more accurately you are able to quantify your ability to retire. The chapters on investments show you that you do not want to risk your ability to retire by exceeding the "speed limit" of how a portfolio should be managed consistent with the risks of investment.

Some of my happiest clients were able to retire years ago but are still working and enjoying it. Their jobs are fulfilling even though they have the option of retiring. They have a dependable staff that can handle everything at work if they choose to take time off. Work is fun, especially with a solid retirement plan in place.

Long-Term Care Insurance: Not Necessary

In retirement, long-term care insurance is usually unnecessary. When a physician or his or her spouse goes into a nursing home or extended care facility, the expenses often go down. It is reasonable to factor in the effects of age on your body and mind. The exercises in this chapter assume you will someday need a nursing home. When you are both sick, traveling and other activities are restricted, and if only one is disabled, the other tends to spend the time caring for the ill spouse. In your retirement budget and as part of your estate planning, expect to have $700 to $2,500 monthly in healthcare expenses for each of you. You should discuss with your spouse and have a game plan for long-term care should one of you become unable to live in the home.

$10,000 Windows, $1,000 Chairs, and $20 a Month for Starving Children

Around 300,000 new nonprofit organizations were formed in the United States in the last 20 years. The giant nonprofits are staffed by hundreds and have specialists in marketing, e-mail solicitation, direct mail solicitation, and phone solicitation, and they even have specialists to call on physicians. When they call Amy or me, we used to have a lot of trouble saying, "No." Now I have found some ways to get around the constant donation solicitation, such as for the new emergency room fund, the local church, the local school, the homeless shelter, the women's center, the children's crisis center, or the African epidemic.

This section gives coaching on how to weave through the maze of charitable giving. Here is some advice: First, be conscious and intentional about your charitable giving. Know if you want to help, who you want to help and how you want to help them. Second, have a plan that is based on a budget; for example, 5% to 10% of income to charitable concerns with perhaps half of that fixed to a certain charity that you favor to help long term with the balance going to other concerns that you want to support. Assume that you will buy the Boy Scout popcorn, stationery, and $10 boxes of $2 candy; all told at about $50 to $100 per month. Just put this in the budget with a smile and say, "Fine."

Larger Donations: One-on-One Solicitation

My suggestions for larger donations are as follows: First, have convictions about what you stand for in your charitable giving. For example, if you feel that it is silly to pay $10,000 for a new stained glass window at your church when there are people starving in Guatemala or Africa, keep that to yourself, but use that feeling to realize your giving goal might be to help people in developing nations. Even so, it can be hard to say "No," regardless of your convictions. To say, "Nearly all of the charitable contributions I make are confidential," can be helpful in one-on-one solicitations. With the contributions I make, often I send a letter or talk with the director of the foundation or endeavor and say, "Please keep all of my giving confidential. I prefer to not even have it discussed at the board level or at any level." Periodically, I am approached to be on a charitable board. My reply is, "Are you asking me because you want me to donate money and figure that if I'm on your board, I'll see the need and donate? If so, then let me look at the need now, and perhaps I will be a donor only." There is a saying in the nonprofit community: "Ask for help and get money, ask for money and get advice." Asking for help is a common way to get people to donate to charitable work.

Many organizations desperately need physicians' skills. Many organizations ask for doctors to fly all over the world to help the severely disadvantaged. This is wonderful. See pages 202 to 208 for a listing of healthcare volunteer organizations.

Some physicians start their own foundation or charities or have used an independent charity as a conduit for personal giving. They can then say, "All of my charitable contributions are funneled through The *XYZ* Foundation." The bottom line is that it is really hard to say "no." When turning down a solicitation, first, as they taught us in communications school, repeat the pitch, showing that you have understanding; second, acknowledge that you feel it is a valid endeavor; then if you do not plan on helping, say, "You know, I really am concentrating my charitable contributions to other endeavors. I look at this once per year. If you want to write a letter to me next December describing your cause, I will sit down with my spouse and look at whether we want to include you in our charitable giving for next year." If you are not interested, just say, "You know, this is just not where I tend to concentrate my giving." Many people who are charitably inclined concentrate gift investments on a very few organizations. Therefore, this is an appropriate answer and one the solicitor will have heard more than once.

One of the largest financial plans I did was for a former board member of an automobile company who left everything to charity except for a set amount of $500,000 to each child. He and his wife could not agree on the charities they thought the money should go to. While she said, "Save the Whales," he thought "human needs" were more appropriate. If you have trouble agreeing with your spouse on whom to give to, I would suggest that each give half to the chosen fund.

The charity industry, like politics, is a huge entity that knows where our buttons are and pushes them. We need to be knowledgeable about ourselves and what is important to us and have conviction that our values are appropriate and consistent and be comfortable with them. If it is not about money, it is about values. If it is not about values, it is about money.

Estate Planning

Event-Driven Dispositions

I come from a big family; mom's mom had six children; so did dad's. I grew up with lots of cousins and family everywhere. I have coached, raised children, and managed people. From my contact with and observation of many different types of people, I believe in event-driven dispositions. I also believe everyone is different; my opinions in this section are only to help you create a thoughtful estate plan. Most important, your plan should be about your values and reflect the legacy you wish to leave.

Most estate plans are boilerplate with slight customization where children are concerned. The plans tend to say, "At my death, pay for my young children's health, education, maintenance, and support [HEMS in lawyer speak]. Then when the children turn 25, they get a third; age 30, one half; and age 35, the rest." The theory is that with age comes maturity, so if the children blow the first third of the estate, they still have two more tries to arrive at their parents' intent. This, for big estates, seems to be simply to make the children financially rich. To me, estate planning for children starts with this question: "If you have young children or grandchildren, what do you want for them?"

Do you wish for them to be happy? To have good relationships? To be productive and self-supporting? To be a good example of your family legacy? To say "No" to drugs? To be able to have more children? To have a happy marriage? I asked this question of Martin Seligman, president of the American Psychological Association; his answer is on page 94 ("Inheriting Great Wealth: Two Cautions"). The way children are parented has the biggest impact on their success in life. It is easy to infer from common sense and Dr Seligman's comments that the legacy we create through our children has more to do with how we parented them than with the money we gave them.

Your estate plan is about your values and what you want your legacy to be. Money influences lives, and it can do great things; my only hope is that you will take your plan seriously.

Following are some life events that you might consider including in your plan to help empower and guide your heirs and give them the confidence and skills to succeed in life:

- Present the trustees with a bachelor's degree: $50,000
- Master's degree gets $100,000
- Doctor's degree gets $125,000
- Get accepted into medical school: $30,000
- Spend 2 years in the Peace Corps or equivalent: $25,000
- Additional payments if degreed from international university: $25,000

- Travel around the world visiting Third World countries: $25,000
- Stay off drugs for right to receive funds from trust
- Present trustees with approved business plan after master's in business administration degree complete: $100,000 to start business
- Gift matches to charitable causes of up to $15,000 annually
- Match dollar-for-dollar earnings from job to maximum of $5,000 monthly
- Horse and horse maintenance and lessons for granddaughter who averages at least a B in school

Events should be customized by you and clear to the trustees. Most physicians retire with substantial estates, complex family situations, and changing circumstances. If your wealth is greater than what you need to support your lifestyle, then the events can be triggered during your lifetime.

A grandmother could pull her grandson aside at his high school graduation and say, "Grandpa and I set aside money for your college. We just wanted you to know that once you graduate, our trust will pay you $50,000. That should help pay off your student loans and get you started." However, from my experience, the best thing a grandparent can give the grandchildren is time. One woman I know gives each grandchild three travel options for a 1-week vacation with her on his or her 16th birthday. She tried leaving it up to the children, but their choices got outrageous. Her grandchildren will probably remember those weeks with her much more than an inheritance of money.

Budget Busters

What busts a budget in retirement? Children and grandchildren, brothers and sisters, mothers and fathers, and divorce. Budget-busting events need to be factored in your retirement budget. If you want to help your children from your retirement savings, you need to make sure to put it in the budget. If you budget $20,000 per year to help your children, you need to stick to the $20,000. Retirement budget mistakes do not show up right away. They are cumulative, like the effects of smoking or alcohol abuse. The first few years you do not notice that you are eroding your financial security by exceeding your portfolio's ability to keep up with your spending patterns. The mistakes we make by drawing too much on our investments now do not affect us for 15 to 20 years. It is okay to help our children as they need it. What is most important, however, is to be conscious of the consequences of the choices you are making. You should discuss any of these extra outlays with your financial advisor, not whether they are the right value decision, but so you understand the consequences. If the advisor says, "Well, the consequence is that in 15 to 20 years, if your investment returns are less than, for example, 5%, you should expect to have your income drop by 10% to 15%. This means you would not be able to travel as much, or you might have to let go of the second home or take some other action." Those are acceptable decisions if you are conscious of them and know the consequences.

If you have trouble saying "no" to friends and your children before retirement, realize that it will not get easier afterward. This is where a good, solid financial planner can help. You will be able to respond to requests for money like this: "You know, my money is held in trust and retirement plans. I'll need to call my advisor to see whether I have adequate resources to help you out." In that way, it allows the financial planner to be the bad guy if, for example, a request is denied to pay off the children's credit cards for the third time in 3 years.

Synergy and Tax Planning for Retirement

Tax-qualified retirement plans are usually the most efficient of all the avenues physicians have at their disposal to create significant wealth. Tax-qualified retirement plan benefits and attributes are so compelling that you will find that insurance agents, annuity salespeople, stockbrokers, Realtors®, and others will expend great effort to keep you from realizing the importance and beauty of the tax-qualified retirement plans. These plans have three significant tax advantages: (1) contributions are currently tax deductible, (2) the earnings in the retirement accounts grow tax-deferred, (3) the synergy between the tax-deductible contributions and the tax-deferred earnings of the retirement plan is truly a remarkable way to compound returns. The plans also create wealth efficiently to use for children's education, to pass on to heirs, or to just build net worth so you will have the option of retirement. Your number one goal and priority should be to fund the maximum tax-favored retirement plan that you can. See "Retirement Plan Synergy" on page 123 for an illustration of the tremendous tax savings possible with a retirement plan.

Retirement Plan Synergy

Asset Values				Plan Income Difference	
$2,000,000			$2,009,000*		
			Retirement plan assets from qualified plan		$10,000
$1,000,000		$1,007,070†			
	$720,000	Taxable returns at 30% tax rate equals net 4.2% on net $1,400 monthly $2,000 gross		$5,000	Monthly from qualified plan
$500,00	Net deposits at $2,000 monthly			Monthly from taxable plan	

*$2,000 monthly deposit for 30 years at 6% return.

†$1,400 monthly equals $2,000 − 30% tax = $1,400 net deposit.

Income difference assumes all taxable income from qualified plan or nonqualified plan. Individual retirement accounts, 403(b), 401(k), pension plans, all have tax advantages similar to those illustrated here for qualified plans. For illustration only, to show the synergy of tax benefits for retirement plans.

Source: Financial and Investment Management Group, Retirement Planning Services.

Retirement Plan Specifics

401(k), 403(b), Profit Sharing, Money Purchase, Individual Retirement Accounts, and More

As this is being written, George Bush is staking his political capital on pushing through significant tax and Social Security funding reform to help shore up the nation's basic retirement plan. One key element of safe and secure retirement for all Americans is, according to politicians, tax-qualified retirement plans. This is the one area in which Congress and Capitol Hill have consistently liberalized and given incentives as the ideal way to save for wealth accumulation. They have put significant limitations on other forms such as annuities, life insurance, real estate, oil, and gas tax shelters. Congress has made the tax-qualified retirement plan the most robust and flexible area to find the right prescription for wealth accumulation for retirement and financial independence. The plans are now so flexible that they can often be used effectively to help pay for children's education, a home, or other things. You can start drawing on retirement plans at any age, as long as you take the money out for at least 5 years or to age 59 and one half, whichever is longer.

The first job in retirement planning is getting your budget in order so that you have adequate cash flow for savings to fund a retirement plan at the maximum level. This means getting your debts and personal budget under control so that you can save in tax-qualified retirement plans. Once you have the cash, every personal savings dollar should be allocated first to your qualified retirement plan. When you are young, usually it is a profit-sharing plan combined with a 401(k) that allows you to put nearly $50,500 away. And if your spouse is eligible and works even part time, depending on your circumstances, you could put away up to another 100% of his or her earned income up to $15,500. If you have 401(k) provision, there is significant flexibility. When you are young and have little discretionary income to save, there are simple individual retirement account (IRA) plans that you can use. If you work for a hospital or nonprofit research organization, you may be eligible for 403(b)s—all of which are described in the chart, "Retirement Plan Comparison" on page 127. In most physicians' practices today, you will find a profit-sharing plan combined with a 401(k) because the 2007 contribution limits are up to $45,000 ($50,000 over age 50) annually. Profit-sharing/401(k) plans tend to be the workhorse of retirement plans. For older physicians who have a significant ability to save up to $180,000 annually, the defined benefit plan can be ideal. Your retirement plan consulting firm or financial advisor will be able to assist you in this regard.

The maximum annual contribution limitation table on page 133 illustrates the different types of plans and how much can be put in at different participant compensation systems and ages. You can use this table to get a ballpark idea of what you can put into retirement plans on behalf of yourself and your employees. Your financial planners retirement team or consultant will look at a number of factors in order to design a plan that is ideally suited for you, including (1) age and compensation of all employees; (2) your goals; for example, to maximize tax shelter advantage of the retirement plan, optimize flexibility, or something else; (3) stability of the practice; (4) employer goals such as employee retention, rewarding of employees, ability to borrow on the plan to use for down payment on homes, educate children, and so forth. Plans usually have complete investment flexibility except those sponsored by institutions that have specific investment programs that go

IRS Retirement Plan Limits	2005	2006	2007
DC Plan Annual Addition	$42,000.00	$44,000.00	$45,000.00
DB Plan Annual Benefits	$170,000.00	$175,000.00	$180,000.00
Maximum Compensation Limit	$210,000.00	$220,000.00	$225,000.00
401(k), SARSEP, 403(b), and 457 Plan Deferrals/Catch-up	$14,000.00/$4,000.00	$15,000/$5,000	$15,500.00/$5,000.00
SIMPLE Deferrals/Catch-up	$10,000.00/$2,000.00	$10,000/$2,500	$10,500.00/$2,500.00
IRA Contributions/Catch-up	$4,000.00/$500.00	$4,000.00/$1,000.00	$4,000.00/$1,500.00
HCE (for use of following yr. tests)	$95,000.00	$100,000.00	$100,000.00
Key Employee (Officer) Comp.	$135,000.00	$140,000.00	$145,000.00
SSTWB	$90,000.00	$94,200.00	$97,500.00

DC = Defined Contribution
DB = Defined Benefit
HCE = Highly Compensated Definition
SSTWB = Social Security Wage Base

along with their plan of administration or design. It is important to separate plan design from plan investments, and often those attributes can be blurred.

First, design an ideal plan for you, which is the first leg in the retirement plan journey. The second leg is to find a good investment advisor for your plan and not just default to what is simple. The financial firm may have robust plan designs, but it may dumb down the portfolio options by allowing you to "be your own manager by using indexed or benchmark-oriented funds." You should have three or four nonindexed funds that are globally managed for total absolute returns, encompassing a range of risk tolerances. The third leg is retirement plan administration. Retirement plan administration cannot be overemphasized, because when you set up a tax-qualified retirement plan, you often become a fiduciary and must comply with many Department of Labor regulations. It is important for your retirement plan administrator to understand these obligations and to keep your plan consistent with current best practices.

If you are using a bank, a bank trust department, or a trust company, understand that it does not mean you are delegating your fiduciary obligation. If your bank trust company has a plan with poor or mediocre investment options, do not assume that you have delegated your fiduciary obligation to them. The onus is on you, because there are thousands of trust companies throughout the United States to choose from. Nor should you assume the brokerage firm has done the due diligence and has the expertise to absolve you of your fiduciary obligations under your plan. Make sure you have a registered investment advisor who has had above-average consistent returns and whose investment philosophy and principles you understand and believe make sense so that you can honestly say you have great management of your funds.

Just because a firm has a trillion dollars under management does not mean it is the suitable one for you or that you have done your due diligence because 12,000 other plans are administered or managed by that plan sponsor. You need to come to your own conclusion as to whether it is the appropriate investment advisor for you based on your own criteria. The bottom line is that the retirement plan must be designed consistent with what is optimal for your unique

Manage Your Portfolios Like You'll Live Forever*

Annual Income Needed	Lump Sum Needed for Retirement Income			
	6% Draw Aggressive	5.4% Draw Balanced	4.8% Draw Yield	3.6% Draw Capital Preservation
$ 50,000	$ 833,333	$ 925,925	$ 1,041,666	$ 1,388,888
75,000	1,250,000	1,388,888	1,562,500	2,083,333
100,000	1,666,666	1,851,851	2,083,333	2,777,777
125,000	2,083,333	2,314,814	2,604,166	3,472,222
150,000	2,500,000	2,777,777	3,125,000	4,166,666
175,000	2,916,666	3,240,740	3,645,833	4,861,111
200,000	3,333,333	3,703,703	4,166,666	5,555,555
225,000	3,750,000	4,166,666	4,687,500	6,250,000
250,000	4,166,666	4,629,629	5,208,333	6,944,444
300,000	5,000,000	5,555,555	6,250,000	8,333,333
350,000	5,833,333	6,481,481	7,291,666	9,722,222
400,000	6,666,666	7,407,407	8,333,333	11,111,111
450,000	7,500,000	8,333,333	9,375,000	12,500,000
600,000	10,000,000	11,111,111	12,500,000	16,666,666
700,000	11,666,666	12,962,962	14,583,333	19,444,444

*Naturally, the future is unknown as are future returns on assets. The above is a best-guess analysis of reasonable returns to expect to keep you retired. The main risk is your long-term portfolio results and the effects of inflation/deflation on your income needs and portfolio. This table assumes your portfolio principal will grow and your income will increase over the years to help offset inflation. Retirement portfolios should be managed for long-term predictable income with, ideally, some growth in that income from investment of excess returns over the draw rate.

Retirement Plan Comparison Chart 2007

Plan Type	Contribution Limits	Who Should Consider	Administrative Requirements Fiduciary Responsibility	Key Advantages	Key Disadvantages
Traditional IRA Individual Retirement Account providing a tax savings through a deduction while benefiting from tax-deferred compounding interest.	Individual limit is $4,000.* catch-up $1,000 contributions, if over 50. Contributions may be tax deductible.	Physician in residency, fellowship program, or who has limited ability to save.	Very easy to establish. May be established by the due date of your tax return for the year.	May contribute to other retirement plans. Can convert to a Roth IRA. Current-year deduction. Investment flexibility. Tax deduction. Tax-deferred growth.	Pay taxes on your earnings upon withdrawal. Withdrawals made prior to age 59 may be subject to a 10% IRS penalty. If non-systematic benefit stream for 5 yrs or to age 60, whichever is longer.
Roth IRA Individual Retirement Account providing a tax savings while benefiting from compounding interest and possible tax-free withdrawals.	Individual limit is $4,000.* $5,00* catch-up $1,000 contributions, if over 50.	Physician in residency, fellowship program, or who has limited ability to save. Younger physicians in a lower tax bracket.	Very easy to establish. May be established by the due date of your tax return for the year.	Contributions are allowed after age 70 with earned income. Certain circumstances allow distributions to be tax-free if you are at least 59½. Investment flexibility tax-deferred growth.	Contributions are not currently deductible. Withdrawals made prior to age 59 may be subject to a 10% IRS penalty.
SEP IRA Simplified Employee Pension. Employer contributions are made to IRAs established for employees.	Contributions are limited to the lesser of 25% of the employee's compensation or $45,000.* All contributions are 100% vested.	New and/or smaller practice wishing to offer retirement benefits.	IRA must be established for all who are eligible. Certain plans must provide a minimum contribution. Minimal fiduciary responsibility. May be established by the due date of your business' tax return for the year (including extension).	Choice of allocation formulas. SEP does not require IRS reporting. Easy to establish and administer. Contributions are flexible. Investment flexibility. Tax deduction. Tax-deferred growth.	Cannot sponsor any other qualified plan. All employees earning $450 annual compensation are eligible. All participants are 100% vested. Does not permit allocation formulas. Does not permit loans.

(continued)

Plan Type	Contribution Limits	Who Should Consider	Administrative Requirements Fiduciary Responsibility	Key Advantages	Key Disadvantages
Simple IRA Savings Incentive Match Plan tax-favored retirement plan. Corporations, partnership, and sole proprietorship make contributions to IRAs established for employees.	Deferral limit $10,500.* $3,000* catch-up $2,500 contributions, if over 50. All employees are eligible if compensation is at least $5,000 during the year and the 2 prior years.	Newer practice or practice with fewer employees wishing to provide retirement benefits and allow for both salary deferral and employer contributions.	Annual notification to all eligible employees. Mandatory employer contribution for all eligible participants. IRS forms 5498, 1099-R. Maintained on a calendar year. Requires timely deposits. Must be established prior to October 1. Low fiduciary responsibility.	A simplified way both owner and employees can make contributions for retirement future. Employer contributions are deductible. Few administrative requirements. Easy to establish and administer. Investment flexibility. Tax deduction. Tax-deferred growth.	Generally must be the only retirement plan to which individuals make contributions. A greater amount of IRS reporting. Low annual limits. All participants are 100% vested. Does not permit loans.
Simple 401(k) Savings Incentive Match Plan tax-favored retirement plan. Corporations, partnership, and sole proprietorship establish IRAs for employees.	Deferral limit $10,500.* $3,000* catch-up $2,500 contributions, if over 50. Eligible if compensation is at least $5,000 during the year and prior years.	Newer practice or practice with fewer employees wishing to provide retirement benefits and allow for both salary deferral and employer contributions.	Annual notification to all eligible employees. An employer contribution provided to all eligible participants. IRS forms 1099-R, 5500. Prior to October 1 Moderate fiduciary responsibility.	Plan is not subject to discrimination testing. Employer contributions are deductible. Easy to establish and administer. Fewer administrative requirements. Investment flexibility. Tax deduction. Tax-deferred growth.	Generally must be the only retirement plan to which individuals make contributions. IRS reporting requirements. All participants are 100% vested.

Solo 401(k) with Profit Sharing Plan Owner only Sole proprietorship, partnership, LLC, can establish a tax-favored retirement plan.	Deferral limit $15,500.* Individual limit is 100% of compensation up to $45,000.* Employer contribution limited to 25% of total eligible compensation. $5,000* catch-up contributions, if over 50.	Sole owner practice. Earning less than $164,000 and seek to maximize contributions (*could be used as spouse's plan*).	Plan document IRS form 5500-EZ when plan assets reach $100,000 December 31 or by employer's tax year end. Moderate fiduciary responsibility.	Deductibility of employer contributions. Low administrative costs. Maximize contributions. Investment flexibility. Tax-deferred growth. Loans: up to $50,000 or ½ of vested account balance.	Must not employ common law employees. IRS reporting requirements.
401(k) Tax-favored retirement plan with deferral arrangement allows for pre-tax contributions.	Deferral limit $15,500.* Overall individual limit 100% of compensation up to $45,000.* $5,000* catch-up contributions, if over 50.	Thriving practice wishing to maximize retirement future while maintaining flexibility. Can be combined with other plans.	Plan document IRS forms 1099-R, 5500. Compliance testing. Participant reporting requirements December 31 or by employer's tax year end. High fiduciary responsibility.	Plan design to maximize contributions. Deductibility of employer contributions. Investment flexibility. Tax-deferred growth. Loans: up to $50,000 or ½ of vested account balance.	Administrative costs. IRS reporting requirements. Ongoing compliance. Fiduciary obligation.
Profit Sharing Plan Tax-favored retirement plan incentive for employees to increase profitability.	Overall individual limit 100% of compensation up to $45,000.* Employer contribution limited to 25% of total eligible compensation.	Ideal for thriving practice seeking discretionary contributions. Plan design can maximize your retirement future. Can be combined with 401(k) plan.	Plan document IRS forms 1099-R, 5500. Compliance testing. Participant reporting requirements December 31 or by employer's tax year end. High fiduciary responsibility.	Plan design to fit practice. Deductibility of employer contributions. Investment flexibility. Tax-deferred growth. Loans: up to $50,000 or ½ of vested account balance.	Administrative costs. IRS reporting requirements. Ongoing compliance. Fiduciary obligation.

(*continued*)

Plan Type	Contribution Limits	Who Should Consider	Administrative Requirements Fiduciary Responsibility	Key Advantages	Key Disadvantages
Age-weighted/Class-Based Plan Tax-favored retirement plan strategically designed to benefit specific group.	Employer contribution limited to 25% of total eligible compensation. Allocation methods allow an individual to receive up to the lesser of 100% of compensation or $45,000.*	Thriving practice wishing to favor either older employees or a specific "class" of employees. Plan design can maximize individual retirement future. May be combined with 401(k) plan.	Plan document IRS forms 1099-R, 5500. Compliance testing. Participant reporting requirements December 31 or by employer's tax year end. High fiduciary responsibility.	Custom-designed plan. Deductibility of employer contributions. Allocation can favor older and/or key employees. Investment flexibility. Tax deduction. Tax-deferred growth. Loans: up to $50,000 or ½ of vested account balance.	Administrative costs. IRS reporting requirements. Ongoing compliance and amendments. Fiduciary obligation.
Money Purchase Plan Employer-sponsored retirement plan with an annual contribution formula that allows employees to accrue a benefit.	Overall individual limit 100% of compensation up to $45,000.* $5,000* catch-up contributions, if over 50.	Thriving practice wishing to establish retirement benefits for employees. Can be combined with 401(k) plan.	Plan document IRS forms 1099-R, 5500. Compliance testing. Participant reporting requirements. Mandatory employer contribution December 31. High fiduciary responsibility.	Can establish other retirement plans. Employee retention. Investment flexibility. Large tax deduction. Tax-deferred growth. Loans: up to $50,000 or ½ of vested account balance.	High administrative costs. 10% excise tax applies if minimum funding is not satisfied. Inflexible funding requirements. Fiduciary obligation.

Defined Benefit "Traditional Pension" Employer-sponsored retirement plan with strict contribution formulas that allow eligible employees to accrue a benefit.	Benefit based not to exceed 100% participant's highest 3-year average compensation, up to $180,000.*	Thriving practice wanting to offer a fixed benefit that favors older employees. Ideal for owner at least 50 years of age who has never sponsored any type of retirement plan.	Plan document IRS forms 1099-R, 5500 and schedules. Compliance testing. Participant reporting requirements. Actuarial calculations and PBGA. Insurance. Very high fiduciary responsibility.	Promised specific level of benefit. Individual benefit up to $170,000.* Investment flexibility. Very large tax deduction. Tax-deferred growth. Loans are permitted.	Strict funding formulas. High administrative costs. Ongoing compliance and amendments. Fiduciary obligation.
403(b) Plan "Tax Sheltered Annuities" flexible retirement vehicle for IRC 501(c)(3).	Deferral limit $15,500.* Overall individual limit of compensation up to $45,000.* $5,000* catch-up contributions, if over 50.	Usually the only plan available to physicians working for not-for-profit such as hospitals, churches, and charities that wish to provide retirement benefits through employee salary deferral.	December 31 or by employer's tax year end. Minimal reporting requirements. Low fiduciary responsibility. Deadline depends on sponsor.	Individual contributions can be excluded or deducted from income. Investment flexibility. Tax deduction. Tax-deferred growth. Loans: up to $50,000 or 1/2 of vested account balance.	Loose ERISA requirements may cause relaxed administration. Possible 5500 filings. Investment options limited to mutual funds, annuities, and certain credit union accounts.

*2005 limitations as indexed
http://www.irs.gov/

Source: FIM Group Retirement Planning Team: This comparison chart is general in nature and should not be considered advice specific to your situation. Use it as a guide in working with your advisors or source provider.

situation. In addition, retirement plan administration is more than merely complying with the Internal Revenue Service, Department of Labor, and other regulatory bodies. Retirement plan administration includes communicating to each employee the benefits of the retirement plan and how that plan fits into the financial life and goal of each of your employees and your partners. Retirement plan sponsors should use an independent, fee-only investment manager who has expertise in managing retirement plan assets. Asset allocation, diversification, individual investment choices, which funds are best, and other vital investment decisions should be made by a full-time experienced investment team, not your physician's group. The team's job is to understand risk and manage those portfolios consistently with appropriate, prudent investment management techniques. See "Long-Term Retirement Investment Policy Strategies" on pages 212–214 for a sample investment policy statement with goals for your plan.

Other chapters in this book describe investment management styles. It is important to understand that just because there are more choices for the retirement plan participant, allowing individuals to choose any type of investment they want does not necessarily mean that the plan is better. Plan sponsors have a responsibility to give their plan participants options that are managed, suitable, appropriate, and prudent. Usually that means access to a good, solid investment manager. There are 50,000 stocks to invest in, thousands and thousands of mutual funds, hundreds of thousands of bonds, and many other products. Just allowing the employee to have access to all of those is like sending a child with a headache to the drugstore to choose the best analgesic. A plan sponsor (ie, the employer) and those who work for the plan sponsor have a fiduciary obligation to the employees to make sure their portfolios are managed appropriately and well. Be wary of firms that charge additionally for consulting and trustee work and add marketing fees on top of investment management fees. This is common with retirement plans sponsored by insurance companies, trust companies, brokerage firms, and some financial planners. Make sure your controlling cost is consistent with quality, excellence, and common sense. Many firms add a consulting fee or trustee's fees on top of already high fees. Although this may allow the physician to feel comfortable and that he is getting another layer of advice, often these fees are unnecessary. It can be more cost-effective to hire a firm on an hourly basis once per year or every 2 years to go over your plan than to pay them to look over your shoulder.

You are ultimately responsible, so you need to make sure the investment manager works consistently with what you think is appropriate and that you are not irresponsibly delegating this important task. Whoever manages your retirement plan should have the training, education, temperament, experience, long

2007 Annual Contribution Limits for Qualified Plans	
Annual Compensation	$225,000
Defined Benefit Basic Limit	$180,000
Defined Contribution Plans Basic Limit (415)	$45,000
DC Deferral Limit (402)	$15,500
DC Catch-up Limit	$5,000
Simple Plans Deferral Limit	$10,500
Simple Catch-up Limit	$2,500
Highly Compensated Definition (prior year comp.)	$100,000
Key Employees Compensation	$145,000

*The investment climate is chaotic, complex, and ever-changing. Your portfolio manager's goal should be to construct and manage portfolios that are ideally constructed (at every moment) to provide peace of mind, reliability, and long-term security. The management of retirement portfolios is by far more complex and important than any other type of portfolio management. The manager's key tools of security selection, asset allocation, and macro-/microeconomic analysis must be skillfully applied with sustainable diligence and forethought. At minimum, three of the above five options should be available in any retirement plan that allows investment flexibility.

Source: Financial and Investment Management Group, retirement plan team. A printable copy of this worksheet is available at www.fimg.net.

track record, and resources available to them to successfully continue taking care of your retirement plan. It should be a stable firm of sufficient size to assure your employees that someone is going to take care of them now and into the future. While the one-man or small shop that works out of your certified public accountant (CPA) firm may seem good on paper, often it is not ideally suited for the long term of your plan. Also, the fact that it is your golf buddy at the local brokerage firm should have no bearing in your choice of retirement plan administrator, investment manager, or plan design consultant.

Investment Options for Retirement Plans

Most plans should have at least three investment options. Each option should be designed to meet a specific investment goal and value at-risk matrix as described in other chapters. Each investment strategy should be a long-term retirement investment strategy based on the goal of great income from your retirement plan. The "Long-Term Retirement Investment Policy Strategies" listed in the table on page 212 should be a core to any investment policy that you have for your employees. Hire a skill-based investment manager who believes in management. By hiring an indexing-oriented investment manager is equivalent to basically transferring the investment management to the employee. If your investment manager's options are primarily to invest in only stocks or only bonds, this is being passive index–oriented and leaving the most important decisions to your employees. If your employees choose stocks or bonds for their portfolio, they are making the most important investment decision a person can make. The timing of a decision could be a disaster for their retirement security (see "What It Takes to Recover from Declines" on page 192). A skill-based investment manager who manages those portfolios, as illustrated in the "Long Term Retirement Investment Policy Strategies" table (page 212), should be hired.

It's Simple

If your goal is to retire, then the first objective of the financial planning process is to add efficiency so you can get to retirement more quickly. Second, increase your probability of retiring with ease. Third, decrease your possibility of not being able to retire because of financial trauma or some

Adjusted Roth's Gross Income Phase-Outs

As a physician, chances are your income will disqualify you from establishing a Roth individual retirement account (IRA) with annual contributions or a Roth conversion from a traditional IRA. Roth contributions are phased out between $150,000 and $160,000 of adjusted gross income (AGI). In addition, eligibility for Roth conversion is dependent upon an AGI under $100,000.

Adjusted Gross Income Phase-Outs

	Single	Married Filing Jointly
Roth IRA conversion	$100,000	$100,000
Roth IRA contributions	$97,000 to $114,000	$156,000 to $165,000

Generally, contributing to a Roth is not a good planning tool for physicians. However, if you qualify for a Roth conversion because of low income for a year caused by disability, a fellowship, childcare time off, volunteer work, or any reason (under $50,000 AGI or so), a Roth conversion should be considered. Funding a Roth for your teenage children is a great start for them. Your fee-only financial planner can run the numbers for you.

other reason. Using tax-qualified plans helps leverage your income, grows your wealth more quickly on a better risk-adjusted basis, and helps you to be efficient about the way you manage your financial affairs.

I remember talking with the editor of a financial journal for physicians who also did financial planning for physicians. He said, "Face it Paul, all physicians need to do is (1) have good, adequate casualty insurance with high deductibles and high coverage limits; (2) have term life insurance to take care of their family; (3) have disability insurance to make sure that if something happens to them they will have income security; and (4) fund the maximum they possibly can in their retirement plan, and they can spend the rest and have a great life." Any financial plan needs all those elements plus an estate plan (will and/or a trust), and you are often all set. The editor's summary is the essence of this chapter, if it includes budgeting and understanding insurance and taxes to create excess income to put toward savings and retirement plans.

Retirement Planning

Beware Rules of Thumb

Everyone's financial situation is different. However, our brains are wired to oversimplify complexity into rules of thumb and apply them to all situations. With financial planning, this can be disastrous. Some rules of thumb sound good on the surface but belie common sense and wisdom. Three common retirement plan rules of thumb you will hear are (1) at retirement, you will need 80% of your pre-retirement income; (2) 100 minus your age should be your percentage in equities; and (3) the more investment options your retirement plan has, the better. These statements, like folk wisdom, are full of contradictions, just as "look before you leap," contradicts "he who hesitates is lost," and "you can't teach an old dog new tricks" contradicts the fact that "it's never too late to learn."

According to the book *Nibbling on Einstein's Brain* (Swanson, D. Toronto, Canada: Annick Press. 2001), lightning does strike the same place twice; in fact, lightning bolts once struck the Empire State Building in New York City 15 times in 15 minutes. With investments, you are better off safe than sorry, but then again, nothing ventured, nothing gained. Like anything in life, we can always find a phrase or behavior to justify what we do. Wall Street and investment marketers in their zeal to sell can oversimplify with phrases that sound wise, correct, and appropriate that can derail your financial plan.

Dismantling the three common but bogus rules of thumb is as easy as the following three principles: One, at retirement, you will need what you will need. Two, what if the average yield on stocks is 7% and on bonds is 4%? What if you are 100 years old? What if stocks are overvalued and you are 50? Third, if I am a size nine and I have 100 size twelve's to choose from, am I better off?

Tax Strategies

"The Congress shall have the power to lay and collect tax on incomes from whatever source arrived without a proportionate among the several states and without regard to any census or enumeration." (16th Amendment to the Constitution, 1913).

Taxes are usually the largest budgetary item in a physician's financial life. Thus, tax avoidance can often be overemphasized in planning. Many people do almost anything to avoid paying taxes, even risking their financial health. In the 1970s, many risked their financial well-being by investing in leveraged oil deals. In the 1980s it was leveraged real estate deals, and in the 1990s, tax credit technology. In this decade it appears to be all three. The best tax shelter is good advice that fits you well. The second best is a tax-favored, tax-qualified retirement plan as discussed in this chapter. Tax-qualified retirement plans, however, are not discussed here in the context of tax influences on investing. A good CPA and financial planner working together can help minimize your taxes while helping to grow your net worth.

When looking at your investment portfolio, it is reasonable to figure net risk adjusted after tax returns. However, many financial advisors and investors are spending more time worrying about taxes than total returns. It is always better to have a 15% return, pay 5% of that return in taxes, and end up with 10% net after taxes than it is to be in an investment that will earn maybe 7% to 8% and eventually have capital gains (5% to 15% at the current rate) plus state rate; that capital rate could go up, and people end up with net 6% or so. Often, financial planners and writers naively talk about the benefits of tax advantage accounts, not realizing that eventually you do have to pay taxes. The key focus should be total return, because the difference between 8% and 6% net return over a 25-year period is over $275,000 on a $100,000 initial investment. Personally, I will pay a few dollars more in taxes today to end up with more net dollars. Taxes should never preempt an investment strategy. They are merely input to the investment process. Too many investors concentrate only on avoiding taxes.

Tax Deals

Usually when somebody thinks of tax-favored investments, they think of oil and gas, real estate, technology, and research and development deals. Tax-favored investments are not supposed to be poor investments that lose money. Tax-favored investments need to be very profitable investments that compensate you for significant risks. You should expect to make significant economic gains, therefore tax savings should be part of the decision process. If you want to buy a tax-sheltered investment through a limited partnership, hedge fund, or limited liability pool or limited liability company (LLC), the questions outlined under the next heading (page 138) should be asked to make sure you have a good understanding of your potential investments. Conceptually, when you are investing in a tax shelter you are investing in a business entity, so you can use business analysis tools to determine whether it is an appropriate investment; in other words: Is it managed well? What is the expected return on an investment? What are the costs and fees to manage that business? Often, these investments are expensive to manage, and as one advisor joked, "Tax-sheltered investments are where the limited partners, ie, you, have all the money in the beginning and the general partner has very little. At the end, the general partner has all the money and the limited partner has very little." In many cases this is true.

There are war stories about the physician who bought silly tax shelters, not having a clue he was being ripped off. The tax shelter questions on page 138 will help so you do not get fooled and instead will be assured that you are making good, concrete investment decisions.

There are basically four entities involved in tax-sheltered investments. The first is the investor, which is usually you. The second is the manufacturer of the investment, or the promoter. This includes the people who put the deal together. Often, they are entrepreneurs. The third entity is the business manager. The business manager operates the business: perhaps the research scientist, oil people for oil deals, or a real estate development company for property deals. The fourth player is the salesperson. There are hundreds of tax shelter salespeople out there. The salespeople are usually affiliated with brokers or commission financial planning shops. The commissions can be significant on tax-sheltered deals. Often, commissions are 5% to 10% of what you invest. People will use titles such as *financial planner*, *financial advisor*, *financial consultant*, *tax shelter specialist*, or *retirement tax-sheltered specialist* to hide their job, which is selling tax shelters. The fifth party that should be involved is the advisor to the investor. This is a fee-only objective person who has the background, experience, and training to evaluate the deal for you and give you a letter that states that it is suitable as an investment for you and has investment merits, it is not unreasonable to have in your investment portfolio, and the tax benefits can be used by you and are consistent with current tax laws.

Tax-Sheltered Investments

All investments need to be made on the merit of significant returns. Tax-sheltered investments tend to be sold as a tax-planning vehicle or a vehicle to reduce taxes. It is very easy to pay no taxes: do not make money. Or, to reduce taxes, you can give up to half of your income to charities. If you compare these two options with what the economic returns are on most tax-favored or tax-sheltered investments, you probably would be ahead and do more for society if you donated the money to a charity than to the general partner, the tax-sheltered promoter, or the salesperson who brokered the deal.

Following are specific questions to ask someone who proposes a tax shelter or tax-favored investment under limited partnership, LLC, or some other formula:

1. What will the partnership or entity own?
    a. Are there appraisals on those properties, and has the entity paid a fair price?
2. Are the assets being purchased from the general partner or an entity that is affiliated with the general partner?
3. What did the general partner or the entity affiliated with the general partner or promoter of this pay for those investments being transferred into the partnership or LLC?
4. What investment assumptions are made about the economic benefits, for example, tax-savings appreciation of income, and are they reasonable?
    a. Why are they reasonable?
    b. Has an objective third party reviewed this investment?

5. Is the partnership structured so that I will participate in the effective tax benefits and appreciation in addition to income and other benefits?
6. Does the investment have the potential to throw off phantom income? How much and why? (Phantom income is income that you have to pay taxes on without receiving any cash.)
7. If the partnership is a blind pool, who will make the investment decisions, what is their background, and what is their track record?
8. Who will manage the partnership, what is their background, what is their track record, and are they financially strong?
9. What is my total limit of liability on the investment?
   a. Is there any chance that I will need to add more cash to this deal?
   b. If so, how much?
   c. Do I have unlimited liability with regard to this investment? For example, if it is an oil well, could I lose all of my investment and risk other assets if it blew up and destroyed the local elementary school that was next to the well?
10. What is the expected life of this investment in years?
11. If the investment is a disaster and does not work, does the general partner/manager have the staying power to manage the programs to the best (tax) advantage of the limited partnership, or would the general partner/manager walk away?
12. After fees, commissions and markups, interests, and other financial expenses, how much of each of my dollars is going to be invested?
    a. First in the percentage of equity, and second as a percentage of the total deal including debt.
    b. How will I participate in profits, cash, or appreciation of this program after it is up and running? For example, how much will I get, and how much will the general partner get?
13. Is the general partner taking the substantial risks for his or her contribution to the partnership?
    a. Will the general partner have a strong incentive to make the program work both economically and to maintain its good reputation?
    b. What specific economic incentives does the general partner have to make this deal work?

c. Is the general partner just in the business of coming up with many partnerships, hoping that some will succeed and get extreme economic returns while others may fail in a "throw a deal at the wall and see what sticks" management process?

14. Do I fit to a tee the offering memorandums explanation of who should invest in this deal?
    a. Do my CPA, lawyer, and financial advisor agree with that statement?
15. Why is this better for me than another deal, another investment idea, or just paying off my mortgage?
16. If this is a multiple write-off deal, $2 for $1, do I have a letter addressed to me from a major CPA or tax law firm stating that they feel the tax benefits will flow to me as advised?
17. Did a CPA review this to make sure that it will not throw me into an alternative minimum tax situation?
18. Does this investment fit into my overall financial plan?
19. Are my tax-qualified retirement plans fully refunded, and thus am I already maxing out on them and is my investment portfolio very liquid? If not, why would this be a better deal than funding a tax-qualified retirement plan?
20. Have my tax-sheltered salesperson and financial planner gone over this questionnaire with me?
21. Do I have a letter from my tax-sheltered salesperson or promoter answering each of these questions in writing?

A printable copy of this form is available at www.fimg.net.

Fixed Immediate Annuities

Fixed immediate annuities have a possible place in retirement planning and financial planning. Deferred or variable annuities generally do not. When you are retired and close to drawing on investment principal or you have started using principal and income from your portfolio over a consistent period, then you will need to consider an immediate life annuity that will pay you no matter how long you live and that guarantees that you will not outlive your retirement investments. Immediate life annuities transfer the risk of living too long to an insurance company or companies. If you need

> **Annuities and Life Insurance as Tax Shelters**
>
> Annuities and life insurance have some tax benefits. These tax benefits are of consequence only in that they help offset the terrible financial deal that cash-value life insurance and annuities are, so as to make them only horrible, not totally horrible. Annuities are by far the most over-sold so-called investment products around. They pay nearly the highest commissions of any investment product in general and are by far the worst deal for investors and the best deal for brokers and commission financial advisors and for the insurance companies and mutual fund companies that promote these investments. They are a rip-off.

to do this in retirement, always do it under the advice of a fee-only registered investment advisor. Then, you will want to diversify your immediate annuity policies among a number of insurance companies to reduce risks. Immediate life annuities have tax advantages, and they are designed primarily to help people avoid outliving their income.

Congress, in its great wisdom, gave annuities tax advantages to help people achieve retirement security. However, the tax benefits of a deferred annuity mean that you give the money to the insurance company 20 to 30 years before you retire. The length of deferral period has severely eroded the tax benefit because of abuses by certain industry which took a product that was designed to keep people from outliving their income and promoted the tax-advantages as immediate tax benefits. There is immediate tax benefits, ie, no current tax on the income or growth within the annuity product; however, it's at a huge cost. See "Variable Annuities: Can't Live With 'Em" by my colleague, Jeff Lokken, on page 142 to learn more about variable annuities.

I have seen annuities sold as mutual funds with a tax-free wrapper or mutual funds with tax-deferred components. These are basically insurance companies' products with generally high commissions and high expenses hidden in ledger after ledger of manipulated data to make them look better than other alternatives. If you use assumptions similar to those the annuity company uses, compare them with mutual funds, an actively managed portfolio of municipal bonds, real estate, or any other investment outside of an annuity wrapper. When you add the fees, commissions, and expenses objectively into the equation, rare is the case in which you will be able to justify a variable or fixed annuity. Deferred annuities can be tax bombs destined to blow up. Many physicians have naively purchased deferred annuities, and they are sometimes difficult to get out of.

Variable Annuities: Can't Live With 'Em

I recently read an article in the MSN Web site's money section: "The Worst Retirement Investment You Can Make" by Liz Pulliam Weston. (Available at: http://articles.money-central.msn.com/RetirementandWills/InvestForRetirement/TheWorstRetirementInvestmentYouCanMake.aspx. Accessed August 4, 2006.) Shockingly, Weston noted that "variable annuities posted their second-highest sales ever in 2003" with sales of $124.6 billion. Given their cost and recent tax law changes, variable annuities are, at best, ineffective investment vehicles for creating wealth. Additionally, they significantly complicate estate-planning options. Despite this, Americans have almost $1 trillion invested in variable annuities. This makes annuities one of the most common products sold by stockbrokers and insurance agents.

An annuity, according to *The Portable MBA Desk Reference* (Nohria N. Hoboken, NJ: John Wiley & Sons; 1998), is a "contract sold by life insurance companies that guarantees periodic payments to the buyer (annuitant) at a future point in time, usually upon retirement" (p. 38). There are two types of annuities: fixed and variable. Fixed annuities provide future payments of an equal amount and variable annuities provide future payments that change based on the underlying value of the investments within the annuity. Variable annuities provide investors with separate account options in the annuity, much like mutual funds.

Most investors should not purchase variable annuities. Why? Here are a few reasons:

- Although the accumulation of an annuity grows, tax-deferred gains are taxed at ordinary income rates when withdrawn, which may be as high as 37.6% federal tax. This compares to the maximum current tax rate of 15% on long-term capital gains and certain qualified dividends.

- Variable annuities are expensive, often costing as much as 3% annually when you add up administrative charges, contract fee, separate account management fees, and mortality charges. Given the low current investment environment, variable annuity investors could loose money after paying these expenses.

- Not only are ongoing expenses high, but also most annuities have huge penalties for early withdrawal. These surrender fees are usually 5% to 7% initially and decline annually. This seriously affects investment flexibility should tax laws or your planning situations change.

- At death, variable annuities may guarantee the original investment; however, the heirs are denied the benefit of step-up in tax basis. In effect, a step-up is when the asset's tax basis is valued as of the date of death for the heir and eliminates taxation on the pre-death growth when the asset is sold. In contrast, an heir must pay high ordinary income taxes on the taxable death benefit of a variable annuity.

- An investment in a variable annuity within a tax-sheltered account such as an individual retirement account or 401(k) makes no sense at all. Because annuities are already tax-deferred, you are placing a shelter within a shelter. This reduces your compounded return by the higher fees in the annuity. This could be as much as 2% per year paid to the insurance company instead of compounding your wealth.

It is imperative that owners of annuity policies seriously consider the effectiveness of annuities for achieving their financial planning objectives. In many situations, the sooner the annuity can be efficiently surrendered, the better.

Despite the fact that annuities are a popular investment product sold by brokers and insurance agents, a wise investor should not invest in them. (Should you currently own a variable annuity, get advice about what to do with it from a fee-only advisor.)

By Jeff Lokken, Financial and Investments Management Group.

There are a number of ways to get out of a high-cost annuity. One is through the advice of a fee-only advisor to switch to a product that has very low expenses and fees such as those offered by Charles Schwab (www.schwab.com) or Vanguard (www.vanguard.com). If you have annuities, you can manage them in a way similar to the do-it-yourself portfolio in which you move the money from stocks to bonds to money market as needed. This can allow the annuities to grow tax-free. One way to get out of deferred annuities is to draw on them first in retirement. Even if someone offers you a low-cost deferred annuity, it is probably not in your best interest. If someone sold you an annuity in the last 10 years before the tax reform act that made annuities a bad deal, fire the person, hire someone else, and realize that the advice was tainted by commissions.

If you do have an annuity and are interested in its benefits, then the following questions in "Variable Annuities: Can't Live With 'Em" (page 142) should be asked of your annuity company in a letter (see page 196 for suggested wording of the letter).

> **Two Annuity Questions**
>
> Did you know that deferred variable annuities estimated before October 31, 1979, are eligible for a step-up in basis at your death? However, if these annuities were 1035-exchanged since then, they loose the eligibility.
>
> Did you know that using your retirement annuity as collateral for a personal loan will destroy the tax deferral of the annuity and will trigger taxable income? **Did the guy who sold you that policy tell you this?**

Wealth-Destruction Products

Imagine if, as a physician, you could earn an extra $100,000 per year if you counseled your patients to smoke cigarettes. Not many cigarettes, perhaps just 7 to 10 per day, so that it would be unlikely to cause premature aging or premature death. Your patients trust you and know you would not lead them astray, and thus would faithfully smoke the cigarettes. Visions of the vital Marlboro® man would appear in your patients' minds as you describe the benefits of American-grown and union-made tobacco products that enhance health. Perhaps $100,000 is not enough to cause or entice you to violate your ethics and to counsel people to smoke; perhaps it is $200,000, or $1 million, or maybe no amount. Maybe you would re-read the Hippocratic Oath and say, "Even recommending one cigarette is inconsistent with this."

In the financial industry, however, there are many wealth-destruction products that are sold by institutions purely driven by commissions. Those who sell them are as ruthless as the physician telling a patient that cigarettes are healthy. These destructive products include both fixed and variable deferred annuities and any cash-value life insurance used for accumulating wealth. Add to this group almost any oil or gas drilling, oil and gas income, cattle breeding, research and development, equipment leasing, and real estate partnership in which the front expenses, commissions, and fees exceed 3% to 5% of your investment and ongoing costs exceed 2%. Leveraging off their industries good reputations, some hedge funds and high-load indexed mutual funds also might look very sinister if held up to the light of comparative analyses. Nevertheless, there are some good, well-structured oil, gas, real estate, R&D analyses and I have some friends who are spectacular managers that manage well-run hedge funds. There are many fine no-load and even a few load funds available as very low- or no-load funds.

"Mind you, only <u>one</u> doctor out of ten recommends it."

© The New Yorker Collection 1992 Ed Fisher from cartoonbank.com. All Rights Reserved.

People will do almost anything to avoid paying taxes, and tax shelter salespeople know this. They know the full risk to financial health, and they know exactly what to say to sell their products. Their sales slicks, phone solicitations, and luncheon interviews contain terms like *tax-deferred*, *tax-sheltered*, *tax-favored*, and *tax-enhanced*. They ask probing questions such as, "Well, you don't want to pay more tax than you have to, do you?" And, "Would you like to reduce your taxes?" I would like to wash down a hot fudge brownie with something stronger than coffee; however, I know this is not good for me, is it?"

In God We Trust; Others Provide Data

As we have seen in previous sections, rules of thumb can create havoc in financial planning. For another example of this, look at the "80% of pre-retirement income to retirement" rule of thumb. It assumes that your life after retirement will look similar to your life before, which is as ridiculous as saying that at age 65 you will look like you did at 35. Everyone's retirement lifestyle looks different. Many people sacrifice and work long hours during their work years,

"You don't know how lucky you are! A quarter of an inch either way, and it would have been outside the area of reimbursable coverage!"

© The New Yorker Collection 1991 Al Ross from cartoonbank.com. All Rights Reserved.

saving significant amounts of their income, but need even more money in retirement because they chose a robust retirement lifestyle. For some, their pre-retirement income may be two to three times what they need for retirement. It all depends on how much income you will need to support the lifestyle you want. If a financial planner says, "You will need 80% of what you needed before retirement," without asking you to do a retirement budget, find someone else to give you advice and do not look back, because the person is oversimplifying a complex subject. If he or she is nonchalant about planning for retirement, this attitude will spill over into his or her insurance recommendations, investment recommendations, and other related areas.

The rule of thumb to "take your age, subtract it from 100, and that is how much you should have in stocks" is debunked by the investment information I have given in this book. What if bonds yield 2% and stocks yield 7%? Once again, oversimplifying can have disastrous outcomes on your retirement goals.

Now, Not Later, Gifting Guidelines

After they retire, most physicians settle into a routine budget after 1 to 4 years. By looking over a few years' income and expenses, future income can be projected. When you know what you will need, you can estimate how much you can gift. Following are my gifting rules of thumb:

1. No debts.
2. Good hospital/medical insurance.
3. Money for major purchases or expenses such as second home, to fix up home, etc, should be set aside for those needs.
4. Any commitments to family that might be a call on your wealth are accounted for (mother-in-law expenses, children's special needs).
5. Your portfolio supports 120% of your most outrageous budget at a 4% rate of return.

For example, if your home is paid off, your second home is free and clear, you have set aside $50,000 to add a mother-in-law apartment or support her if need be, and you need $100,000 living expenses above your Social Security, you will need to have $3,050,000 in financial assets ($100,000 × 120% = $120,000 annually ÷ 0.04 = $3,000,000 + $50,000 for mom = $3,050,000).

If your investment assets were significantly in excess of the $3,050,000, then it would be reasonable to consider a gifting program, charitable bequeaths, and other forms of transferring assets to reduce your estate (and thus potential estate taxes) and help your beneficiaries now rather than later. Everyone's goals and needs are different and the amount of income-producing assets needed to produce a secure and safe retirement is also different. Usually, because of the cost of long-term care facilities and nursing care, gifting should not be done unless income-producing, marketable investment assets are in excess of $1 million. Any gifting program should be with the guidance of a fee-only qualified financial advisor who is trained in budgeting and working with high-income/high-net worth individuals and families.

The third harmful rule of thumb is that you have to pay for investment services, so you might as well hire a commission-based or fee-based financial advisor who can receive the commissions you would pay anyway. As a portfolio manager, we can purchase $1 million worth of investments for a portfolio and the total cost is $10. Yes, we had to pay a commission, but it was $10. Financial salespeople might say, "Yeah but . . . ," but the truth is, we have our own trading mechanisms that tie right into Wall Street and pay roughly $9.95 for securities transactions. If the broker says, "You will have to pay a commission anyway," realize that you could pay $10 or $500

Sample Insurance Letter

Dear Insurance Company,

Regarding my policy #_____, I have the following questions:

1. What is my exact beneficiary designation and ownership registration on this annuity product?
2. What is the financial strength of your company based on Standard & Poor's, Best's, or other rating agencies?
3. If it is a variable annuity, what are the investment options of this annuity? What are the total fees, expenses, and commissions paid on each of these investment options including internal fees and expenses paid on any mutual funds, separate accounts, or other products? For example, the annuity wrapper fee, any mortality fee, any 12b1 or marketing fees, commissions paid internally to the investment that the annuity invests in, kickbacks, referral fees, or expenses paid to brokers or any interested parties. Please itemize these in a list and state this as a percentage of total investment and total I paid for this annuity as a dollar amount.
4. What was the total commission paid to the broker, the brokerage firm, or the agent regarding this annuity when I purchased it? What are the ongoing commissions paid regarding this annuity?
5. What are the surrender fees on this annuity if I were to move it to a no-load or low-load annuity product with different fees, commissions, or expenses?
6. How is my annuity currently invested?
7. Does your company sell or have available any products with significantly lower expense ratios than what I have with my current product? For example, do you have another product that has lower mortality insurance or other expenses than this product?
8. I am having trouble understanding the specifics of why my insurance agent, stockbroker, or financial advisor recommended this product to me. Does your company have any third-party material, articles, etc, that describe why this product would be better than other investment options (such as owning plain mutual funds, government bonds, CDs, managed accounts, tax-free municipal bonds, etc)?

Please give me this information in writing and be as specific as possible. I want a thorough understanding of exactly what I have with this annuity product. Additional information would be greatly appreciated. Also, if possible, please send me a copy of the original application I signed to get this annuity and any subsequent forms I have signed regarding this policy.

Sincerely Yours,

[Your name]

A printable version of this letter is available at www.fimg.net.

or more for the same trade. There are mutual funds within the same firm that have a multitude of different commission and fee schedules. I have seen up to 23 different commission amounts that could be paid on one fund. The large investor gets deal "#1," the less sophisticated gets commission and fee schedule "# 23." Yes, you have to pay a commission or fee, but if you pay 1.7% in fees and expenses instead of 0.17%, you pay 10 times more. Yes, you had to pay, but is 10 times more reasonable?

Many brokers and investment people who receive commissions say, "It's all built-in, or 'baked in.'" When a commission-based person tells you this, say, "Exactly how is that baked in, and exactly how much is backed in? Am I paying more than if I would have gone directly to this company? What substitute investment could I make to get this at a bargain price?" Ask for their reply in writing, and then you can decide if it was worth paying that broker $25,000 instead of paying a fee-only advisor $1,000 to give you the same advice in a few hours. So, when someone gives you a rule of thumb, please make sure that you look before you leap, read the writing on the wall, open your eyes to see what is there, and don't count your chickens before they hatch.

Disguised Annuities

Often, annuities are disguised with new names such as nonqualified retirement plans; also, they are labeled by what they fund, for example, IRAs, 403(b)s, pension plans, tax-favored deferred compensation. None of these entities have anything to do with the investment. The annuity is used to fund them. Any time someone asks you to use an annuity to fund a retirement plan, they are asking you to put a tax shelter inside of a tax shelter, which is inefficient and a bad deal.

Cash Value Life Insurance

Physicians add great inefficiency to their financial plan by owning commissionable cash-value life insurance. Older physicians seem compelled by the idea that life insurance products can help them save estate taxes, which is untrue. To say that life insurance saves estate taxes is like saying *donuts-washed-down-with-whiskey-in-your-coffee-while-you-smoke-cigarettes* is a healthy diet. It is impossible for life insurance to reduce estate tax. Life insurance can create an estate. It can increase the size of an estate. It can create wealth outside of an estate, but it does not save estate taxes. Life insurance, low-cost term life as discussed earlier, can be used as a tool in estate planning and, in some circumstances, can be helpful for families with young children who need to create an instant estate to protect the children and the surviving spouse. As stated in other chapters, life insurance is to carry you until your net worth is sufficient. It is not to be purchased for estate tax–paying planning reasons, except in rare circumstances in which perhaps your spouse is the insurance agent and needs the commission!

Life insurance is not designed to be an investment! It is about insurance and death! Policies are probably the most inefficient wealth accumulator around, even worse than sticking the money in your mattress. If an insurance agent recommends that you buy any insurance product for wealth accumulation, ask, "What is my exact cash value after I put in the premium the first year if I cash the policy in?" If the cash value is less than the pure term cost less the premium, you know you are getting a raw deal. If the cash value is not significantly better than what you get with any other investment product, then you should look at alternatives.

Life insurance should not be combined with investment elements, regardless of whether there is a variable product inside the policy (a so-called life insurance wrapper). Life insurance, no matter how it is disguised, is a product designed to provide a benefit should someone die. The only significant cost of life insurance should be the cost of the pure term component of the policy. That component goes up every year, and whole life insurance just levels the premium to something you could call whole life term to age 100.

Reprinted with permission from *Stu's Views* © 2002 Stu All Rights Reserved www.stus.com

It cannot be overemphasized that cash-value life insurance is probably one of the biggest scams around and should not be purchased under any circumstances, unless you get advice from a fee-only advisor and stick to low load or no load products.

If the only information you get is from your insurance agent or an insurance agent who has an attorney in his pocket, use the common-sense test and ask, "What are the alternatives?" Get an objective opinion from a fee-only advisor. Life insurance does have some tax advantages; however, they are significantly mitigated by the fees, commissions, tax issues, and expenses imposed on the insurance policy. If you need a no-commission policy, cash-value policy, or a policy that would go on forever because of certain trust, business, or other needs, then call Low Load Insurance Services (www.llis.com) or other companies listed in Chapter 4 to obtain proposals.

CHAPTER 6
Invest Wisely

Investing with Confidence and the Paradox of *If*

In 2004 I was approached by a potential client looking for someone to manage his money. From his flurry of questions I inferred that others had previously shown him indexes, Standard and Poor's 500 charts, asset allocation, bond ladders, and growth and bond mutual funds, all prefaced with "*if*." I believe their pitch was, "*If* you had or did this, then you would [have this return]." Well, *if* I had someone buy me a lottery ticket and if I won, I would have a winning lottery ticket, right? My point is, many money managers armed with fancy charts and graphs based on what looks like rational thought and logic show returns based on *if*. From our conversation, it seemed that none of the presentations that this prospective client had heard were about investing, but rather, they were about *if*.

My beef with this approach is that it is not straightforward or intellectually genuine. Many trust officers, mutual fund salespeople, and Wall Street brokers sell and promote anything and say it is reasonable. I have yet to find a Wall Street broker, trust company, or mutual fund company that called clients regarding their growth or balanced portfolios near market peaks and said, "We think the market is so expensive, sell everything or 90% of everything." How do I know this? Before Black Monday in 1987 and before "the bubble" burst in 1998 and 1989, their clients held lots of expensive, overvalued, and ridiculously priced investments. Most investors do not seem to understand the difference between a bargain investment and an expensive investment and, to their peril, often erroneously think that their broker, trust officer, or financial manager is protecting them against heavy losses or bad investments.

Investing is about making consistent, real returns that can be used to support lifestyle, children, loved ones, or charities or to buy items like a second home. Investing is about feeling secure that the outcome of your investing is known. Investing is about having confidence in the expected return of each specific investment in your portfolio. If, for example, you own and hold to maturity a 5% government bond, you can depend on the fact that before taxes and inflation you will have 5%. If you own a diversified portfolio of companies with an earnings yield of 10% that is growing with the economy, you should feel safe that over a long cycle of 5 to 10 years your total returns will be around 10% from dividends and the reinvestment of those earnings by the company to compound returns. It is hard to find companies today that have earnings yields of 10% or more that we feel merit an investment. When I came into this business in the early 80s before the big run-up in stocks, it was hard to find companies that had less than a 10% expected earnings yield. Today, the average earnings yield is around 5.5% on US stocks, so they would need to drop in price (by 45%!) to get to a 10% earnings yield. Or, of course, earnings could nearly double to get to the 10% earnings yield, which would be very unlikely in a world economy that is growing 2% to 4%.

Expected Returns Based on Price and Value

Asset prices go up and down, but the value that comes from expected cash from the investment over time, discounted mathematically to today, can be calculated using math and judgment. Every investment from gold to housing to stocks can be analyzed to get to a real value and expected future returns.

Common sense and review of history teach us that past returns on specific investments like IBM, the stock market, or classes of investments such as stock or bond indexes are a poor way to forecast the specific investment's expected future performance. I find it a paradox that so-called investors make decisions on their investments on the basis of past price action rather than on real, expected future total returns based on sound financial analysis. Successful investing is making sure you own investments that you expect to have great performance going forward, not backward. Managing a portfolio requires knowing what each investment in the portfolio is worth or, in other words, its intrinsic value and thus its expected return over time. This expected return should not come from looking at an investment's past performance. Eventually, a market will find the value in an investment whose price is too low compared with its value and bid it up. But participating in such gains

Market's Risks

Bull and Bear Markets

	Bull Markets	Bear Markets	Current Bull Market (Since October 9, 2002)
Median duration	614 days	363 days	881 days
Median advance/decline	+65%	−27%	+57%

* Dow Jones industrial average since 1901

Ratios at Market Bottoms and Tops*

	Market Bottoms	Market Tops	Now
Median dividend yield	4.81%	3.58%	1.97%
Median earnings yield	7.38%	5.69%	4.96%
Median price/earnings ratio	13.55	17.57	20.15
Median price/book ratio	1.29	1.93	2.88

*Standard and Poor's 500 since 1929

Conclusion: By all of these measures, the US stock market, as measured by the Standard and Poor's 500 and Dow Jones industrial average, is late in its current bull market and is priced well above its median levels at historic market tops. From levels this high, history, fundamental analysis, and common sense tell us that the market could fall more than 30% and that such a decline could take more than a year to reach the bottom.

Median Price Movements

12 Months Before and After Market Bottoms Since 1929*

	12 Months Preceding Market Bottoms	12 Months Subsequent to Market Bottoms
Large-cap stocks	−9.5%	+33%
Small-cap stocks	−16.3%	+58%

*Large stocks represented by Standard and Poor's 500 total return index; small stocks represented by Ibbotson small company total return index.

Conclusion: It is impossible to pick exact market bottoms, but the risk/return characteristics of buying too early (before market bottoms) are much better than buying too late (after bottoms).

takes patience. It also takes guts and understanding to buy investments when they are bargain priced because, paradoxically, usually they get there by performing poorly.

Many people have trouble understanding the common-sense facts about investing or, as Einstein might say, the relative value of those facts. To better understand this value/price concept, take a look at American housing prices. In many areas of this country, house prices have gone up a gazillion percent over the past few years. Many would conclude that housing is a good investment. But if something was a good investment, does that mean it still is? Housing prices have gone up as interest rates have dropped from 15% to 5%. In addition to much lower interest rates that have allowed us to buy more house for the same payment, demographic shifts such as maturing adults, families with two incomes, human migration to more desired areas, immigration, and the growth of our economy have all contributed to housing's price appreciation. To assume prices of houses will grow at rates similar to the past few years would require interest rates going down to nearly 0% as well as assuming that more and more people will be able to afford more and more house (in terms of dollars, not size). In addition to interest rates, a slew of factors influence house prices including rents to value, cash returns on rented homes, supply and demand, employment, and wages. Whatever happens in the future, rest assured that house prices, like any asset price, will end up at the right "real" level. All investments are influenced by cyclical shifts with causes that are usually identifiable.

If you take an investment and look at it critically with the goal of a high probability of making money, you need to be forward-looking. What I know about successful investing is that it is hard! It takes skill, intelligence, common sense, experience, goals, guts, leadership, an understanding of risk, an eye to find value, and the ability to find the expected returns.

Investing is about making money. Realistic return expectations can be established if you avoid using the rearview mirror "if" method of financial projections so common today among naive investors, financial advisors, brokers, certified financial planners, mutual funds, and trust companies. Price matters, and market bottoms are knowable based on price earnings, price to dividends, price to book, and other factors that represent bargain prices. If you buy when prices are cheap, you can average out to become fully invested, as prices are bottoming out.

"Frankly, Mr. Poole, I would strongly suggest you make one last, desperate bid for happiness."

©The New Yorker Collection 1984 Gahan Wilson from cartoonbank.com. All Rights Reserved.

Bottoms and Tops

"Heal thyself" does not mean "be your own doctor." It means taking responsibility for one's own health by engaging the help of physicians and others. Investing self-sufficiency is similar; it requires you to take responsibility for your investment management decisions, processes, and, ultimately, outcomes.

Investing is not simple; it is about management and making good decisions. All investment decisions are made with incomplete information about an uncertain future. The methods, systems, and philosophy of you, the investor, are all-important. As an investor, there is only one goal: Invest to make money, not lose it. This is unlike a typical stock manager, real estate expert, or bond manager's goal. The typical stock manager's goal is to win the relative performance game. If stocks go down 74.85% for his or her index and "only" 70% is lost, the manager might say, "Look how well I did for you. I did nearly 5% better than the index." (See "Worst Declines" table below.)

If you are hiring a stock manager who believes that he/she must remain at least 70% invested in stocks at all times either through investment management policy or practice philosophy, then it is your job and no one else's to decide when to fire the person, sell those stocks, and get out of the stock market. Many stock, bond, and real estate managers seem to think their job is merely to own the best of the investment arena they favor or must own. Such a rigid and narrow philosophy or constraint creates a huge risk to wealth, especially with stocks, real estate, commodities, corporate bonds, and other narrow-asset class- or index-oriented investing.

Worst Declines Over 10-Year Period Ending December 31, 2004*

	Worst Actual Decline	Period Ending	Length of Period
INDEXES[†]			
NASDAQ	−74.85%	9/30/2002	31 months
S&P 500	−44.71%	9/30/2002	25 months
Dow Jones industrial average	−30.74%	9/30/2003	33 months
Dow Jones Stoxx 50 Global	−46.98%	3/31/2003	35 months
Russell 2000	−34.80%	2/28/2003	36 months
EAFE	−50.65%	3/31/2003	39 months
Balanced index	−22.43%	9/30/2002	25 months
Long-term bond index	−8.94%	12/31/1999	11 months

*Worst declines are peak-to-bottom declines or "draw-downs." They are representative of the worst possible losses that would have resulted from investing and selling at the worst possible points during the period. They are calculated using month-end levels only. This table is one input in an investment management process.

[†]10-year data for Stoxx 50 Global, Russell 2000, and EAFE indexes do not include dividends.

NASDAQ indicates National Association of Securities Dealers automated quotation; S&P indicates Standard and Poor's; EAFE indicates Europe, Australia, and Far East index.

Compiled by Barry Hyman, Financial and Investment Management Group.

Peaks Down/Bottoms Up

Asset	Price at Peak	2 Years Later	Percent Change	Period Beginning
		Bottoms Up		
Gold	666.75	397.00	−40.5%	9/30/1980
Oil	39.60	21.71	−45.2%	9/28/1990
Commodities	291.90	220.80	−24.4%	3/30/1984
Dollar	117.64	91.11	−22.6%	5/30/1986
Large Stocks	1517.68	916.07	−39.6%	8/31/2000
Internet Stocks	628.34	110.41	−82.4%	2/29/2000
NASDAQ	4696.69	1731.49	−63.1%	2/29/2000

Asset	Price at Bottom	2 Years Later	Percent Change	Period Beginning
Gold	287.75	405.85	41.0%	2/28/1985
Oil	11.26	33.82	200.4%	11/30/1998
Commodities	213.30	306.02	43.5%	8/29/1986
Dollar	81.57	99.55	22.0%	7/31/1995
Large Stocks	815.28	1114.58	36.7%	9/30/2002
Internet Stocks	62.74	146.40	133.3%	9/30/2002
NASDAQ	1172.06	1896.84	61.8%	9/30/2002

*Month-end values for all indexes; large stocks represented by Standard and Poor's 500. Internet stocks represented by IIX Index. This table is one input in the investment management process.

NASDAQ indicates National Association of Securities Dealers automated quotation.

Compiled by Barry Hyman, Financial and Investment Management Group.
Internet stocks represented by IIX Index.

Compiled by Barry Hyman, FIM Group. This chart is one input of the investment management process. Financial & Investment Management Group is the manager of the Utopia Funds.

The risk of loss is great when you own overvalued investments. The "Worst Declines" table on page 157 shows some of the peak-to-trough declines of major stock market indexes along with the duration of those declines. Ask each investment manager you are considering hiring, "What percentage of your portfolio was in stocks in 1998 and 1999?" Also find out in writing how they did yearly in 2000, 2001, and 2002.

The point is, before one can evaluate so-called money managers, a lot needs to be known, first about investing successfully, then about the investment business. To my dismay, few managers invest for consistent, absolute, total return rather than for relative returns. Investing is about owning assets that should perform going forward. The "Peaks Down/Bottoms Up" table on page 158 shows the 2-year performance of various asset classes based on an investment's performance coming out of extremely under- or overvaluation situations.

The challenge is to ignore emotions and allow common sense to guide you through times when markets are crashing and things look bleak. Common sense says that cyclical downturns give us low price opportunities to invest in securities such as stocks that are tied to economic robustness. When you buy stocks when things look bleak and prices are down, you can be confident that prices will recover because (1) people will continue to engage in economic activity, (2) money will eventually go where it thinks it will have the best returns, (3) markets are cyclical in part because of psychology, and (4) manias will happen.

Indexing? Asset Allocation? Run!

"The operation was a success, but my patient died." Nothing is more prevalent today than the new, improved, proprietary, holistic asset allocation investment process, which is a reworking of the basic risk management tool of investing diversification! Some major global financial service firms have dozens of people in their asset allocation division squinting at statistics to say, "If you increase your large-cap allocation to 32% from 30% you will end up—probably, statistically (based on historical performance) albeit with slightly more risk—with the chance to earn one 100th of a percent of additional return." So they hand you 10 pages of their analysis and charge you 100/100ths of 1% for their work, and you sleep better thinking you are in good hands paying perhaps $1 to save or earn 10 cents.

If your advisor believes asset allocation is the way, ask two simple questions: First, "If every asset in my portfolio went to its 60-year historic valuation low, by approximately what percentage would my whole portfolio decline?" And, "What did your portfolios do, exactly, from February 29, 2000, to September 30, 2002?" The buzzword of Wall Street financial planners and the like is "asset allocation," which is a very useful investing tool.

But if it is relied on as *the* way in investing instead of just one of many investing tools, mediocre returns are guaranteed at best and failure at worst. Many advisors suggest low-cost index funds, or ETFs, showing a cost savings but then layer fees over those funds that negate the savings. Usually, you are better off hiring a real money manager. All investment strategies, to be successful, at their core must first make common sense, second, be rooted in owning assets at bargain levels, and, third, not own expensive assets. If your manager pretends to manage by using an asset allocation indexing system, run!

I once met a lawyer who told me, "My defense was perfect, the trial was a great success for my career, but my client got life without parole." Success, of course, depends upon where you stand. Investing is complex; it is art as well as science. Do not let anyone oversimplify it or make easy-to-understand process tools, like asset allocations, complex. Asset allocation may look perfect, but do not be suckered; asset allocation is merely one of the tools of investing. The caveat is that it must be combined with diversification, security analysis, management, research-driven securing selection, and, of course, common sense. This means you should own bargains, not expensive assets—even ones that look good in an asset allocation model.

Diversification Demystified

How do you tell when markets are at bargain prices? When your friends and colleagues are complaining about the bad investments they made, apply the common-sense test. In investing, method and philosophy are everything. To be successful you limit mistakes by applying common sense and limit the effect of the inevitable mistakes in the name of blind faith and over reliance on diversification.

At our firm, we have strict constraints on our portfolios to limit risks through diversification. Why diversify? To avoid "being right but investing wrong." Here is a hypothetical example of being right but investing wrong: Diligent research tells you that the economy is entering an expansionary phase. With clear signs the recession is over and the shock of the terrorist attacks has subsided, you make the logical assumption that as the economy strengthens, people will travel more. However, rather than diversifying across many travel-related industries such as resorts and other lodging, travel-related real estate, regional or international airlines, cruise lines, and the like, you instead decide that major airline stocks are the way to go. You make the decision to invest a large part of your portfolio in what you think is a diversified portfolio of four airline stocks. Although stocks in the other aforementioned travel industries thrive in the subsequent expansion, the airlines wane because of competition, regulation, and a spike in oil prices causing several to declare bankruptcy. You were right about the excellent prospects for travel, but you invested wrongly when you did not diversify into many travel industries.

As a real-world example, in 2003 at our firm, we felt that the US stock market would be stable or increase somewhat, the US dollar would be weak, and interest rates would remain benign. In addition to these factors, valuations of securities outside the United States were better than in the United States. So, common sense told us that the best investment opportunities were in Asia, Europe, and other countries that export to the United States, countries with strong currencies (Yen/Euro) or those with expectation of strong currency. We felt it would be logical to invest in companies in those countries with domestic-oriented businesses such as real estate, retail, services, and others that were similar. From there, we constructed diversified portfolios, owning 0.5% to 1% of the total portfolio in each individual security. Those securities were diversified across several industries, countries, and security types.

If you wish to own Japanese real estate, for example, own four different Japanese Real Estate Investment Trusts (JREITs) at 1% each of your portfolio's value to reduce risk. That way, if you later discover that one of the JREITS uses the accounting principles similar to those of an MCI, Enron, Parmalot, (or the US government), you have limited your losses by diversifying your risks. No one's financial security should ever be in jeopardy because the "books were cooked," management was mishandled, or fraud was committed.

The Dalai Lama, Tenzin Gyatso said, "When a faulty deed has been done, after learning it was wrong, one can be engaged in disclosure of the faulty deed. . . ."

If an investment's management team is fraudulent or is driving 100 miles per hour in a 55-mile-per-hour financial reporting limit, sell. If it is 3:55 p.m. and the market is closing in 5 minutes and you find out that the company is run by crooks, dump your shares without hesitation and do not look back. Usually, unethical management is not limited to a few. If you know your boss is messing with the books and you do nothing about it, by inference you are saying it is okay. Often in companies, if you find one bad apple, more will show up.

Some managers own big investment positions in concentrated portfolios and that is okay, but you should look at them as specialty managers and put no more than 20% of your money with them, because that will make a 5% position 1% of your overall portfolio. But in general, diversify among bargain priced investments until it hurts, then monitor each investment vigilantly and continue to act logically on pertinent information as things change! And remember, each investment should stand on its own merits. Do not use diversification as a crutch or excuse for neglecting to understand and continually research each investment or for owning overvalued investments. Ideally, you should own 70 to 150 investments, each of which is so compelling that you cannot stand not to own it. As I said at the beginning of this chapter, investing is not simple.

Hedge Funds

Management Is Management

The hot topic today in doctors lounges is hedge funds. Hedge funds have grown to nearly $1 trillion, nearly double from 4 years ago. The number of funds has risen from about 2,500 10 years ago to nearly 6,000 today. Wall Street's marketers have noticed this huge passion that investors have for hedge funds, and they are taking advantage of their popularity by coming out with products and services to sell under the guise of hedge funds. Often, these hedge fund managers and Wall Street firms that are pushing hedge funds show that they have recorded annual gains in excess of gains on the Standard and Poor's 500, mutual funds, certificates of deposit at 9%, or other comparisons. The problem is, as with any statistic, you need to look at the source. The public information on hedge funds is skewed in favor of those selling them.

On February, 19, 2005; pp. 13–14, the *Economist*'s lead section began with the following:

> When an opaque investment fund that does no hedging (in other words, it takes no position to offset other bets) calls itself a hedge fund, charges the sky-high fees of a typical hedge fund and has wannabe customers banging on its door, it's time to ask: "What is going on?"

What is going on?

First, some basics. A hedge fund is a legal entity that is usually a partnership with general partners managing the assets and collecting fees and incentives. If the fund does well, the limited partners who take substantial risks (ie, potential losses) share in a portion of the gains the fund earns.

A hedge fund does not add value per se to the investment process. Hedge funds may use leverage, in other words, borrow to invest more assets than they manage, increasing risks and return potential over those of non-leveraged investment entities. Because of its ability to pool assets, it can get to an efficient investment size to effectively hedge investments and do some of the complex investment strategies that can work at the right time. (See "Investment Strategies Explanation" on page 000 by my colleague, Suzanne Stepan, certified financial officer, who managed hedged convertible portfolios for 14 years.)

Hedge fund fees are generally structured to charge an ongoing "administration fee," plus, they take a percentage of new profits. A selling point of hedge funds is that most only take the percentage of profits above the high-water mark, meaning the fund must regain all prior losses first before receiving a percentage of profits. However, hedge funds are not required to continue their existence once they are under water, so to speak, and many fold after a period of losses rather than earning them back.

The key to understanding any investment strategy is that it works best when it works best. For example, leveraged long stock portfolios will do best when coming out of a bear market. (*Leveraged long* simply means that the investor borrows to invest.) History shows that if you were fully invested coming out of the average bear market, in other words, if you were 100% invested at the market's bottoms, the average returns would have been 47% over the subsequent 12 months. The problem is that in a bear market, most investors ride the wave all the way down to the bottom, and that 47% generally does not get them even again. (See the chart "Double Your Pleasure" on page 70, which illustrates this concept, and the chart "Peaks Down/Bottoms Up" on page 158 that talks about bear markets.)

An investment strategy that uses leverage could borrow to invest and, if they did it right, would make much greater returns, "doubling their pleasure." The problem is that if you have a strategy of always being in long stocks, or in any other investment class for that matter, and expect to enhance returns by leverage, you can have a big disaster if you do not use common-sense valuation analysis. If you use leverage, only use it when markets are at bargain prices.

Hedge funds have risks. The risks are mostly embedded in the strategy, management's execution of the hedge fund strategy, or execution risks for the "funds of many hedge funds" that are so popular today, and the biggest risk is human nature. Hedge funds at their core skew rewards in favor of the manager and magnify risk to the investor. Most hedge funds pay the general partner (manager) a 1% to 2% annual administration fee plus an incentive fee of 20% of profits. So a manager with a $100 million fund gets $1 million to $2 million no matter what, and if the fund makes money, the returns to the hedge funds manager can be extraordinary.

Keep in mind that hedge funds can be appropriate tools for futures-only strategies or strategies in which there is a desire to keep it simple with a few investors. My main issue with these funds is twofold: First, the performance fee does not contain a "bad performance expense." One example is a hedge fund that makes a gross gain of 25% on its $100 million pool, or $25 million. The manager gets $1 million at 1% for administration plus 20% of $25 million, or $5 million. The next year his fund bombs down 50%. Most funds have a high-water–mark system that makes it so the manager "only" gets his or her 1% or 2% until the fund gets back to its old high. Lose 50%, and you must double to get back to a participation in profits. What can happen? The fund manager can close down the fund, wait a few years (2002 until 2005, for example), and start anew. Some sophisticated investors will not invest in a hedge fund unless it has a financial incentive to be in business at least 5 years.

The second beef I have with the hedge fund system is the concept of paying a manager more to do better. If I pay a surgeon $100,000 or $10,000 or $0 to cut open my heart, the person will do his or her best no matter what. Yet hedge fund managers effectively say, "I'll do better if you pay me more." The hedge fund system rewards speculative "up" returns or even mediocre returns, and it gives little incentive to avoid failure.

Hedge Funds: "Regulation Light"

Picture the drug industry without the Food and Drug Administration, universities, and other watch guards to challenge their findings or assure that their science is truly science-based and not statistical manipulation. At the very least, the public would be bombarded with unsafe products. The financial industry has the oversight of the Securities and Exchange Commission

(SEC) and other agencies that try to make sure that the information given to the public is appropriate and true. However, hedge funds historically have flown below the radar of the SEC because they tend to be unregulated entities. Unregulated funds' use of statistics leaves enormous room for statistical manipulation.

With regard to hedge funds, the SEC states the following (Registration under the advisers act of certain hedge fund advisers. *Federal Register*. 1994; 69[237]:72054):

> Advisors taking advantage of this private advisor exemption must nonetheless comply with the Act's antifraud provisions, but do not file registration forms with us identifying who they are, do not have to maintain business records in accordance with our rules, do not have to adopt or implement compliance programs or codes of ethics, and are not subject to commission oversight.

The comments go on to explain:

> Today, however, a growing number of investment advisors take advantage of the private advisor exemption to create large investment advisory firms without being registered with the commission. Instead of managing clients' money directly, these advisors pool clients' assets by creating limited partnerships, business trusts, or corporations in which clients invest.

It is extremely important to work with an investment advisor who is registered under the Investment Advisors Act of 1940. This act requires that the registered investment advisor is held to the standard of a fiduciary to his or her clients. As the SEC states, the fiduciary duty requires advisors to manage their clients' portfolios in the best interest of their clients while not in any prescribed manner. Fiduciary obligations to clients include the duty to fully disclose any material conflicts the advisor has with clients, to seek best execution for clients' transactions, and to have a reasonable basis for client recommendations.

But with hedge funds, largely you are on your own. Often, hedge funds are pushed by brokerage firms because they are one of the more lucrative investment products—both for the manager and the salesperson. Because of naiveté or greed, many brokers and individuals sell and buy hedge funds that they do not understand. The "Hedge Fund General Partner Letter" on page 166 should be used to help you evaluate a hedge fund you own or are thinking of buying.

Hedge Fund General Partner Letter

Dear Mr/Ms: [name of senior person in hedge fund group, ie, general partner]

[Name of person who recommended hedge investment] recommended that I invest in your hedge fund. I have some questions that I wish answered in writing before I invest. I am very interested in your fund and just need to do some final due diligence to assure that I am making an investment in an entity that I fully understand. I do understand that all investments have risks and that hedge funds often try to mitigate this risk through different techniques such as those perhaps employed by your fund. Here are my questions:

1. What is your investment fund's investment policy?
2. Where are my funds held?
3. What is the investment philosophy of your firm?
4. What is your firm's code of ethics?
5. What is your firm's soft-dollar policy and the amount of soft dollars that you receive annually to pay your rent, hard research costs, computer systems cost, etc?
6. Can money come out of the fund to your firm without a "noninterested party" letter, for example, your lawyer or the fund's accountant signing off for amounts over your normal fees?
7. Do you make payments to those whom refer clients to you?
8. How much do you pay them?
9. Do you pay them commissions based on the amount of trading done in the fund, or do you pay them a commission out of your fees received from the fund?
10. What are the exact fees, commissions, and expenses paid by this fund based on the last 12 months? (It is okay to give us this information on a calendar basis or an accounting basis to make it simple for you.) Please break out exact amount of commissions, exact amount of administrative fees, exact amount of incentive compensation paid, etc.
11. If your fund is still trying to get to a high-water mark before being compensated for prior investments, how much total performance will you need before you reach your prior highest water mark?
12. My investment in your fund is being recommended by [name of whoever is recommending the fund]. What would his or her compensation be if I invest in this fund?
13. Please send the resumes, names, experience, and time with your firm of the key employees of your firm. What is most important is their time spent managing portfolios where they are making investment decisions specific to client assets.

14. Have you or your firm ever wound up, closed, or merged an investment pool, or fund, or so-called hedge fund? If so, why?
15. What was the performance of the funds that were wound up, closed, or merged?
16. Can I have performance statistics on all of your investment pools and the fee schedule on each?
17. How will you communicate with me? E-mail, US Mail? How often?
18. Please send samples of your communication material.
19. Do you allow your investors to see what is in the investment pool at any time they wish? Please explain.
20. How do I get out of your fund?
21. Is there a lock-up period?
22. Has your firm ever been involved in any complaints or in any investment disputes of consequence? Please explain.
23. When will I get my tax information regarding my investment in [name of fund]?
24. Who is the legal advisor for your firm?
25. Who is the accounting advisor for your firm?
26. Who is the auditor of your firm?
27. Also, would you send three references of clients or investors of yours who have been clients or investors for at least 10 years that I may contact?
28. Do you have a mutual fund or private management division that manages investments similar to your hedge fund division? If so, please explain.

Once I receive the above information, I would like to see your operation and perhaps meet or have lunch with you or one of your senior people. Please give me possible dates that might work for me to visit your firm.

I am very excited about possibly investing in your fund, subject to the due diligence. From all that I have seen it looks like an appropriate investment for me, and I am definitely a suitable investor for your fund. I look forward to meeting you. Thank you for providing me with this information.

Sincerely Yours,

[Your name]

NOTE: Please keep my inquiries regarding my possible investment in your fund confidential.

CC: [Copy your advisors, certified public accountant, lawyer, financial planner, and the person who recommended the fund]

Note to user of this letter: Photocopy this letter and modify it to make it more pertinent to the exact specifics of the hedge funds you are considering. If you do not have time to see the hedge fund manager, then at least set up a phone conference call so you can go over these and other questions regarding the fund. Perhaps your spouse, brother-in-law, or one of your children could go and do the due diligence and meet with the possible advisor. If you are using a fee-only advisor, he or she probably has done significant analysis on the fund. If your fee-only advisor recommended it, it is still good to do your own analysis. Needless to say, your advisor should be able to give you all this information from his or her file, and you should have it in your file. You are responsible for your investment outcomes. They are not.

Source: © Paul Sutherland, Financial and Investment Management Group, All Rights Reserved.

Peter with Misguided Principals

We think the best way to minimize risks is to think. The idea that minimizing risk is taking a portfolio that was 60% in stocks and 40% in bonds—and then making a big announcement that "we are moving our allocation to 65%/35%"—as some strategist, or whatever they call them on Wall Street, do—is pure nonsense. I mean 60/40 or 65/35—it just doesn't make much difference.

Source: Buffett W, Munger C. *Outstanding Investor Digest*, December 31, 2004: p. 32.

CHAPTER 7
Guided Do-It-Yourself Portfolio Management

The Importance of an Investment Philosophy

We all have friends or have known people who are quick to adopt whatever the new hot idea is, whether it is a new religious organization or a happiness philosophy. We see them jump from Christianity to Buddhism to New Age philosophies. They attend seminars and read New Age Christian and self-help books from the shelves of the local bookstores. They seem to come up with new resolutions every 6 weeks. We want to sit those people down and say, "Just take one of those philosophies and get deep enough so that you have an understanding of it instead of staying on the surface and moving from one to the next. You'll never get anywhere unless you really understand the intimate spirituality embedded in that religion or philosophy." Often, investors make mistakes similar to the people who are perpetually searching for something new but never get past the guru's or preacher's personality.

With investments, nothing is more important than having a philosophy built on solid factual historic correlations, common sense, science, and art. The philosophy must make sense to the person who will implement it. If a physician's philosophy is that there is no way he or she will get clients to quit smoking, drinking, and eating 4,000 fat calories per day, the practice will reflect it. A physician who has given up on healthy habits will find it difficult to advise the patient who is conscientious about calorie intake, exercise, and maintaining a healthy lifestyle. Likewise, the physician who counsels clients specifically about diet and lifestyle in a firm but gentle way often finds likeminded clients in his or her reception area—people whose philosophy is consistent with the physician's.

On page 172 is a "Financial and Investment Management Group Philosophy Statement." Financial and Investment Management (FIM) Group (www.fimg.net) is the manager of the Utopia Funds and private portfolios. Use this philosophy and belief system statement as a guide to come to a philosophy that works for you. Other philosophies include:

- Index (and don't manage).
- Have a core portfolio of index funds, and explore a few return-enhancing options; often called "core and explore."
- Asset allocate as the "Way" to invest.
- Buy and hold: An investment strategy in which stocks, for example, are bought and then held for a long period, regardless of the market's fluctuations. The buy and hold approach to investing in stocks rests upon the assumption that in the very long term (over the course of 10, 20, or 50 years) stock prices will go up, but the average investor does not know what will happen tomorrow. Another name for this could be the "buy and put your head in the sand" approach; its success depends on when and what you buy. If stocks (especially overvalued ones) are purchased after the markets have risen to unsustainably high levels, history tells us that the returns are dismal at best. However, if stocks (especially undervalued ones) are purchased when markets are at or below reasonable levels, this approach has worked.
- Sector rotate: This approach involves shifting investments, a portfolio, or part of a portfolio from one sector of the economy to another. Not all sectors of the economy perform well at the same time. Sector rotation is an attempt to profit through owning investments priced right for a particular economic cycle.
- Large-cap stocks: These are stocks with the largest market capitalization. Although the exact level can vary, the term usually refers to companies having a market capitalization between $10 billion and $200 billion. Sometimes the largest of these stocks are called *mega-caps*. These represent the biggest companies of the financial world. Examples include Wal-Mart®, Microsoft®, and General Electric®. Keep in mind that classifications such as large-cap and small-cap are only approximations that vary from source to source and change over time. As with any investment, large-cap stocks

CHAPTER 7 Guided Do-It-Yourself Portfolio Management

work if bought at the right price and sold when expensive and overpriced.

- Balanced indexing: Indexing is constructing a portfolio that matches the performance of a specific securities index including stock indexes, bond indexes, sector indexes, and foreign indexes. Balanced indexing uses a blend or balance of equity and fixed income indexes as the benchmark. The concept in indexing is that it is a very low-cost (although perhaps unprofitable) way of attaining the returns of those benchmarks. The presumption is that the future returns on the index being simulated will be satisfactory. Often, managers charge fees to put a blend of low-cost funds together. The fees can often offset the return gains, so beware of layering high fees on top of low fee funds.

- Top-down: An investment approach in which an investor first looks at a country's economy before considering an industry to invest in; next, determines what industries or sectors will return well because of the economic conditions; and then, buys stocks that are attractive within that industry. Top-down investing can be used to find the hot sectors in the hot markets, or it can be used to find the undervalued sectors or those that are out of favor.

- Bottom-up: An investment strategy in which companies are considered based simply on their own merit without regard to the sectors they are part of or the current economic conditions. A person following this strategy looks closely at the company's management, history, business model, growth prospects, and other characteristics; he or she does not consider general industry and economic trends and extrapolate them to the specific company. Followers of this strategy believe that some companies are superior to their peer groups and will therefore outperform regardless of industry and economic circumstances (www.investorwords.com).

- Do the "hokey-pokey": The hokey-pokey is a game that teaches children to fall in line and do what everyone else is doing. It is a useful visual for understanding how the Wall Street sellers of financial products get the investment crowd to behave like lemmings and follow popular approaches to sell the products or investment approaches that benefit those companies and their salespeople.

If you are delegating your portfolio's management, get the real return performance of the actual portfolios that the manager had under his or her supervision as opposed to an "*if*" portfolio.

Financial and Investment Management Group Philosophy Statement

1. Our primary goal is to maintain the highest degree of integrity, ethics, and quality in working with our clients, employees, business partners, and service providers.

2. No perfect investment exists for all investment cycles. To reduce risk, assets should be reallocated as appropriate to avoid overvalued assets and own undervalued assets.

3. It is important for a money manager to remain flexible, creative, and disciplined. At Financial and Investment Management (FIM) Group, we use fundamental, behavioral, global, quantitative, and sustainable business-school methodology analysis in making our investment management decisions.

4. Diversification should be used carefully to reduce risks and increase rewards by allocating investment portfolios as follows:

    a. Among asset classes, ie, stocks, bonds, money market funds, etc.

    b. Within each asset class, through owning different investments within each asset class or through the use of diversified companies, mutual funds, closed-end trusts, or other investments with built-in diversification.

    c. Through management style, by using information from outside advisers and consultants.

    d. Globally, through exploring investment opportunities worldwide.

5. Patience and perseverance are essential qualities of a money manager. A successful investor keeps a long-term horizon and avoids getting caught up in the mania of the markets. Manias are caused by rapid changes in investor psychology because of real or perceived economic, societal, or world events.

6. Emphasis on long-term capital and income predictability is always important; however, during some periods, greater emphasis must be placed on capital growth and/or purchasing excellent income investments. A manager should carefully search the world for risk-adjusted bargain investments.

7. It is important for a money manager to minimize all costs associated with investing. At FIM Group, we achieve cost-effectiveness by trading at substantially discounted commissions, using no-load funds with low expense ratios, allocating trades to brokers specializing in certain investment areas, and being sensitive to taxes.

8. To be totally objective, a money manager must be compensated on a fee basis only. No commissions or any other transaction-related remuneration should be received by the manager. Financial and Investment Management Group is strictly a fee-only firm.

9. Financial and Investment Management Group is a skills-based portfolio manager that believes in management. We are not passive, nor do we believe in benchmark indexed–based management. We are dedicated to providing real, absolute, positive returns for our clients. The investment world is dynamic. A passive approach is inconsistent with reality and common sense.

10. A money management team should have the training, education, temperament, experience, long track record, and resources available to promote success. Each manager must manage, enjoy the process of management, and have passion and commitment for the investment management business.

11. Money managers making specific investment decisions regarding client portfolios should be accessible to their clients to discuss strategy, outlook, conditions, and so on.

12. We honor client confidentiality and have a firm "no exceptions" policy stating that no information will be sold or shared with anyone except as required by law or with the clients' express permission.

Note: We will not purchase investments in companies primarily dealing in tobacco, alcohol, or pornography or in other companies that produce products that hurt people. We want to own financially strong companies with ethical, skilled management and good products.

Sustainable Portfolios

Two monks were traveling to a desert monastery. They fashioned a canoe and paddled it across a great sea to the desert's edge. They had started on their journey across the desert when one monk turned to the other and said, "Why, young friend, are you carrying the canoe?" To which the young monk replied, "We may need it once more." The elder monk smiled and picked up a handful of desert sand and rocks and threw them at the youngster saying, "Put the canoe down. We won't need it again! It is dry desert for the rest of our journey."

Investments are tools that can help us with our life's financial journeys. Some are designed to provide sustainable, long-term income like bonds, long-term bank certificates of deposit (CDs), preferred stocks, income-oriented stocks or mutual funds, and trusts designed to own such investments. Other investments might be designed for growth in capital only, and yet others need to maintain their set value, such as short-term CDs and bonds.

Each investment has benefits, risks, and perils. I am sad to say that even if an investment seems right, no investment is ever the best investment to have all the time, even if it seems like the right tool for your goal.

The monk's small canoe would be little help in a violent storm at sea, and yet, with some reengineering, it might provide shelter from the desert cold or sun. All investment markets are cyclical, bond yields and values fluctuate wildly over time, stock prices act likewise, and CDs and short-term money-market–type investments also will have huge swings over time in their yields depending on the financial landscape.

The investment chapters of this book are to help you make better choices with your investments. But, they will only work if your mind is open and you are not striving to find a simple key or oversimplified solution to the complexities of investing. Many insurance agents, investment brokers, trust officers, and professionals take on an educated aloofness and fashion simple solutions to your investment needs. Such "experts" or salespeople, no matter what they are called, should be avoided unless they have 10 to 15 years of investment management experience minimum. Not experience selling investments or advising investors, but real in-the-canoe, paddling-across-the-great-investment-sea experience. How do you find these people?

First, you need to know what you are looking for. At a minimum, whomever you find to help you, either directly through referrals, mutual funds, or through the Internet or over the telephone, should be fee-only all of the time. Their contractual relationships with all their clients should be 100% fee-only. Their practice style should forbid them from receiving any commissions, fee kickbacks, or compensation from anyone but you.

Second, managers should have 15 years of experience making real discretionary investment decisions on behalf of clients' needs consistent with a client's contract and risk tolerance.

Third, they should have the ability to provide references for clients who have been clients for at least 10 years whom you can call. For mutual funds and larger firms, often their marketing and disclosure information will contain the needed information.

Fourth, the firm should have at least audited financial statements, and your accounts should be held in your name or your trust's name in an insured brokerage or corporate and trust account that is fully regulated by securities exchanges or banking regulators with insurance to protect your account from fraud, bankruptcy, thefts, and the like.

Doing it Yourself

Most experienced managers will not take on clients unless they have a minimum of $500,000 to $5 million in investable assets. In addition, most might not meet your criteria for ethics and sustainable investing. Thus, you might be on your own to construct your portfolio. Thankfully, there are many resources that you can access through the Internet, libraries, or bookstores to get you on your way. You can construct a portfolio of mutual funds and individual investments on your own if you are disciplined and guided by common sense. Common sense says the investor's goal should be to make money and not lose it. It should not be to own stocks, mutual funds, bonds, or CDs; it should be to make money and not lose it. Your portfolio must be guided at its core by this simple common-sense approach: to make money—don't lose it!

So total returns are what you want. Naturally, taxes are an input, and you need to factor them into your investment returns. And do not get attached to formulas or strategies that often are driven by tax savings instead of "make money don't lose it." Tools like diversification, indexing, dollar cost averaging, asset allocation, security analysis, behavioral investing, leverage, buying real estate, selling short, and the like are merely tools that can be used when appropriate to help you achieve investment success consistently and with lower risk.

My industry (fee-only included) has done a great disservice to clients by making asset allocation the primary way of investing. Asset allocation has been combined with indexing primarily through mutual funds to the great detriment of investors. Mutual fund companies, bank trust companies, and many financial planners have made asset allocation the way of investing, and it can work well if applied appropriately but will be a disaster if not applied with a disciplined approach designed to make money and not lose it.

Asset allocation and indexing can work well if they are combined with the premise that price matters. Most asset allocation and indexing strategies are based on an oversimplified misuse of modern portfolio theory, the premise of which is that price does not matter, and if it did, you cannot tell if an asset or asset class is a bargain and should be bought or if it is expensive and should be sold or avoided. Statistically, modern portfolio theory makes sense, but of course, statistics are truly the most misused, manipulated sales tools ever used by the legions of mutual fund sales people, booksellers, and so-called point-the-way experts.

It is common sense that if you buy an investment for $100 and it goes to $1,000 that it can lose more value and have more risk at $1,000 than it did at $100. At best, if your $100 goes to zero, you only lost $100. At $1,000, you lost 10 times as much on the way to zero. Modern portfolio theory is statistical mush. The trick is judging an investment's worth.

Dividend yields are a good start in judging worth. The "Dividends in History" table below can be studied to learn how bargain stock market investments

Dividends in History*

Date	Standard and Poor's 500 Dividend Yield	Subsequent Standard and Poor's 500 Change
August 31, 1929[†]	2.87%	−59% over 21 months
May 31, 1946	3.55%	−30% over 19 months
March 31, 1961	2.98%	−20% over 15 months
January 5, 1973	2.96%	−43% over 22 months
August 25, 1987	2.78%	−33% over 3½ months
July 16, 1990	3.28%	−19% over 3 months
August 30, 2000	0.73%	−45% over 25 months

*Dividend yields throughout history have been a good indicator of future stock market performance. This table illustrates how massively overvalued the stock market is as reflected through the Standard and Poor's 500 Index in 2000. What is interesting about this table is that it shows that bull market manias can go on for a long time and the consequences can be disastrous. If a portfolio drops 50%, it must double to get even again. This table illustrates also how much risk can be embedded in an investment because of complacency and mania behavior. Avoiding big losses is key, and the key to avoiding big losses is to use common sense and not own investments that are not priced at bargain levels. Thus, when dividends are low, look out! This table should be considered one input to the investment process.

[†]In the crash of the 1930s it took until 1957 to get even with the prices of 1929 once again (28 years).

Source: Sutherland, PH. *Zenvesting, The Art of Abundance and Managing Money*. Suttons Bay, MI: Financial Sourcebook, 1998. Bloomberg, Ibottson, S&P, and Financial and Investment Management Group.

Standard and Poor's 500 Dividend Yield and (Future) Stock Performance*

Standard and Poor's 500 Yield	6 Months	1 Year	2 Years	3 Years	Rational Portfolio Action
Below 3%	−1%	−5%	−10%	−1%	Reduce equity exposure to minimum at 3% or below
3 to 4%	+1%	+4%	+9%	+12%	Equity exposure in a neutral area 3 to 4.5%

*Because one individual stock pays a 6% dividend does not mean it is a bargain. When the average yield of the Standard and Poor's 500, which is composed of 500 of the world's largest companies, is at or above 5% to 6%, stocks are a bargain and equities should be favored. This table illustrates the importance of buying investments at bargain values. With indexes, dividend yields are reflective of the overall stock market's price as it relates to value. Naturally, things change, and this should be considered one input in the investment process.

Zenvesting, Bloomberg, Standard and Poor's, and Financial and Investment Management Group.

can be identified by simply knowing the yields on the markets. Of course, dividend yields are one tool of identifying whether markets are expensive or bargains; earning yields, price-to-book, and price-to-growth in earnings are other tools a manager will use.

Do-It-Yourself Formulas

This is my third book in the past 15 years in which I have offered a do-it-yourself formula to help individual investors manage their money. The problem with my past do-it-yourself portfolios is that most found them hard to implement. Some even kept the mutual fund idea and hired managers who charged them to purchase and manage a portfolio of mutual funds. They all had their reasons to *not* do it themselves. Many investors were seduced by the new-paradigm bull market of the late 1990s and threw caution to the wind. In this book, I introduce three formulas for those of you who want to do it yourself with the help of professionally managed mutual funds. Of course, you could also use an experienced, quality investment manager.

Strategy #1: Pile On Income Investments

This strategy is for the investor who realizes that investing is about accumulating money for use in the future, be that a major purchase or perhaps to fund a retirement plan.

A. Short-term income investments (10%–25% of portfolio)

   Prime rate/treasury bills, CDs, floating rate short-term income investments, and open-end mutual funds such as

   Vanguard Short-Term Investment Grade (VFSTX)

   Schwab Short-Term Bond (SWBDX)

   Northern Institutional Short Intermediate Bond (BSBAX) PIMCO Low Duration III Institutional (PLDIX)

   Others from list on page 185

B. Income/some growth (20%–25% of portfolio)

   Actively managed income and growth, investments, convertibles, preferreds, and income equity–oriented mutual funds such as

   American Advantage Balanced Instl (AADBX)

   Dodge & Cox Balanced (DODBX)

   Berwyn Income (BERIX)

   Vanguard Wellington (VWELX)

   Others from list on page 186

C. Long-term fixed income/predictable income (20%–45% of portfolio)

   Actively managed bonds or fixed income mutual funds such as

   Fidelity Advisor Strategic Income Ins (FSRIX)

   GMO International Bond III (GMIBX)

   Loomis Sayles Bond Instl (LSBDX)

   Others from list on page 188

D. Balanced total return mutual funds or actively managed "total return" funds (10%–25%)

   Funds such as

   Bruce (BRUFX)

   Leuthold Core Investment (LCORX)

   Vanguard Wellesley Income (VWINX)

   FPA Crescent Fund (FPACX)

   Others from list on page 189

E. Global equity funds actively managed (10%–30%)

Funds such as the following (½ global and ½ resource funds):

Templeton Global Smaller (TGSAX)

UBS Global Allocation Y (BPGLX)

USAA Precious Metals and Minerals (USAGX)

Others from list on page 190

Procedure: Maximum draw on this portfolio is 4% annually; in other words, each $100,000 investment equals $4,000 annual income. As a long-term strategy, it is okay to start drawing 6% initially and then work down over the years to annual withdrawal rates of 3% to 4%.

Strategy #2: Hot Fad Du Jour

This strategy is for those who choose to be self-defeating or want an excuse to work the rest of their lives.

1. Buy mutual funds featured in *Money* magazine or by Morningstar that have had the best recent performance. Get disenchanted.

2. Buy mutual funds or hire a manager after reading how well their recent performance has been in a *Fortune* or *BusinessWeek* article. Get disenchanted.

3. Do it yourself by subscribing to Morningstar's mutual fund monitor. Get disenchanted. (Morningstar can help in the process, however.)

4. Give up doing it yourself, call a brokerage firm, and have a commissioned broker or commissioned financial advisor guide you. Get disenchanted.

5. Try buying individual stocks and bonds because everyone else is doing it and 1 through 4 did not work. Get disenchanted.

6. Hire a professional fee-only investment advisor with experience, training, a long track record, and education or use do-it-yourself Strategy #1 or #3.

Strategy #2B: Hot Fad Du Jour Express

Skip steps 1 through 5 and jump directly to step 6!

Strategy #3: Total Return

Sample Portfolio Adjusted For Investors With 15 Or More Years Until Retirement.

Short-term income investments (0–10%).

Prime rate/floating rate short-term income investments, open-end funds (1 to 3 year funds) such as

T Rowe Price Short-Term Bond (PRWBX)

Schwab Short-Term Bond (SWBDX)

Income/some growth (10%)

Actively managed income and growth, mutual funds, convertibles, preferreds, and income equities oriented such as

American Advantage Balanced Instl (AADBX)

Dodge & Cox Balanced (DODBX)

Berwyn Income (BERIX)

Vanguard Wellington (VWELX)

Long-term fixed income/predictable income (10%).

Fixed income mutual funds or actively managed bonds such as

Fidelity Advisor Strategic Income Ins (FSRIX)

GMO International Bond III (GMIBX)

Loomis Sayles Bond Instl (LSBDX)

Balanced total return mutual funds (35%–60%); actively managed "total return," mutual funds such as

Utopia Core Fund*

Utopia Core Conservative Fund*

Bruce (BRUFX)

Leuthold Core Investment (LCORX)

MainStay Balanced I (MBAIX)

FPA Crescent (FPCAX)

Greenspring (GRSPX)

Global equity funds actively managed (10%–35%; no more than 15% in natural resources) such as

Utopia Growth Fund*

Scudder Gold & Precious Metals (SCGDX)

Templeton Global Smaller (TGSAX)

UBS Global Allocation Y (BPGLX)

USAA Precious Metals and Minerals (USAGX)

Vanguard Global Equity (VHGEX)

Blackrock Global Resources Instl (SGLSX)

Excelsior Energy & Nat Resources (UMESX)

T Rowe Price New Era (PRNEX)

Sample Portfolio Adjusted For Investors With 5 Or More Years Until Retirement.

Short-term income investments (10%).

Prime rate/floating rate short-term income investments, open end funds such as

Blackrock Interm Govt Instl (PNIGX)

Classic Institutional Interm Bond I (SAMIX)

CMG Short-Term Bond (COTBX)

Income/some growth (25%).

Actively managed income, and growth, mutual funds, convertibles, preferreds, and income equities–oriented funds such as

Berwyn Income (BERIX)

Dodge & Cox Balanced (DODBX)

Vanguard Wellington (VWELX)

Utopia Core Conservative Fund

Utopia Yield Income Fund

Long-term fixed income/predictable income (20%).

Fixed income mutual funds or actively managed bond funds such as

Evergreen International Bond Instl (ESICX)

Fidelity Strategic Income (FSICX)

GMO International Bond III (GMIBX)

PIMCO Global Bond (unhedged) Instl (PIGLX)

Balanced total return mutual funds (20%; no more than half in natural resources funds) or actively managed "total return," funds such as

FPA Crescent (FPACX)

Bruce (BRUFX)

Leuthold Core Investment (LCORX)

Vanguard Wellesley Income (VWINX)

Utopia Core Fund*

Global equity funds actively managed (20%):

Scudder Gold & Precious Metals S (SCGDX)

Templeton Global Smaller (TGSAX)

UBS Global Allocation Y (BPGLX)

USAA Precious Metals and Minerals (USAGX)

Vanguard Global Equity (VHGEX)

Blackrock Global Resources Instl (SGLSX)

Excelsior Energy & Nat Resources (UMESX)

T Rowe Price New Era (PRNEX)

Utopia Growth Fund*

Total Return Portfolio Adjusted For Investors With Less Than 5 Years Until Retirement Or Are Retired.

Short-term income investments (15%).

Prime rate/floating rate short-term income investments open end funds such as

Blackrock Interm Govt Instl (PNIGX)

Classic Institutional Interm Bond I (SAMIX)

CHAPTER 7 Guided Do-It-Yourself Portfolio Management 183

CMG Short-Term Bond (COTBX)

PIMCO Low-Duration III Instl (PLDIX)

Schwab Short-Term Bond Market (SWBDX)

Vanguard Short-Term Investment Grade (VFSTX)

Income/some growth (15%).

Actively managed income, and growth, mutual funds, convertibles, preferreds, and income equities–oriented funds such as

Berwyn Income (BERIX)

Dodge & Cox Balanced (DODBX)

Vanguard Wellington (VWELX)

Utopia Core Conservative Fund*

Utopia Yield Income Fund*

Long-term fixed income/predictable income (40%).

Fixed income mutual funds or actively managed municipals or bonds such as

Evergreen International Bond Instl (ESICX)

Fidelity Advisor Strategic Income INS (FSRIX)

PIMCO Global Bond (Unhedged) Instl (PIGLX)

T Rowe Price Spectrum Income (RPSIX)

Balanced total return mutual funds (15%)

or actively managed "total return" funds such as

Utopia Core Fund*

FPA Crescent (FPACX)

Bruce (BRUFX)

Leuthold Core Investment (LCORX)

Vanguard Wellesley Income (VWINX)

Global equity funds actively managed (15%; 7% in natural resource funds) such as

Templeton Global Smaller (TGSAX)

UBS Global Allocation Y (BPGLX)

T Rowe Price New Era (PRNEX)

Utopia Growth Fund*

Historically, Bull Markets Follow Bear Markets*
Strong advances have historically followed multiyear weakness and vice versa

Year	Return†	Year	Return†	Year	Return†	Year	Return†
1929	−8.8%	1939	−1.1%	1973	−14.8%	2000	−9.1%
1930	−25.0%	1940	−10.1%	1974	−26.6%	2001	−11.9%
1931	−43.1%	1941	−11.8%	1975	+37.2%	2002	−22.1%
1932	−5.3%	1942	+21.4%	1976	+23.6%	2003	+28.3%
1933	+55.1%	1943	+25.7%			2004	+10.7%

*All investments have bull and bear markets. They are as natural as the seasons. Stocks, bonds, real estate, gold, oil, art, and antiques are all affected by investor psychology and mania cycles. The goal of this table is to illustrate the importance of, first, buying low at bargain prices; second, selling when investments are expensive; and third, patience. This chart is one input to the investment process.

†Return reflects the return of the Standard and Poor's 500 Index for that particular year.

Source: Ned Davis Research, Inc., Bloomberg, Financial and Investment Management Group.

Be Early*

	Average Annual Return Following Bear Market		
	12-Month Period	24-Month Period	36-Month Period
If fully invested after bear ends	47%	28%	20%
1 month of cash after bear ends	33%	22%	17%
3 months of cash after bear ends	18%	16%	12%
6 months of cash after bear ends	11%	13%	10%

*This table illustrates the importance of "being there" when stocks (or other assets) are bargain priced. The key is to start buying when stocks are cheap using **price/earnings**, dividend yields, **price/earnings** to expected growth, **price/earnings** to inflation, and **other valuation techniques;** to *buy* when the investments are bargains**;** and **to** be well-invested when the bear market ends. This, of course, is only known after it ends, so you must invest as the investments become bargains over time, using judgment. The term *fully invested* is represented by total monthly returns of the Standard and Poor's 500 Index, January 1926 through December 2002. Cash is represented by total returns of the 30-day Treasury bill. The 14 bear markets analyzed are defined as periods with cumulative declines greater than 10% and duration of at least 6 months and do not include the current market. Past performance is no indication of future results. This **table** is one input to the investment process.

Source: Schwab Center for Investment Research with data from Ibbotson Associates; Financial and Investment Management Group.

Asset Classes

Short-Term Income Investments

Interest rates are especially sensitive to inflation expectations, the economic realities of currency values, Federal Reserve policies, supply and demand, and other factors. Short- and long-term rates are volatile and tend to rise when economies expand and especially when they overheat, which causes inflation expectations. Likewise, interest rates usually drop during recessions or periods of moderating growth. Once you reach $10,000 in one fund, start adding to another.

- Blackrock Interm Govt Instl (PNIGX)
- Classic Institutional Interm Bond I (SAMIX)
- CMG Short-Term Bond (COTBX)
- Delaware Limited Term Government Ins (DTINX)
- Dryden Short-Term Corporate Bd Z (PIFZX)
- Evergreen Limited Duration Instl (ESDIX)
- Fidelity Advisor Short Fixed Inc I (FSXIX)
- Northern Institutional Sh-Intm Bond A (BSBAX)
- Payden Short Bond (PYSBX)
- Phoenix-Kayne Interm Tot Ret Bd (KATRX)
- PIMCO Low-Duration III Instl (PLDIX)
- Schwab Short-Term Bond Market (SWBDX)
- T Rowe Price Short-Term Bond (PRWBX)
- Vanguard Short-Term Investment Grade (VFSTX)
- Weitz Fixed Income (WEFIX)

Income With Some Growth (Total Return)

Risk is tricky to analyze, but in investing, it is strictly a judgment measurement of the certainty or uncertainty an investor places on the probability of an investment not reaching a set goal. In retirement, current income is usually the number one concern, namely, that it rises over time to help offset inflation and preserve purchasing power.

Mutual funds or money managers that specialize in this style of investing typically balance three objectives: (1) income, (2) capital preservation ("don't lose it"), and (3) growth. They attempt to accomplish these goals by using the favored tools of all good managers: judgment honed by experience and education, security analysis, asset allocation, and diversification.

Listed here are candidates to diversify among. As you reach $10,000 in any one fund, start adding to another.

Alliance Bernstein Balanced Shares Adv (CBSYX)

American Advantage Balanced Instl (AADBX)

Dodge & Cox Balanced (DODBX)

Vanguard Wellington (VWELX)

Berwyn Income (BERIX)

Bruce (BRUFX)

Compounding Returns

$1,000 monthly at various return scenarios (hypothetical scenarios for a 35-year period).

$1,000 monthly at 10% for 25 years then
   8% for 5 years then
   6% for 5 years = $2,835,000

$1,000 monthly at 8% for 25 years then
   6% for 5 years then
   4% for 5 years = $1,717,000

$1,000 monthly at 4% for 25 years then
   6% for 5 years then
   8% for 5 years = $2,111,000

$1,000 monthly at 15% for 3 years then
   −15% for 2 years then
   6% for 10 years then
   0% for 5 years then
   10% for 5 years then
   6% for 10 years = $1,446,000

The future is unknown; therefore, the importance is to first save and invest and second to strive for good risk-adjusted returns. Paying attention to returns earned early is especially important, as is avoiding large losses.

Source: Paul Sutherland, chief investment officer, Financial and Investment Management Group; manager of the Utopia Funds.

Inflation and Stocks*

Inflation	Average P/E	Peak P/E (Mania Overvaluation)	Trough P/E (Mania Undervaluation)	Possible Peak P/E to Trough P/E Loss on Standard and Poor's
<2%	21.4	46.5	13.1	−72%
2–3%	20.3	36.8	12.5	−67%
3–4%	18.4	33.3	11.0	−66%
4–5%	14.8	20.3	9.4	−54%
5–6%	14.4	19.2	8.9	54%
6–7%	11.4	15.9	7.7	−52%
>7%	8.8	12.0	6.7	−44%

*Inflation has a dramatic effect on all asset class returns: stocks, bonds, real estate, and commodities. Many do not realize how rising and high inflation is especially detrimental to stock prices. Many advisors actually say stocks are a good inflation hedge. They certainly are not if you squint at this chart. The bottom line is, favor stocks or any asset when prices are low and at bargain levels. The possible peak P/E to trough P/E loss on Standard and Poor's is to illustrate the loss possible and does not include dividends that would reduce the total loss somewhat. P/E indicates the price you pay for earnings. Low P/E equals low price. P/E is often substituted for *earnings yield*, which is the actual yield that can be compared with bonds, certificates of deposit, etc. A P/E of 6.7 equals a 15% earnings yield, and a P/E of 46.5 equals an earnings yield of 2.15% or a speculative valuation extreme. Price matters with investing. This table shows by ranges of inflation the corresponding average historical P/E ratio, peak P/E ratio, and trough P/E ratio for the Standard and Poor's 500 Index companies. P/Es are based on trailing 12-month earnings. This table is one input to the investment decision process.

PE indicates price/earnings.

Source: Ned Davis Research, Inc, Bloomberg, Financial and Investment Management Group.

Long-Term Fixed Income/Predictable Income

Imagine an opportunity to earn a fixed return on your whole portfolio of 14% per year over many years. This rate of return was available on US government–guaranteed bonds that returned all of your money back in 10 to 30 years. Such a dream investment existed in 1983. Of course, it was shunned by the media, investors, and others who believed that double-digit inflation was a long-term reality and that short-term investments were always going to return 12% to 20%. Again, we can point out the cyclical nature of markets now that 30-year bonds have paid as little as 5% since their high in the mid 1980s. My hat is off to those investors who locked in that 14% long-term annual rate.

In contrast, look at Japan, which currently has long-term government bonds with rates under 2%; rates that the United States has not seen since the

Depression years. Short-term government bonds, CDs, and other investments are well under 1% in Japan. Imagine the unfortunate US investor who retired in 1983 with what he felt were reasonable expectations of rolling CDs every 1 to 5 years at those hefty 12% to 17% rates. Today, that investor would be rolling to 2% to 4% CDs and living on one quarter of his or her prior income, not even factoring in the effects of inflation.

The moral here is that in retirement, you must have a rational, long-term income strategy. Very low interest rates are a risk and long-term income investments help lock in predictable, long-term income.

As you reach $10,000 in your first fund, start adding to another.

Total return fixed income:
Fidelity Advisor Strategic Income Ins (FSRIX)
Fidelity Strategic Income (FSICX)
Loomis Sayles Bond Instl (LSBDX)
PIMCO Global Bond (unhedged) Instl (PIGLX)
T Rowe Price Spectrum Income (RPSIX)

Total Return Global Income:
American Century International Bd Inv (BEGBX)
Consulting Group International F/I (TIFUX)
Credit Suisse Global Fixed Income (CGFIX)
Delaware Pooled International Fix Inc (DPIFX)
Evergreen International Bond Instl (ESICX)
FFTW International (FFIFX)
GMO International Bond III (GMIBX)
Northern Institutional Intl Bond A (BIBAX)
Western Asset Non-US Opp Bond Instl (WAFIX)

Balanced Total Return Management Style

Careful studies of history show that all investments are affected by cycles and the manic behavior of investors. Inherent to economics and financial markets is the continuous circulation of events; periods of growth are inevitably followed by recessions, which eventually give way to episodes of expansion. Elemental. And, as a whole, investors can be counted on to bid investments up to manic, overvalued bubble-like stocks as in 1999 and 1929, gold in 1983, Japanese real estate and stocks in the 1980s, Florida and California real estate in 2005, and on and on. When investments become overvalued, they should be sold. When markets reach bargain levels like stocks and bonds did in the early 1930s and 1980s and like gold did in the early 1970s, they should be purchased. The key is that real money is made by a strategy based upon the fact that investments get overvalued. When investments are overvalued, they should be sold and avoided until, through the cyclical influence of markets, they return to an undervalued state in which they are priced right, at which time they should be bought. This is not simple stuff; it takes experience, talent, training, and education to recognize and act on all of the variables. Yet there are generally opportunities somewhere to create, preserve, and grow wealth, and a strategy that heeds the lessons of cycles and manias is well-situated to discover the hidden gems.

The following funds have characteristics I desire in this balanced total return style of management. Many of them are encumbered by silly rules regarding geography, asset allocation, indexes, leverage, concentration, and the like, so diversify well among them.

Bruce (BRUFX)

Leuthold Core Investment (LCORX)

MainStay Balanced I (MBAIX)

Vanguard Wellesley Income (VWINX)

FPA Crescent (FPACX)

Global Equity Funds/Natural Resource Funds

Historically, financial markets have rewarded investors for taking prudent, appropriate, thoughtful risks far more often, and reliably, than those who choose speculative investment opportunities. Even equity investors have found consistent year-to-year success as long as they adhered to a "price matters," common-sense approach to the stock market. In fact, during the difficult 1970s, one of my investment gurus often began his mutual fund reports with, "Another good year."

After over 20 years of managing money, I see my job as co-manager of the Utopia Funds and manager of my clients' wealth as looking everywhere for opportunities to preserve and grow wealth, and I look for a similar discipline in the managers I favor.

Place a third of your portfolio in each group, with no less than $10,000 in any one fund. My favorite in this group is the UBS Global Allocation. Balance between precious metal funds and global funds with no more than 10% of your portfolio in natural resource funds.

> UBS Global Allocation Y (BPGLX)
> Scudder Gold & Precious Metals S (SCGDX)
> Templeton Global Smaller (TGSAX)
> USAA Precious Metals and Minerals (USAGX)
> Vanguard Global Equity (VHGEX)
> Blackrock Global Resources Instl (SGLSX)
> Excelsior Energy & Nat Resources (UMESX)
> T Rowe Price New Era (PRNEX)

100% Funds

The Utopia Funds, which are managed by my team at Financial and Investment Management Group, are no-load, no 12b-1 global total return-oriented investment funds designed to be used as complete all-season lifetime investment portfolios. In other words, each of the four Utopia Funds is designed as a tool for investors at different stages of life who simply wish to retire or accumulate money—those who wish to delegate the management of their money to a professional, experienced management team with a good performance record and a disciplined, total-return-in-all-economic-seasons approach. The Utopia Funds are long-term funds most suitable for income retirement plans or as an accumulation vehicle. Any one of the four funds may be the right prescription to make deposits into until your portfolio is of a sufficient size to hire a private money manager who is tax-sensitive. I have, of course, a conflict of interest in recommending the Utopia Funds because my company manages them and uses them for our clients when the fit is right. Also, these funds are where most of my family's long-term investments are. Your financial advisor will be familiar with these funds, and for an objective second opinion, ask him or her about them. Investigate Utopia Funds prospectus before you invest by visiting www.utopiafunds.com or by calling 888-Utopia3.

Nobody's Perfect

Nobody's perfect, or so go the words to the famous song, but we can all try to be perfect and set a goal of maximizing our positive impact on our portfolio returns, society, the environment, and our world. So nobody's perfect! Doesn't that justify selling the pleasures of smoking to children? Or glamorizing alcohol to teens and promoting as the norm a diet rich in fats, sugars, animal meat, and other manufactured foods as the norm?

Do *Playboy* magazine and Hooters® restaurants exploit and promote the objectification of women? Do Wal-Mart® and Home Depot® destroy small towns, ruin entrepreneurship, and promote mass culture and mass products at the expense of innovation, uniqueness, individualization, customization, and art?

I have used every oil company's products and have shopped at Wal-Mart. In Buddhist literature you can read about how our very nature of being [alive] uses up resources! As investors who hold ethics and sustainability as important, we can practice investing behaviors that reduce our harmful impact on society and the environment while, it is hoped, nurturing positive returns and positive impact. Many investors today (including my company, which manages the Utopia Funds) believe that it is appropriate to invest consistent with our values. For example, we tell some companies that we own to edge toward more sustainable ethical practices, and we won't own companies that are in the business of making products that kill the people who use them. Not owning tobacco companies is easy if you think cigarettes kill, but after that it gets hard. Beer, gambling, abortions, weapons, polluters, French-fry sellers, drug companies, retailers buying from exploitative companies; where does what a company does become something you are not comfortable with? It is a judgment call on the part of each investor to determine the right way to invest, but of course no one and no company is perfect! I believe that to do the right thing is economically responsible and appropriate for any long-term investor.

Market Timing

One popular study showed that an investor would have underperformed the buy-and-hold strategy by missing just a few key "up" months in the market. We verified that if an investor had missed 50 of the largest up months since 1926, the portfolio would have gained only 0.4% per annum versus the Dow's 9.6% per annum buy-and-hold return. But to be fair, if we exclude the largest up months, then should we not also exclude the largest "down" months? When we excluded both the largest 50 up and down months (100 in all), we found the gain per annum to be 12.0% or somewhat above the buy-and-hold rate. Furthermore, when we just show the effect of taking out the largest 50 losing months (what market timing ideally should do), the gain per annum jumps to 22.1%. At that rate of gain, an investor's portfolio would double in just over 3 years. At the very least, we felt this illustrated that there can be considerable margin for error in market timing.

Source: Ned Davis Research.

What Does It Take to Recover from Declines?*

Original Principal	Percentage Decline	Dollar Decline	Remaining Principal	Percentage to recover	Years to recover at 7%
$1,000,000	10	$(100,000)	$900,000	11.1	1.6
$1,000,000	20	$(200,000)	$800,000	25.0	3.3
$1,000,000	30	$(300,000)	$700,000	42.9	5.3
$1,000,000	40	$(400,000)	$600,000	66.7	7.6
$1,000,000	50	$(500,000)	$500,000	100.0	10.2
$1,000,000	60	$(600,000)	$400,000	150.0	13.5
$1,000,000	70	$(700,000)	$300,000	233.3	17.8
$1,000,000	80	$(800,000)	$200,000	400.0	23.8
$1,000,000	90	$(900,000)	$100,000	900.0	34.0

*This table illustrates unleveraged declines in value.

Source: Performance Report: a contextual presentation. *Traverse City*: Financial and Investment Management Group; 2004.

CHAPTER 7 Guided Do-It-Yourself Portfolio Management

Pulling It All Together

The first century Jesuit monk Gracián (circa 1500s) started his book about heroes discussing his trust that the reader of his writings would favor and embrace the brevity of his words and be satisfied with him providing enough for understanding, but not so much as to be cumbersome and wordy. He trusted his readers to use common sense, intelligence, and instincts to help them make good choices.

My goal in this guide is to give enough information so that each reader is well-equipped with understanding and information to make good choices. For the old or young physician, by now it is apparent that good financial planning comes from the ability to allocate time and assets toward fulfilling goals based on commitments, priorities, and intentions.

For a young physician with children who is just starting out, usually a financial plan emphasizes risk management, career, debt management, housing, and budgeting. This makes wills (possibly trusts), life insurance and disability insurance, employment issues, smart budgeting, and debt management the main attributes of a solid plan.

As those areas are addressed, capital accumulation for retirement, education of children, second homes, and the like are layered over the risk management and budgeting issues to build a more comprehensive plan. The use of tax-qualified retirement plans is the bedrock of the savings- and net worth–building component of a My Way/Our Way Life Plan.

Taxes, of course, are always an input to the planning process, but they should never drive it. The driver of your plan must be common sense along with your goals, values, and commitments. A financial planner's job is to add financial efficiency and economic security to this process.

If you are married with children and for whatever reason or excuse have not taken the time to have wills or trusts created or have not had your insurance reviewed, go see a fee-only financial advisor, because you cannot do it yourself! If you have not reviewed your debt situation or do not have your tax returns reviewed periodically by a fee-only financial planning firm, you most likely need a planner. Planners come in all shapes and sizes and practice styles. Some will only do expensive, many-paged written financial plans. Others feel that a book-sized plan adds little value to the planning process and would rather sit with you and give you guidance and a legal pad–sized to-do list that might look something like this:

1. Call Low Load for two $500,000 10-year term policies and American Medical Association (AMA) for one $500,000 5-year term policy. Spouse as beneficiary, children secondary beneficiary until trust is set up.
2. Call an attorney to get wills and event-driven disposition trusts set up for children.
3. Change disability policies to 1 year, wait, and make benefit period life instead of age 65. Call AMA to layer on $3,000 monthly policy.
4. Call bank to change mortgage to 30-year fixed (no points) and pay off car loans and second mortgage with proceeds.
5. Fund 401(k) to maximum and hire manager to manage existing assets.
6. Discuss with partner idea of changing 401(k) investment options to include "make money, don't lose it" management style.
7. Send tax returns and employment agreement to advisor for review.
8. Not time for children's education 529 plans yet.
9. Hedge funds: probably not for me.
10. Family limited partnership and offshore trusts probably not for me now (maybe in future).
11. Buy *Physician's Guide to Financial Planning* for partner.

I believe in financial "do-ing" and feel the key financial plan is the implementation of it. I do not believe that the 50- to 100-page written plans add much value. I think the financial planner's job is to guide you with his or her words, to-do lists, meetings with your other advisors, phone calls to your other advisors, and the like. To get something done is the key in the process toward financial well-being—not volumes of pages that say "save for retirement." You know you need to save and invest wisely, so do it.

Delegation of the components of your plan can save you time and money and add great efficiency in accomplishing your goals with greater security and less time. This delegation should be done competently. The easy part is narrowing down the key attributes you want in anyone you delegate to. These qualities should include the following:

Independence: Not affiliated with a bank, broker, or insurance agency.

Objective and fee-only all the time: Not able to receive any commissions, kickbacks, or compensation of any kind from anyone but you through fees. The National Association of Personal Financial Advisors (NAPFA) has more on fee-only.

Competence: The training, experience, and education to help you.

Track record: No one advising you should have less than 10 years experience (or be well supervised by someone with 15 to 20 years experience).

Ethics: Do they believe in honesty? Do they believe it is okay to hide things from the Internal Revenue Service (IRS)? Do they talk about their "creative" tax deals and investment plans that are not backed up by the IRS, private letter rulings, or large certified public accounting or law firm opinion letters because they do not want to let anyone know about the fine loopholes in case they might close? If someone is dishonest, if they want to hide things, if they won't give it to you in writing, then look elsewhere for an advisor.

Common sense: Do they meet the common-sense test? Are their words consistent with their actions and life?

Firm structure/practice style: Everyone is different, and each firm has a different style based on the collective values of its senior people. For example, my firm has 30-plus employees all devoted to serving our clients. No one is assigned a client, although, naturally, West Coast and Hawaii's clients tend to talk with Barry, Judy, and Alice in Hawaii, but if they call us in Michigan, we are able to help. Our firm is built on a belief that we are a team serving our clients because that is best. I travel, I have family obligations, and no one should wait until I get back from Australia to find out if they should go with a 30-year or 15-year mortgage or buy or lease that new car. Three of our senior people came from one- or two-person office backgrounds and realized early that a deep bench was in the client's interest. Also, for the sake of perpetuities, a firm large enough to continue indefinitely is in a client's best interest. Some firms revolve around a single person. To me, this is not ideal; what if the person dies, becomes disabled, or goes through a life trauma, divorce, sickness of a child, alcoholism, or something else? Also, who is looking over the person's shoulder to give a second or third opinion? Often, one person oversimplifies the process because of his or her own biases and limitations.

The bottom line is to have committed, ethical people to help you; people who have a practice style, competency, education, and experience to meet your needs well. They should have experience in working with physicians and high-income professionals and enjoy working with doctors. The letter on page 196 should help you in finding a firm to fit your needs.

Dear [name of planner/group],

We are possibly interested in hiring your firm to help us with financial planning. We assume you are a firm with all employees recovering 100% of their income from fees and receiving no commissions, a registered investment advisor with the Securities and Exchange Commission (SEC), have your firm's books audited annually by an independent certified public accounting auditing firm, and have staff with the training, expertise, education, and experience to work with physicians and high-income professionals. If you do not meet the above criteria, then we are not interested in working with your firm and it is not necessary to read this letter further. If you do meet the above criteria, please explain the following in writing:

1. Why people hire your firm.
2. What you consider your core competencies.
3. Your firm's financial planning philosophy.
4. Criteria for hiring of employees.
5. What you consider your firm's culture. In addition to the above questions, could you please send us the following:
    a. Fact sheet/resumes of your planning team.
    b. Philosophy statement for how you manage portfolios.
    c. Recent newsletters to clients.
    d. Client service agreements.
    e. Privacy statement.
    f. SEC form ADV (complete form).
    g. Any other information that you feel we should have to help us evaluate your firm.

Once we review this information, we would like to meet you in person or by phone to talk about your vision, practice philosophy, values, and what we can expect as a client. After we have interviewed you, we will ask you to provide us with two or three references to clients who have been with your firm for over 10 years. Please keep our inquiry confidential.

Sincerely,

[Your name]

Note: For a printable copy of a letter similar to this that can be tailored to your situation, visit truthinperformance.com.

Sample Letter for Investment Management

If you wish to use your planning firm for investment management as well as financial planning, here is an additional questionnaire you should have answered. Or, if you are going to hire a firm just for investment management, this letter will help get you the information you need:

Dear Sirs and Madams,

We are considering hiring [name of firm] to assist in managing our investment (pension) accounts. We have the following questions we would like answered in writing:

1. Has anyone in your firm ever been convicted of insider trading, front running, or other serious securities violation?

2. Was your firm or anyone in your firm ever fined (or through an arbitration process forced to pay) for breach of fiduciary duty, self-dealing, or excessive commissions (churning)?

3. When you show performance, is it with actual performance for all clients you have or have had, or is it someone else's performance that your firm is now endorsing? What actual client outcomes have you had (for your clients, in other words) over the past 10 years?

4. In 1989, 1999, 2000, and 2001, what percentage of all your clients' holdings were in US stocks, global stocks, convertible bonds, and preferred stocks?

5. What was your worst 12-month period client investment group's performance in the past 3, 5, and 10 years?

6. Does your firm manage any annuity accounts that have commissions layered over your fees? Does your firm manage mutual funds that pay sales commission loads to brokers or charge 12b-1 fees?

Please give this information, even if those who managed these portfolios are no longer part of your firm. If you used outside managers or mutual funds but no longer use them, please give actual performance of your clients. We wish to evaluate your client outcomes because we are looking for a firm to guide our investments and our investment policy and help us manage risk. We want to know how your clients' actual investment accounts have performed over the past 1, 3, 5, and 10 years and beyond.

Please provide net returns, after all fees, commissions, and expenses, of your portfolio management style that you feel is best for us or a category with approximately 35% value at risk (VAR), 25% VAR, 15% VAR. These numbers do not need to be audited but should be representative of all of your clients' actual experience. If possible, fill in the following table:

Performance over last 10 years ending: [Date]

	Worst 12-Month Period	Best 12-Month Period	3-Year IRR	5-Year IRR	10-Year IRR
Value at Risk					
35%/40%					
25%/30%					
15%/20%					

Internal Rate of Return (IRR) indicates.

Could you also be so kind as to send us a snapshot of all your managed holdings for a specific period in 1998, 2000, 2002, and 2004?

Also, please send marketing materials with your investment team members' qualifications, experience, and service time with your firm as well as your firm's investment philosophy, values statement, mission statement, and other pertinent materials for our review.

Please keep this inquiry confidential.

Sincerely,

[Your name]

cc: CPA (if possible); other advisors (if possible); lawyer (if possible)

Note: Visit truthinperformance.com for a printable copy of this letter.

Not Leaving It to Chance

You will need to rely on others to help you in your planning. Whether you have a Charles Schwab (www.schwab.com) manager help you implement a do-it-yourself portfolio strategy or hire a fee-only advisor, you need to understand the process and rely on solid, time-tested advice that meets the commonsense test. Charles Schwab and Fidelity have many of the investment products discussed in this book (mutual fund services, for example), so you may get more favorable rates through their services. TD Waterhouse, Scottrade, Vanguard (www.vanguard.com), and many other discount brokerage and mutual fund groups also have systems for you to work through.

In working with any firm, you need to understand their weaknesses and strengths. For example, with some science, let us take apart the mutual fund industry. From its noble beginnings as a way for the small, average investor to afford professional management, tax ease, diversification, and cost savings, mutual funds have grown to an $8 trillion business with 92 million Americans owning shares. Most fund holders, it seems, are unaware that they are often investing in expensive, lightly managed funds. To illustrate, a full 80% of fund shareholders bought their funds (often paying unnecessary commissions) through brokers, banks, or commissioned financial planners. Around 11% directly purchased funds through a discount broker or by doing their own research on which mutual fund tool was best for them. Collectively, the 53 million homes that have mutual funds have $48,000 in four different funds equaling just under 50% of the financial assets. Of those families, 80% own equity or stock-oriented funds. What is interesting is that while the average investor plans to hold those funds 5 years, over the past 4 years, investors have annually redeemed funds for a high of 41% in 2002 to a low of 24% last year. Any study shows that sound investing takes patience, buying investments at the right price, and understanding their characteristics and use. It is estimated that over the past 5 years, over 40% of growth mutual funds paid their managers more in fees than they made for their shareholders.

The investment and mutual fund industry has morphed from tried and true to allowing investors to speculate on or invest in everything from Standard and Poor's indexes to gold stocks to Internet plays to biotech and health-related investments. Some fund marketers and salespeople have leveraged this great product's reputation and stacked the deck so that it appears that shareholders are investing in stodgy, safe, rational, long-term investments, and in some cases they have (there are many fine funds), but in many cases, they have not. As mentioned previously, at least 80% of funds are "sold," not bought. They are sold by marketing organizations that "allow investors," as a manager of a large college fund said in a seminar that I had attended a few years back, "to have their 401(k)s become 201(k)s by letting shareholders be guided by what's hot, what sells well, and what looked good in the past" (ICI.org). It is like basketball team A that played only one game all season against team B. Team A lost, of course, but sent out two press releases. One said, "Team A loses only one game all year." The other said, "Team B won only one game all season."

Banks, brokers, and many financial advisors, who are driven by commissions, naiveté, or greed and not common sense or ethics let their clients bet on a team that "lost one game!" The investment industry is under scrutiny today even by its most stalwart supporters. Insider buying, hidden commissions, hidden kickbacks, after-hour trading, and hiding the truth about a company's total track record of all their client investment funds, even the ones that "failed," are causing a backlash that, it is hoped, will allow new groups to emerge that will be guided by ethics, transparency, and virtue. The fund group that I started, Utopia Funds,* I believe will be a part of this trend.

If your advisor has no incentive to sell you this or that to make money, at least his or her advice will not be tainted by commissions or money. Feeling competent about your advisor is key, so dig deep into your advisory firm's belly to see what is real.

Advice given in this book is general in nature and may not pertain to your specific needs. If you have any doubt as to whether the information pertains to your situation, you should seek competent financial planning advice.

Mutual funds service providers and companies listed in this book are not necessarily endorsed by the author, editor, or publisher. Inflation, taxation, and a host of new investment and tax law changes occur almost daily. Also, companies change focus, are bought out, sell out to the big guys, or lose key employees, all of which can change their character. The reader's responsibility is to assess the risk or appropriateness of any investment or strategy on his or her own or with guidance from competent advisors.

I wish to provide the most objective and purposeful information possible. I believe there is no substitute for integrity when it comes to serving readers. I expect a degree of criticism based on my sharp commentary on commissioned salespeople such as stockbrokers selling load and commissionable mutual funds, insurance agents pushing insurance products for large commissions, and inept, unqualified people with little experience giving financial advice. I also expect that some companies will be put off by my sharp

---

*The Utopia Mutual Funds are managed by Financial and Investment Management Group. Of course I am biased, so investigate before you invest. The funds are offered only by a prospectus, and truly, you need to read it before investing. It is available at www.utopiafunds.com, or you can call 1-888-Utopia3 and ask for one. Also, you could ask your fee-only advisor or discount broker's mutual fund specialist his or her thoughts on the Utopia Funds.

critique of their sales practices regarding the fact that they create poor-quality products that add little value or are very expensively priced, such as variable life and annuities, loaded mutual funds with 12b-1 fees, and expensive index-oriented asset allocation wrap programs.

There are fine, good, ethical advisors available who work for solid, integrity-based firms. As a physician, you are smart and you assess people and risks every day, so you have the high-functioning mental and emotional capacity and ability to make good choices. Of course, investigate but trust your judgment, too. Good luck!

APPENDIX A

International Volunteer Opportunities for Physicians

Aloha Medical Mission
1314 South King St., Suite 503
Honolulu, HI 96814
Tele: (808) 593-9696
E-mail: info@alohamm.org
Web site: www.alohamm.org

Commitment of 1 to 3 weeks. Serves Vietnam, Laos, the Philippines, and other countries of Asia to provide care for the poor.

American Refugee Committee
430 Oak Grove St., Suite 204
Minneapolis, MN 55403
Tele: (612) 872-7060
E-mail: archq@archq.org
Web site: www.archq.org

Commitment of 1 month to 1 year. One million people uprooted by war are provided with primary care, medical training, and public health services through the American Refugee Committee. Countries currently being served include Pakistan, Thailand, Guinea, the former Yugoslavia, Rwanda, Sudan, Liberia, and Sierra Leone.

Bridges to Community, Inc
Box 35
Scarborough, NY 10510
Tele: (914) 923-2200
E-mail: brdgs2comm@aol.com
Web site: www.bridgestocommunity.org

Commitment of 10 to 15 days. Serves Kenya, Nepal, Cambodia, and Nicaragua. Primary care physicians, nurses, and medical students are needed to serve in urban and rural clinics.

Canvasback Mission, Inc
940 Adams St., Suite R
Benicia, CA 94510
Tele: (800) 793-7215
E-mail: canvasback1@earthlink.net
Web site: www.canvasback.org

Commitment of 2 to 6 weeks to hospitals in Micronesia and the Marshall Islands. Medical personnel staff outer island clinics and establish preventive programs, and specialty teams provide training, consultation, and surgery where services are unavailable.

Cardiostart International, Inc
6110 Hartford St.
Tampa, FL 33619
Tele: (813) 689-3289
E-mail: info@cardiostart.com
Web site: www.cardiostart.com

Physicians are dispatched to the Caribbean, Eastern Europe, the Middle East, and Central America for 1 week to 1 month with the average commitment being 2 weeks. Cardiostart International provides heart surgery at no cost to people in need throughout the world as well as family, obstetric and gynecologic, and orphanage care. This group is particularly in need of cardiologists, cardiac surgeons, anesthesiologists, and obstetrics-gynecology physicians.

CB International
1501 West Mineral Ave.
Littleton, CO 80120
Tele: (800) 487-4224, ext 2520
E-mail: cbi@cbi.org
Web site: www.cbi.org

Medical personnel are dispatched for 1 month to 2 years to 60 areas of the world located on five continents. Obstetrics-gynecology physicians, ophthalmologists, public health specialists, surgeons, and midwives are needed. Volunteers fund their own work or receive support from friends, family, and churches.

Children's Heartlink
5075 Arcadia Ave.
Minneapolis, MN 55436
Tele: (800) 928-6678
E-mail: info@childrensheartlink.org
Web site: www.childrensheartlink.org

Medical personnel are dispatched for 1 to 2 weeks to Central America, East Africa, China, India, Kenya, Israel, and the Ukraine. The main focus of the organization is to prevent and treat heart disease in children. Experienced cardiologists, cardiac surgeons, anesthesiologists, intensive care physicians, and public healthcare specialists are needed.

Concern America
Box 1790
Santa Ana, CA 92702
Tele: (800) 266-2376
E-mail: concernamerica@earthlink.net
Web site: www.concernamerica.org

Medical personnel are asked to serve a 2-year commitment training local health workers in both preventive and curative medicine and addressing sanitation and vaccination issues. Volunteers must speak Spanish or Portuguese or be willing to learn. Countries currently being served by Concern America include Mexico, El Salvador, Guatemala, Honduras, Columbia, Guinea, and Mozambique.

(continued)

DOCARE International, Inc
430 King Ave
East Dundee, IL 60118
Tele: (847) 836-8022
Web site: www.docareintl.org

Medical personnel serve a 7- to 14-day commitment in an outreach program that brings needed healthcare to primitive and isolated people in remote areas of Western Hemisphere countries. Volunteers work in local clinics and also provide care in makeshift village clinics.

Doctors of the World, USA, Inc
375 West Broadway, 4th Floor
New York, NY 10012
Tele: (888) 817-HELP
E-mail: info@dowusa.org
Web site: www.doctorsoftheworld.org

Medical personnel volunteer for 1 to 12 months. Doctors of the World, USA, is working to treat tuberculosis and human immunodeficiency virus in four regions of the world and plans to significantly expand its efforts. Also, women's health and the needs of survivors of torture and other gross human rights abuses are being addressed by the organization. Children with disabilities, street children, and children in institutions or those separated from their families are served by this organization as well.

Doctors On Call for Service, Inc
Box 24597
Saint Simon Island, GA 31522
Tele: (912) 634-0065
E-mail: docs@docs.org
Web site: www.docs.org

Doctors On Call for Service provides medical professionals the opportunity to mentor and encourage their African colleagues. The organization is looking for health professionals to share insights and practical experience during continuing medical education (CME) trips to Africa. These CME trips typically last for 2 weeks and are scheduled in April and October. Doctors On Call for Service handles all arrangements (air travel, visas, food, housing, ground transportation).

Doctors Without Borders/Médecins Sans Frontières (MSF)
6 East 39th St, 8th Floor
New York, NY 10016
Tele: (212) 679-6800
E-mail: doctors@newyork.msf.org
Web site: www.doctorswithoutborders.org
Contact: Recruitment

For details see "Doctors Without Borders Description and Criteria" on page 10.

Esperanca, Inc
1911 West Earll Dr
Phoenix, AZ 85015
Tele: (602) 252-7772, ext 101
E-mail: info@esperanca.org
Web site: www.esperanca.org

A typical mission lasts 2 weeks. Esperanca is a nonprofit, international health organization working to improve the well-being of children and their families through public health programming and volunteer surgical missions. Services are provided in 14 countries on four continents. Current projects are in Bolivia, Nicaragua, and Mozambique. Esperanca has a need for orthopedic, plastic, urologic, and general surgery teams.

Flying Doctors of America
15 Medical Dr
Cartersville, GA 30121
Tele: (770) 386-5221
E-mail: pittsman54@aol.com
Web site: www.fdamerica.org

Short-term (6-day) volunteer missions are undertaken by private plane. Teams travel to remote clinics to follow the Mother Theresa principle of caring for the poorest of the poor. Volunteers bring medical care to Mexico, Central America, the Caribbean, India, Africa, Mongolia, and Thailand.

Global Volunteers
375 E Little Canada Rd
St Paul, MN 55117
Tele: (800) 487-1074
E-mail: email@globalvolunteers.org
Web site: www.globalvolunteers.org

Physicians and laypersons serve 1- to 3-week missions, providing basic services to developing countries in local homes and outreach clinics. Global Volunteers participates in medical missions to Asia, the South Pacific, Africa, India, the Americas, the Caribbean, and Europe. Host communities often lack modern medical facilities, so volunteers should plan to bring their own instruments and medical supplies.

Health Volunteers Overseas
1900 L Street NW, Suite 310
Washington, DC 20036
Tele: (202) 296-0928
E-mail: info@hvousa.org
Web site: www.hvousa.org

Volunteers train local healthcare providers in developing countries, giving them the knowledge and skills to make a difference in their own communities. Most programs require that volunteers serve for 1 month, but there are some sites where they may serve for 2 weeks. There are opportunities for longer placements if a volunteer has the time available, and in some instances families may accompany volunteers. This organization supports over 60 programs in more than 25 countries in Africa, Asia, Latin America, Eastern Europe, and the Caribbean. Each project is different depending on the educational needs and technological capacity of the country.

Heart to Heart International
401 S Clairborne Rd, Suite 302
Olathe, KS 66062
Tele: (405) 787-5200, ext 104
E-mail: info@hearttoheart.org
Web site: www.hearttoheart.org

Volunteers are sent on missions that average 2 weeks. Heart to Heart International's programs are both relief- and development-focused. Large international airlifts are often accompanied by a delegation of volunteers (medical and non-medical) who build bridges of friendship and understanding between countries that are worlds apart. Heart to Heart also partners with medical teams and other humanitarian organizations, supplying them with medicines and supplies to treat men, women, and children in some of the world's neediest areas. In 2003 Heart to Heart changed the lives of millions of people in more than 50 countries.

(continued)

Helps International
15301 Dallas Pkwy, Suite 200
Addison, TX 75001
Tele: (800) 414-3577
E-mail: rmartin@helpsintl.org
Web site: www.helpsintl.org

Volunteers go from January through May on 12-day missions. The organization believes in providing first-class, US hospital–standard healthcare to the people of Guatemala and tries to provide surgical and general care assistance to as many of the rural population as possible in local and US government–built hospitals.

International Health Service
Box 16149
Saint Louis Park, MN 55416
Tele: (952) 920-0433
E-mail: ihsofmn@hotmail.com
Web site: www.ihsofmn.org

Each year, International Health Service sponsors two medical missions to Honduras. The main mission is in the second half of February and lasts for 17 days. Typically, about 100 people are on this mission. They are broken up into 8 to 10 teams consisting of medical, surgical, or dental personnel. Individual teams consist of one or more of these areas of specialty, depending on the needs of the area that they will be serving. The second mission of the year is in late October and is for 10 days. It coincides with a trip by various members of International Health Service planning for the following February mission. Participation in this mission has been limited and is generally dictated by the amount of interest.

International Relief Teams
3547 Camino del Rio S, Suite C
San Diego, CA 92108
Tele: (619) 284-7979
E-mail: info@irteams.org
Web site: www.irteams.org

International Relief Teams sends medical personnel to developing countries for missions that range from 10 days to 2 weeks. International Relief Teams promotes self-sufficiency and sustainability by training the trainers while establishing a solid foundation upon which healthcare can be dramatically improved in emerging nations. Volunteer teams instruct local healthcare professionals in specialized surgery and maternal and newborn care and run health education programs.

Interplast, Inc
300-B Pioneer Way
Mountain View, CA 94041
Tele: (650) 962-0123
E-mail: Beverly@interplast.org
Web site: www.interplast.org

Interplast partners with physicians in developing countries to provide free reconstructive plastic surgery for needy children and adults who have nowhere else to turn for help. Trips generally last 2 weeks, and teams typically perform approximately 75 surgeries per trip. Interplast's volunteer medical teams include plastic surgeons, anesthesiologists, pediatricians, operating room nurses, and recovery room nurses. Volunteers who do not fit the specialties listed above are not accepted. The organization is active in

Ecuador, Honduras, Peru, the Philippines, Nepal, and Vietnam.

Mercy Ships
Box 2020
Garden Valley, TX 75771
Tele: (800) 424-7447
E-mail: info@mercyships.org
Web site: www.mercyships.org

Short-term volunteers can participate for 2 weeks to a full year with Mercy Ships, whereas others may choose to serve in a career capacity. Mercy Ships welcomes volunteers who would like to give their time, efforts, and expertise to the work of bringing hope and healing to the poor. Mercy Ships is a global charity and has operated a growing fleet of hospital ships in developing nations since 1978, providing cataract operations, orthopedic operations, cleft lip and cleft palate operations, and Vesico-vaginal fistula operations.

MIMA Foundation
Box 7133
Jupiter, FL 33468
Tele: (561) 747-3334
E-mail: mimafoundation@mail.com
Web site: www.mimafoundation.com

A private, nonprofit, nondenominational organization, MIMA sends volunteer healthcare professionals to third world countries and other areas of need for 1- to 2-week medical outreach programs. MIMA is derived from the Spanish mimar, which means "to care for." Since its inception, MIMA has traveled to Bolivia and Peru and hopes to expand to locations in Central America. All the members are volunteers; no one is a paid employee, and the team members raise all funds.

Northwest Medical Teams International
Box 10
Portland, OR 97207
Tele: (800) 959-4325
E-mail: jmckenzie@nwmti.org
Web site: www.nwmedicalteams.org

This organization sends many types of medical teams around the world to assist their international country partners in long-term development projects. Volunteer missions of 1 to 3 weeks provide clinical and disaster relief around the world to such areas as Southeast Asia, Central Asia, Africa, South America, Central America, and Eastern Europe. Surgical teams perform plastic (cleft lip, cleft palate); ophthalmologic (cataract); ear, nose, and throat; and orthopedic surgeries. Medical brigades work in clinics, mountain villages, and places where routine care and assessment are needed.

Orbis International
520 9th Ave, 11th Floor
New York, NY 10018
Tele: (800) 672-4787 or
(540) 261-7737
E-mail: swhitton@ny.orbis.org
Web site: www.orbis.org

The mission of Orbis International is to preserve and restore sight by strengthening the capacity of local partners to prevent and treat blindness. Orbis relies on volunteer ophthalmologists, nurses, and other healthcare professionals to share their knowledge and skills in countries in which access to basic eye care is an uncommon privilege.

(continued)

Volunteers typically commit to a 1-week program, which takes place either at a local hospital or on board the Orbis DC-10 Flying Eye Hospital. Every effort is made to match skills and languages to the countries Orbis visits. Volunteer opportunities exist for ophthalmologists, anesthesiologists, neonatologists, orthopedists, ophthalmic nurses, and optometrists in developing countries.

Physicians for Peace
229 W Bute St, Suite 200
Norfolk, VA 23510
Tele: (757) 625-7569
E-mail: admin@physiciansforpeace.org
Web site: www.physiciansforpeace.org

Physicians for Peace seeks world peace and international goodwill by providing quality medical care to those in need. A typical volunteer mission ranges from 10 days to 2 weeks. The organization works closely with other medical relief and international aid organizations to improve medical education and deliver healthcare services in developing nations around the world. Physicians for Peace serves at the request of a country in a designated medical need area.

Project Hope
225 Carter Hall Ln
Millwood, VA 22646
Tele: (800) 544-4673
E-mail: recruitment@projecthope.org
Web site: www.projecthope.org

Volunteer medical personnel with assignments that range from a week to a year teach the latest in healthcare techniques in developing countries throughout the world. The organization conducts land-based medical training and healthcare education programs on five continents including North America. Volunteer medical personnel are an integral part of Project Hope, and all interested medical professionals are welcomed.

Special thanks to Julie Quinn, MD, Donna Manthei, and *Diversions Magazine* for their help in compiling this volunteer section

APPENDIX B

Resources

Read *MD: Doctors Talk about Themselves*, by John Pekkanen, and *Life After Medical School: Thirty-Two Doctors Describe How They Shaped Their Medical Careers,* by Leonard Laster, editor, then say nothing except, "Honey, for my birthday I'd like you to read these books."

Read *The Optimist Child: Proven Program to Safeguard Children from Depression and Build Lifelong Resilience,* by Dr. Martin E. Seligman, and *Children Are from Heaven: Positive Parenting Skills for Raising Cooperative, Confident, and Compassionate Children,* by John Gray, to your spouse at the breakfast table or before bed if you have children, plan on having children, watch your sister-in-law's children, or tell your parents how they should have raised you.

If you are going to read only one book on investing, read *The Book of Investing Wisdom: Classic Writings by Great Stock Pickers and Legends of Wall Street*, edited by Peter Krass. If you like it, then read *The Intelligent Investor*, by Benjamin Graham. These two books will help you understand investing and give you insight into what your investment manager *should* be doing, which is actually making sure every dollar in your portfolio is invested rationally, appropriately, and consistent with a common-sense approach that favors bargain-priced investments, and avoids overpriced investments.

Following is a list of these and other resources I have found helpful.

These resources are periodically updated at FIMG.NET.

- Brazelton TB, Greenspan SL. *The Irreducible Needs of Children: What Every Child Must Have to Grow, Learn, and Flourish.* New York, NY: Perseus Publishing; 2001.

- Graham B. *The Intelligent Investor.* New York, NY: Harper Business Essentials; July 8, 2003.

- Gray J. *Children Are from Heaven: Positive Parenting Skills for Raising Cooperative, Confident, and Compassionate Children.* New York, NY: Perennial Currents; 2001.

- Krass P. *The Book of Investing Wisdom.* New York, NY: Perennial Currents; 2001.

- Krass P. *The Book of Wisdom: Classic Writings by Great Stock Pickers and Legends of Wall Street.* Hoboken, NJ: Wiley; 1999.

- Laster, L. *Life After Medical School: Thirty-Two Doctors Describe How They Shaped Their Medical Careers.* New York, NY: WW Norton & Company; 1996.

- Lundberg GD. *Severed Trust: Why American Medicine Hasn't Been Fixed.* New York, NY: Basic Books; 2002.

- Nielsen J, Vollers M. *Ice Bound: A Doctor's Incredible Battle for Survival at the South Pole.* New York, NY: Hyperion; 2001.

- Pekkanen J. *MD: Doctors Talk about Themselves.* New York, NY: Dell;1990.

- Rothman EL. *White Coat: Becoming a Doctor at Harvard Medical School.* New York, NY: William Morrow & Company; 1999.

- Seligman ME. *The Optimistic Child: Proven Program to Safeguard Children from Depression and Build Lifelong Resilience.* New York, NY: Perennial Currents, Harper edition; 1996.

- Swanson D. *Nibbling on Einstein's Brain: The Good, the Bad and the Bogus in Science.* Toronto, ON, Canada: Annick Press; 2001.

Meeting Your Fiduciary Responsibilities

Tips for Employers with Retirement Plans

- Understanding fiduciary responsibilities is important for the security of a retirement plan and compliance with the law. The following tips may be a helpful starting point.

- Have you identified your plan fiduciaries, and are they clear about the extent of their fiduciary responsibilities?

- If participants make their own investment decisions, have you provided sufficient information for them to exercise control in making those decisions?

- Are you aware of the schedule to deposit participants' contributions in the plan, and have you made sure it complies with the law?

- If you are hiring third-party service providers, have you looked at a number of providers, given each potential provider the same information, and considered whether the fees are reasonable for the services provided?

- Have you documented the hiring process?

- Are you prepared to monitor your plan's service providers?

- Have you identified parties-in-interest to the plan and taken steps to monitor transactions with them?

- Are you aware of the major exemptions under the Employee Retirement Income Security Act that permit transactions with parties-in-interest, especially those key for plan operations (such as hiring service providers and making plan loans to participants)?

- Have you reviewed your plan document in light of current plan operations and made necessary updates? After amending the plan, have you provided participants with an updated Summary Plan Description (SPD) or Summary of Material Modifications (SMM)?

- Do those individuals handling plan funds or other plan property have a fidelity bond?

Source: US Department of Labor, Employee Benefits Security Administration (http://www.dol.gov/ebsa/)

Long-Term Retirement Investment Policy Strategies

Growth Investment Policy
Emphasis: Equities/Growth
Timeframe: 5 years to 10 years
Maximum Expected Value at Risk
Volatility: ±25% to ±45%

Growth retirement portfolio investment policy statement would emphasize that the trust investments are managed for favorable total returns from an actively managed, global, diversified portfolio of equity (stocks and convertibles) and fixed income (bonds and money market) investments. Growth retirement portfolios may contain up to 100% (or more if leverage is allowed) equity investments with a goal of positive consistent returns over rolling 5 to 10 year periods. A secondary goal of this strategy might be to limit the portfolio's downside volatility in any single year to 35% through active management, careful security selection, hedging strategies, diversification, asset allocation, and other risk management tools.

Balanced Investment Policy
Emphasis: Equities/Total Return
Timeframe: 4 years to 5 years
Maximum Expected Value at Risk
Volatility: ±20% to ±30%

Balanced retirement portfolio investment policy statement would emphasize the investments are managed with an objective of favorable total returns from an actively managed, global, diversified portfolio of equity (stocks and convertibles) and fixed income (bonds, preferred and money market) investments. Over time, balanced portfolios will emphasize equity investments. Balanced retirement portfolios are managed with the goal of positive consistent returns over rolling 4 to 5 year periods. A secondary goal is to limit a balanced portfolio's downside volatility in any single year to approximately 25% through active management, careful security selection, hedging strategies, diversification, asset allocation, and other management tools. Most retirement plans that have only one available strategy will have variations on this strategy.

Appendix B

Balanced Conservative Investment Policy
Emphasis: Income Securities/Bonds/Income Stocks
Timeframe: 3 years to 4 years
Maximum Expected Value at Risk
Volatility: ±15% to ±25%

Balanced Conservative retirement portfolios are managed with the objective of favorable sustainable total returns from an actively managed, global, diversified portfolio of equity (stocks and convertibles) and fixed income (bonds, preferred and money market) investments. Over time, balanced conservative portfolios will emphasize income-oriented securities and equity income investments. Balanced conservative retirement plan portfolios should be managed with the goal of positive consistent returns over rolling 3 to 5 year periods. A secondary goal is to limit downside volatility in any single year to 20% through active management, careful security selection, hedging strategies, diversification, asset allocation, and other management tools.

Yield Income Investment Policy
Emphasis: Income Securities/Bonds/Income Stocks
Timeframe: 3 years to 4 years
Maximum Expected Value at Risk
Volatility: ±15% to ±20%

Yield Income retirement portfolios are managed with the objective of favorable total returns from an actively managed, global, diversified portfolio of equity and fixed income investments. The goal of a yield income portfolio is to provide current, sustainable income, preserve capital and enhance the portfolio's purchasing power and income over time. Over time, these portfolios will emphasize fixed income and income-oriented equity investments. Retirement plan yield income portfolios are managed with the goal of positive consistent returns over a rolling 3 to 4 year periods. A secondary goal is to limit a yield income portfolio's downside volatility in any single year to 15% through active management, careful security selection, hedging strategies, diversification, asset allocation, and other management tools.

(continued)

Long-Term Retirement Investment Policy Strategies (*continued*)

Fixed Income Investment Policy
Emphasis: Bonds/Fixed Income Securities
Timeframe: 1 year to 4 years
Maximum Expected
Volatility: ±1% to ±10%

The goal of the retirement plan **Fixed Income** accounts is to achieve net total returns in excess of Treasuries or Certificates of Deposit over the stated time, through active, careful investment selection and management of fixed income investments.

Note: ERISA holds retirement plan fiduciaries to a high standard of care, prudence and diligence in the management of retirement portfolios. 401(k) and other money purchase plans might have 4 or more "managed" strategies (as above) to chose from plus a do-it yourself option that might include specialty mutual funds, index funds, trust accounts, or the ability to use individual investments in a self managed account.

The investment climate is chaotic, complex, and ever-changing. Your portfolio manager's goal should be to construct and manage portfolios that are ideally constructed (at every moment) to provide peace of mind, reliability, and long-term security. The management of retirement portfolios is by far, more complex and important than any other type of portfolio management. The manager's key tools of security selection, asset allocation, and macro/micro economic analysis must be skillfully applied with sustainable diligence and forethought. At a minimum, three of the above five options should be available in any retirement plan that allows investment flexibility.

Source: FIM Group

Web Site Sources

Socially Responsible Web Sites

Educational information and list of socially responsible mutual funds:
www.coopamerica.org

Information for investors:
www.greenmoney.org

List of socially responsible funds and other information:
www.goodmoney.com

Mutual Fund Performance Chart and news on responsible investing:
www.socialinvest.org

Financial Web Sites

Bloomberg:
www.bloomberg.com

Economist:
www.economist.com

Financial Times:
http://news.ft.com/home/us

The Straits Times:
http://straitstimes.asia1.com.sg/

British Broadcasting Corporation:
http://news.bbc.co.uk/

ABC Australia:
http://www.abc.net.au/

The New York Times:
www.nytimes.com

The Wall Street Journal:
www.wsj.com

The Washington Post:
www.washingtonpost.com

Bankrate:
www.bankrate.com

Fed World:
www.fedworld.gov

Social Security Administration:
www.ssa.gov

Internal Revenue Service:
www.irs.ustreas.gov

Securities Exchange Commission:
www.sec.gov

American Institute of Certified Public Accountants:
www.aicpa.org

Investment Company Institute:
www.ici.com

Money **Magazine:**
www.moneymagazine.com

Mutual Funds **Magazine:**
www.mfmag.com

Investment Advisor Exchange:
www.iaxchange.com

National Association of Personal Financial Advisors:
www.napfa.org

Investorama:
www.investorama.com

Over-the-counter stocks bulletin board:
www.otcfn.com

Kiplinger:
www.kiplinger.com

American Stock Exchange:
www.amex.com

Chicago Board of Trade:
www.cbot.com

Chicago Board Options Exchange:
www.cboe.com

Chicago Mercantile Exchange:
www.cme.com

National Association of Securities Dealers:
www.nasd.com

NASDAQ Stock Exchange:
www.nasdaq.com

New York Stock Exchange:
www.nyse.com

Medical Web Sites

Patient Alcohol Problems: National Institute on Alcohol Abuse and Alcoholism:
http://www.niaaa.nih.gov/publications/physicn.htm

Doctor's Guide Allergy Information:
http://www.pslgroup.com/ALLERGIES.HTM#News

American Academy of Allergy Asthma and Immunology:
www.aaaai.org

Global Anesthesiology Server Network:
http://gasnet.med.yale.edu/

Online Journal of Cardiac Ultrasound:
http://www2.umdnj.edu/~shindler/echo.html

American College of Cardiology:
http://www.acc.org

American Heart Association:
http://www.amhrt.org

Cliniweb:
http://www.ohsu.edu/cliniweb

Drug abuse–related birth defects outcomes:
http://www.health.org

Duke Occupational Medicine:
http://occ-env-med.mc.duke.edu/poem/

Doctor's Guide: breast cancer information:
http://www.pslgroup.com/BREASTCANCER.HTM

National Cancer Institute's late-breaking news:
http://wwwicic.nci.nih.gov/

Cancer treatment information at National Cancer Institute:
http://wwwicic.nci.nih.gov/h_treat.htm

Cancer screening and prevention information at National Cancer Institute:
http://wwwicic.nci.nih.gov/cancertopics

Oncolink Multimedia Oncology:
http://oncolink.upenn.edu/

National Cancer Institute CancerNet search:
http://imsdd.meb.uni-bonn.de/cancernet/cancernet_search.html

Breast Cancer Information Clearinghouse:
gopher://nysernet.org:70/11/BCIC

Prostate cancer home page:
http://www.cancer.med.umich.edu/prostcan/prostcan.html

The Hearing Journal:
http://www.wwilkins.com/thehearingjournal/

Gastroenterology:
http://www.gastrojournal.org/

MedHunters:
http://www.medhunters.com/

World Wide Medical Services:
http://www.wwmedical.com/

Journal of Hepatology:
http://www.munksgaard.dk/hepatology/text.html

Plastic and Reconstructive Surgery:
http://www.wwilkins.com/PRS/

The Quarterly Journal of Medicine at Oxford University Press:
http://www.oup.co.uk/jnls/list/qjmedj/

Abdominal Imaging:
http://link.springer.de/link/service/journals/00261/index.hml

Annals of Hematology:
http://link.springer.de/link/service/journals/00277/index.htm

Archives of Dermatological Research:
http://link.springer.de/link/service/journals/00403/index.htm

Archives of Gynecology and Obstetrics:
http://link.springer.de/link/service/journals/00404/index.htm

Medical jobs/healthcare jobs:
http://www.nationjob.com/medical

Practice opportunities online:
http://www.practiceline.com

Cardiovascular and Interventional Radiology:
http://link.springer.de/link/service/journals/00270/index.htm

Dysphagia:
http://link.springer.de/link/service/journals/00455/index.htm

National Tuberculosis Center at New Jersey:
http://www.umdnj.edu/ntbc/

Combined health information database from US Government agencies:
http://chid.nih.gov/welcome/welcome.html

Nephrology Dialysis Transplantation at Oxford University Press:
http://www.oup.co.uk/jnls/list/ndt/hdb/

American Society for Parenteral and Enteral Nutrition:
http://www.clinnutr.org/index.html

Uroweb:
http://www.bpc.nl/uroweb/

The Online Journal of Cardiology:
http://www.hrt.org

International Journal of Pediatric Hematology/Oncology:
http://biomednet.com/

Advances in Oto-Rhino-Laryngology:
http://biomednet.com

Allergies and environmental health:
http://www.orbital.net/~jmay/enviro.html

HyperMed Pediatrics:
http://www.hm1.com/

Clinical information from the American College of Cardiology:
http://www.acc.org/clinical/index.htm

BreastNet Cancer Institute:
http://www.bci.org.au

Diabetes Monitor:
http://www.mdcc.com/

Doctor's Guide to the Internet: Diabetes:
http://www.pslgroup.com/DIABETES.htm

National marrow donor program:
http://www.marrow.org/

Dysphagia Resource Center:
http://www.dysphagia.com/

Missouri Arthritis Rehabilitation Research and Training Center fibromyalgia resources:
http://www.hsc.missouri.edu/fibro

OncoLink:
http://cancer.med.upenn.edu/

Cholesterol, Genetics, and Heart Disease Institute:
http://www.heartdisease.org/

Hypertrophic Cardiomyopathy Association:
http://www.4hcm.org/WCMS/index.php

Brian's chronic hepatitis page:
http://165.247.177.65/brian/index.htm

State University of New York Stonybrook radiation oncology:
http://www.radonc.sunysb.edu/

University of Michigan Comprehensive Cancer Center home page:
http://www.cancer.med.umich.edu/

Pediatric Leukemias:
http://cancer.med.upenn.edu/disease/leukemia

CancerNet Cancer treatment database:
http://www.meb.uni-bonn.de/cancernet/cancernet.html

Oncology Online Medical Information Services:
http://www.otnnet.com/

Cancer treatment information at National Cancer Institute:
http://wwwicic.nci.nih.gov/h_treat.htm

Leukemia Information Center from Medicine OnLine:
http://www.meds.com

Family medicine information technology:
http://apollo.gac.edu/

Family medicine–related Internet resources:
http://views.vcu.edu/views/fap/volc-r.html

Neonatology online reference materials:
http://www.csmc.edu/neonatology/ref/ref.html

Physician Recruiter Associations

Physician recruiters serve the nation's healthcare providers by matching hospitals, medical groups, private practitioners, and communities with the appropriate candidates. They are relied on for information and advice. To accomplish successful healthcare consulting and recruitment, the physician recruiter must be committed, professional, dedicated, and experienced. These are counselors who should equally represent all parties and who can analyze a situation, develop a strategy, and match the appropriate physician, all the while, striving to perform these services with integrity.

The National Association of Physician Recruiters
222 S Westmonte Dr, Suite 101
Altamonte Springs, FL 32714
(800) 726-5613
www.napr.org

Association of Staff Physician Recruiters
1711 W County Road B, Suite 300
Roseville, MN 55113
(800) 830-2777
www.aspr.org

Sunbelt Management Association
5600 Executive Center Dr, Suite 102
Charlotte, NC 28212
(800) 955-1897
www.sunbeltmgt.com

Stanton Healthcare Group
575 Lexington Ave, Suite 400
New York, NY 10022
(212) 527-7505
www.stantonhealthcaregroup.com

MDR Associates
4000 Ponce de Leon Blvd, Suite 470
Coral Gables, FL 33146
(800) 327-1585
www.mdrsearch.com

The Peterson Group, Inc
1423 E Wells Fargo Dr
Olathe, KS 66062
(800) 669-4804
www.peterson-search.com

Rogo, Inc
1450 E. Boot Rd, Suite 500E
West Chester, PA 19380
(800) 830-7646
www.rogoinc.com

Physicians Search, Inc
5581 E Stetson Ct
Anaheim, CA 92807-4650
(800) 748-6320
www.physicianssearch.com

NES Inc
6477 College Park Square, Suite 316
Virginia Beach, VA 23464
(800) 637-3627
www.neshold.com

Practice Appraisal and Broker Firms

Mercer Capital
5860 Ridgeway Center Pkwy
Memphis, TN 38120
(800) 769-0967, (901) 685-2120

RH Medical
Rick Holdren
PO Box 820889
Houston, TX 77282
(281) 496-7777

California Professional Practices
1224 E Katella Ave, #202
Orange, CA 92667-5045
(800) 748-6320

Private Equities
50 Airport Parkway
San Jose, CA 95110
(408) 295-4299

Howard, Wershdale and Co
4 Commerce Park Sq, Suite 700
23200 Chagrin Blvd
Cleveland, OH 44122-5403
(216) 831-1200

Foti, Flynn, Lowen and Co
PO Box 12765
Roanoke, VA 24028
(540) 344-9246

Broker Disciplinary Associations

National Association of Securities Dealers
(800) 289-9999

National Futures Association
(800) 676-4632

North American Securities Administrators Association
(202) 737-0900

Securities and Exchange Commission
National Headquarters
450 5th St NW

Washington, DC 20549
(202) 942-4108

Information Services
(800) 732-0330

State Regulators

These are government offices that license brokerage firms and financial planners.

Alabama
Securities Commission
(334) 242-2984

Alaska
Department of Commerce
and Economic Development
(907) 465-2521

Arizona
Securities Division
(602) 542-4242

Arkansas
Securities Department
(501) 324-9260

California
Department of Corporations
(213) 736-2741

Colorado
Securities Division
(303) 894-2320

Connecticut
Department of Banking
(860) 240-8230

Delaware
Division of Securities
(302) 577-8424

District of Columbia
Securities Division
(202) 626-5137

Florida
Division of Securities
(904) 488-9805

Georgia
Business Services and Regulation
(404) 656-2894

Hawaii
Department of Commerce and
Consumer Affairs
(808) 586-2740

Idaho
Securities Bureau
(208) 332-8004

Illinois
Securities Department
(217) 782-2256

Indiana
Securities Division
(317) 232-6681

Iowa
Securities Bureau
(515) 281-4441

Kansas
Securities Commission
(913) 296-3307

Kentucky
Department of Financial Institutions
(502) 573-3390

Louisiana
Securities Commission
(504) 846-6970

Maine
Securities Division
(207) 624-8551

Maryland
Division of Securities
(410) 576-6360

Massachusetts
Securities Division
(617) 727-3548

Michigan
Corporation and Securities Bureau
(517) 334-6215

Minnesota
Securities Division
(800) 657-3602

Mississippi
Securities Division
(601) 359-6363

Missouri
Division of Securities
(573) 751-4136

Montana
Securities Department
(406) 444-2040

Nebraska
Bureau of Securities
(402) 471-3445

Nevada
Securities Division
(702) 486-2440

New Hampshire
Bureau of Securities Regulation
(603) 271-1463

New Jersey
Bureau of Securities
(201) 504-3600

New Mexico
Securities Division
(505) 827-7140

New York
Bureau of Investor Protection and Securities
(212) 416-8185

North Carolina
Securities Division
(919) 733-3924

North Dakota
Securities Commissioner's Office
(701) 328-2910

Ohio
Division of Securities
(614) 644-7381

Oklahoma
Department of Securities
(405) 280-7700

Oregon
Division of Finance and Corporate Securities
(503) 378-4387

Pennsylvania
Securities Commission
(717) 783-5177

Puerto Rico
Securities Division
(809) 723-8445

Rhode Island
Securities Division
(401) 277-3048

South Carolina
Securities Division
(803) 734-1087

South Dakota
Division of Securities
(605) 773-4823

Tennessee
Securities Division
(615) 741-3187

Texas
State Securities Board
(512) 305-8300

Utah
Securities Division
(801) 530-6600

Vermont
Securities Division
(802) 828-3420

Virginia
Division of Securities
(804) 371-9051

Washington
Securities Division
(360) 902-8760

West Virginia
Securities Division
(304) 558-2258

Wisconsin
Division of Securities
(608) 266-3431

Wyoming
Securities Division
(307) 777-7370

Social Security, Pension, and 401(k) Information

Many free publications are available through the Social Security Administration that describe their programs. Call your local Social Security office or (800) 772-1213. Your employer should have all relevant plan documents, or contact your regional office of the Pension and Welfare Benefits Administration for additional help.

Pension and Welfare Benefits Administration
(202) 219-8233

Professional Investment Organizations

American Association of Individual Investors (compiles a yearly survey of discount brokers)
(800) 428-2244

The following five organizations provide lists of investment professionals in your area:

American Institute of Certified Public Accountants,
Personal Financial Planning Division
(800) 862-4272

The Institute of Certified Financial Planners
(800) 282-7526

Licensed Independent Network of CPA Financial Planners
(LINC, Inc)
(800) 737-2727

The National Association of Personal Financial Advisors (NAPFA)
(800) 366-2732

Directory of Registered Investment Advisors with the SEC
(800) 977-1450

Mutual Fund Information

Investment Company Institute
(202) 326-5800

CDA/Wiesenberger Mutual Funds Report and Update
(two monthly statistical and performance guides on mutual funds)
(800) 232-2285

Directory of Mutual Funds (annual list of over 5,000 funds)
(202) 326-5800

The Individual Investor's Guide to Low Load Mutual Funds
(analysis on over 800 low-load funds)
(800) 428-2244

Morningstar Mutual Funds
(biweekly reports on individual funds)
(800) 735-0700

Mutual Fund 500
(performance and risk ratings on 500 load and no-load funds)
(800) 735-0700

Quarterly Low Load Mutual Fund Update
(extensive data on 850 load and no-load funds)
(800) 428-2244

Value Line Mutual Fund Survey
(follows over 2,000 funds)
(800) 634-3583

Fundalarm.com (a free, non-commercial web site.
(mutual fund commentary by Professor Snowball)
http://www.fundalarm.com/

Investment Publications and Journals

Barron's
(800) 544-0422

Business Week
(800) 635-1200

The Economist
(800) 456-6086

Financial World
(800) 829-5916

Fortune
(800) 621-8000

Investor's Business Daily
(800) 831-2525

The Wall Street Journal
(800) 568-7625

Financial Analyst's Journal
(804) 980-3668

The Financial Review
(904) 644-4220

Journal of Finance
(212) 998-0347

Journal of Financial Planning
(303) 759-4900

Journal of Investing
(212) 224-3185

Journal of Portfolio Management
(212) 224-3185

Insurance Company Ratings

AM Best Co
(908) 439-2200

Insurance Forum
PO Box 245
Ellettsville, IN 47429

Standard and Poor's Insurance Rating Services
(212) 208-1146

Weiss Ratings Hotline
(800) 289-9222

Quotes and Policy Information

American Council of Life Insurance
(202) 624-2000

Consumer Federation of America's Insurance Group
(202) 387-6121

Insurance Information Company
(800) 472-5800

Life Insurance Advisors Association
(800) 521-4578

National Insurance Consumer Helpline
(800) 942-4242

GLOSSARY

401(k) plan: A type of profit-sharing plan that allows employees to set aside for retirement part of their gross pay (maximum $14,000 for 2005, $15,000 for 2006, and $? for 2007? before-tax, into a tax-deferred trust until it is withdrawn.

403(b) plan: A non-qualified deferred compensation program offered to employees of tax-exempt organizations under Internal Revenue Code (c)(3)501 for employees of certain educational organizations. These are very similar to qualified plans such as 401(k)s but have some important differences.

AARP: American Association of Retired Persons.

absolute total return (investment) management: An investment management style that is not constrained by benchmarks, indexes, asset allocation models, or other investing tools that could impede its ability to perform in any market environment. All investing is really about making money and preserving wealth, absolute managers manage funds with such a mandate, often having only a numerical value as risk measurement or normal investment management, mutual fund or regulatory constraints.

administrator: Individual or entity responsible for reporting to and complying with all Internal Revenue Service and Department of Labor requirements in the administration of retirement plans.

age-driven dispositions: Part of an estate plan that distributes assets once a beneficiary attains a certain age. *See also* **event-driven distributions**.

agent: One who acts for another, also called a *principal*. One who represents another from whom he or she has derived authority.

aggressive growth fund: A stock-oriented mutual fund with an investment objective of substantial capital gains and little income over the long term.

AMT: Alternative minimum tax. This is a tax calculation that uses a separate accounting method with its own unique rules that govern the recognition of income and expenses. It was originally designed to ensure that tax payers with substantial income are not able to avoid paying tax by the inclusion of certain tax preference items.

annual mutual fund expense ratio: Yearly mutual fund fee assessed to cover the fund's expenses including management fees, transaction fees, and marketing expenses. Annual expense ratios usually vary from 0.20% to about 3% of a fund's net asset value. The expense ratio is deducted from each shareholder's holdings.

annual renewable term (ART): A form of pure protection life insurance that guarantees the right to renew coverage each year without evidence of insurability (physical examination), usually to age 65.

annual report: The formal financial and important information statement issued yearly by a corporation, trust, or other entity. The annual report shows assets, liabilities, earnings, standing of the company at the close of the business year, performance of the company with regard to profits during the year, and other information of interest to shareowners.

annuity: An immediate vehicle that provides for the payment of a specific sum of money at uniform intervals (usually monthly). It provides the annuitant with a guaranteed income either immediately or at retirement. Annuities usually pay until death or for a specific period and can provide protection against outliving your financial resources.

arbitrage: Dealing in differences, for example, buying on one exchange while simultaneously selling short on another market at a higher price.

ASCLU: American Society of Chartered Life Underwriters (insurance agents, salespeople, and education association).

asset: On a balance sheet, that which is owned or receivable.

asset allocation: An investment tool similar to diversification that can be used to manage risk (and reward) in portfolios.

association insurance: A form of group insurance. However, instead of being an employee, the insured is a member of a trade or professional association. Associations exist for most professions such as the American Medical Association and for common social causes such as the American Association of Retired Persons. Typically, the member pays dues or membership fees to the association and, as a benefit, the member may purchase various types of insurance such as disability and life insurance at group rate discounts and favorable group underwriting requirements.

back-end load: A commission or fee charged to investors by some commission broker–sold mutual funds when the investors sell their shares in the fund. The fees, which range from about 1% to 6%, typically reduce by about 1% for each year the investor holds the fund. For instance, a fund with a maximum 5% back-end load will charge the full 5% the first year. But the fee normally drops to 4% the second year, 3% the third year, 2% the fourth year, 1% the fifth year, and nothing after the fifth year. The two types of back-end loads are deferred sales charges and redemption fees. Funds with deferred sales fees base charges on the net asset value of the shares when they were purchased, whereas redemption fees are based on the prices of the shares at the time they are sold. Thus, if a fund has a strong gain, much more is paid in redemption fees than in deferred sales charges. Back-end loads are a bad deal; avoid funds with back-end loads. *See also* **load, no-load, front-end load, redemption fee, deferred sales charge.**

balanced fund: A mutual fund that usually keeps within a flexible range of its total assets invested in senior securities such as bonds, stocks, and other assets. Balanced funds have some flexibility and can change their portfolio's characteristics to manage the risk desired by the fund's investment policy.

behavioral finance: A theory stating that important psychological and behavioral variables are involved in investing in the stock market and other investment markets that provide opportunities for smart investors to profit. This theory is in opposition to theories that assert that markets are efficient. Proponents of efficient market theory say that any new information relevant to an investment's value is quickly priced into the market through the process of arbitrage. By contrast, behavioral finance proponents argue that people do not behave rationally and that they let emotions, inertia, and biases affect their investment behavior. Understanding that such effects exist can help investors benefit from the irrational behavior of other participants in the markets. *See also* **endowment behavior and recentcy effect.**

Bond: A fixed income security issued by an entity, such as a government or company, that has a stated maturity date and interest payment.

Bond ladder: A tool in the management of a bond portfolio that can be used to increase rewards or reduce risks by laddering a number of bonds over time to mature at different dates. For example, buying 5-, 10-, 15-, or 20-year maturity bonds of equal value would be a bond ladder. If the manager had ascertained that interest rates would be rising, then she or he might have a ladder equally invested in 1-, 2-, 3-, 4-year maturity bonds. If a manager felt interest rates might be stable or falling and/or because longer term bonds had better yields, she or he might have a bond ladder of investments in bonds maturing in 10, 15, 20, 25, and 30 years.

call: An option to buy a specified amount (number of shares of stock) of a certain investment at a certain price within a specified period of time.

callable: A bond or preferred stock issue, all or part of which may be redeemed by the issuing corporation or government under specific conditions before maturity.

cannibalizing assets: Funds that pay part of their distributions out of principal cannibalize their assets. This depletes the fund's asset base. Funds cannibalize assets to maintain a dividend and keep shareholders happy. However, like feeding a cow its own milk, this practice cannot go on forever.

capital gain or **capital loss:** Profit or loss from the sale of a capital investment asset.

CEBS: Certified employee benefits specialist.

CFP: Certified financial planner.

charitable gift: A contribution of either cash, usually in the form of a check, or capital, often in the form of a security, to a not-for-profit organization qualified under Internal Revenue rules. Contributions to qualified charities are, with some limitations, deductible for income tax purposes.

charitable lead trust: A trust in which excess income is given to a charity and, ultimately, the income and asset return to the grantor.

charitable remainder trust: A trust in which income usually goes to its grantors and, at death, the principal is donated to a charity.

ChFC: Chartered Financial Consultant (insurance, sales, and training association designation).

CIC: Certified Insurance Counselor.

classes of mutual fund shares: Many mutual fund companies issue fund shares with several pricing classifications. For example, the American Funds group has nine levels of sales charges for its class "A" shares, ranging from "0" for the shares brokers can buy for themselves to 5.75% of the sale, their no front end load-back end load funds have a 7 year declining contingent deferred sales charge and they have other iterations of their funds making it so that there are up to 22 different all in fee and commission iterations on their funds. Ethics aside, "Buyer Beware" when purchasing anything from a company that creates a "class" system for their funds. The shares, which normally are referred to as "A" class, "B" class, "C" class, "R" retirement class, levied on the fund's shares. For instance, A shares may have a front-end sales load and a lower annual expense ratio; B shares may have a back-end load and a higher annual expense ratio; C shares may have no sales load but a very high annual expense ratio; and D or R shares may be geared to institutional, large retirement plans and affluent investors with very low fees and may require a minimum investment of $100,000 or more. *See also* **2(B)1 fees, commissions, no–load funds**.

CLU: Charted Life Underwriter (insurance).

COLA: Cost-of-living adjustment.

College for Financial Planning: An organization that offers professional training leading to the granting of the Certified Financial Planner designation. Courses include financial planning, risk management, investments, tax planning, retirement, estate planning, and others.

commission: The salesperson's or broker's fee for purchasing or selling securities, property, or insurance for a client.

commodities: Real or hard assets and other staple products that are usually traded in bulk form. Examples include platinum, corn, copper, meats, and lumber.

common stocks: Certificates representing an undivided ownership interest in the assets of a corporation with no predetermined set rate of return. Ownership of common stock provides for corporate voting rights and an interest or share of the future profit (or loss) of the company. Common stockholders, in short, get what is left.

compensation: In a retirement plan, an employee's compensation is the basic factor that employers use to determine the amount of contributions that will be allocated to a participant's account under a defined contribution plan (eg, a profit-sharing plan) or the amount of benefits that a participant will receive upon retirement. The term is usually broadly defined in the plan and includes, but is not limited to, base salary, commissions, bonuses, overtime, and vacation pay. The Internal Revenue Service requires that the definition used in the retirement plan not be discriminatory (ie, favoring highly compensated employees over lower-paid employees). Further, a ceiling may apply to the amount of compensation that may be taken into account under certain types of plans. For individual retirement account purposes, taxable alimony is treated as compensation.

competitive analysis (investing): The process of analyzing the positioning and comparative strengths and weaknesses of competitors in the marketplace. It may include current and potential product and service development and marketing strategies.

CTFA: Certified Trust and Financial Advisor (estate and trust administration).

currency risk: One of the key risks and potential rewards to consider when investing in foreign stocks or bonds. Changes in the currency exchange rate can have a material positive or negative impact on the return of a foreign investment when the investment is sold and converted back into the original currency.

deferred annuity, fixed: Deferred fixed annuities are insurance contracts (policies) issued by insurance companies usually to individuals. The annuity policies are called *deferred* because income taxes are not paid on the interest earned until it is distributed, usually after many years. Distributions on the accumulated interest of policy values are subject to income tax and, unless certain exemptions are met (death, disability, age 59 and one half, and Rule 72t), may be subject to tax penalties. Additionally, insurance company surrender charges may apply to distributions taken in the early years of the annuity policy. The policies are described as *fixed* because they receive an interest rate declared by the company and do not drop in value.

deferred annuity, variable: Insurance contracts (policies) issued by insurance companies, usually to individuals. They can be issued with very low fees and no back-end fees or contingent deferred sales chares or with significant expenses and commissions represented by a back-end charge. The annuity policies are called *deferred* because income taxes are not paid on the accumulation until it is distributed, usually after many years. Distributions on the appreciation of policy values are subject to income tax and, unless certain exemptions are met (death, disability, age 59 and one half, and Rule 72t), may be subject to tax penalties. Additionally, insurance company surrender charges may apply to distributions taken in the early years of the annuity policy. The policies are described as *variable* because the value of the policies can fluctuate up or down based on the performance of the separate accounts within the policy. The separate accounts are similar to mutual funds, and most variable annuities offer many separate accounts with various investment objectives such as balanced, growth, and income. Shares of the variable annuity are called *units* and are priced each day based on the value of the underlying securities in the separate accounts. *See also* **deferred sales charge**.

deferred sales charge: An unnecessary and some would say unethical commission or sales fee, often called a *back-end load*, charged to shareholders by some mutual funds and annuity companies, when the shareholders sell their fund shares (Deferred sales charges are a way of hiding the commission.) *See also* **back-end load**.

defined benefit plan: A type of qualified retirement plan that determines a participant's benefit based on a preset benefit formula that assumes the participant will continue to work until retirement age.

depreciation: Taxpayers may deduct a reasonable allowance for the exhaustion or wear and tear of property used in a trade or business or property held for the production of income. Depreciation is a bookkeeping entry; it does not represent any cash outlay. It does not apply to stock in trade, inventories, land, or personal assets.

director: A person elected by stockholders or shareholders to establish, monitor, and maintain a company's policies. The directors elect the president, vice president, and all other operating officers. Directors decide, among other matters, if and when dividends will be paid and if the company is being a good corporate citizen.

discount: (1) The amount by which a preferred stock or bond may sell below its par value. (2) Refers to a closed-end fund trading at a market price below its net asset value.

discount broker: A securities or real estate broker who provides lower rates compared with those for so-called full service offerings.

discretionary account/authority: An investment account in which the customer gives an investment advisor, lawyer, broker, or someone else discretion, either complete or within specific limits, as to the purchase and sale of real estate, securities, commodities, or other assets including selection, timing, amount, and price to be paid or received. Discretion should only be given to competent fiduciaries who have experience, training, and education.

discretionary formula plan: A profit-sharing retirement plan that provides for the amount of each year's contribution to be determined by the board of directors (or responsible officials) of the sponsoring employer, in its discretion. (Contributions must be recurring and substantial to keep the plan in a qualified status.)

discrimination: Where a retirement or other employee benefit plan, or employer, through its provisions or through its operations, favors officers, shareholders, or highly compensated employees to the detriment of other employees.

disqualification: Loss of qualified (tax-favored) status by a retirement plan, generally resulting from operation of the plan in a manner contrary to the provisions of the plan or that discriminates against rank-and-file employees. *See also* **discrimination**.

dividend: The payment designated by the board of directors to be distributed pro rata among the shares outstanding. On preferred shares, it is generally a fixed amount. On common shares, the dividend varies and may be omitted if business is poor or if the directors determine to withhold earnings to invest in plant equipment. Sometimes a company will pay a dividend out of past earnings, even if it is not currently operating at a profit. Mutual funds holding dividend-paying stocks pass those dividends on to shareholders in lump sum payments either monthly, quarterly, semiannually, or annually, depending on the fund. Investors in most funds may have the option to have dividends automatically reinvested in additional shares.

dividend reinvestment plan: A mutual fund share account or stock plan for companies. With this type of account, dividends are automatically reinvested in additional shares, as are capital gains distributions.

dividend yield: The annual dividend payment divided by the market price per share. If a stock is trading at $10 per share and it pays a $0.50 dividend, the dividend yield is 5%.

DOL: Department of Labor. The non-tax (regulatory and administrative) provisions of the Employee Retirement Income Security Act are administered by the Department of Labor. The department issues opinion letters and other pronouncements affecting employee benefit plans such as retirement plans and requires certain information forms to be filed.

dollar-cost averaging: A system of buying specific securities at specific, regular intervals with a fixed dollar amount. Under this system, the investor buys by the dollars worth rather than by the number of shares. If each investment is the same number of dollars, you would buy more when the price is low and fewer when it rises. Temporary downswings in price thus can benefit the investor if periodic purchases continue to be made in both good times and bad and if the price at which the shares are sold is more than their average cost.

double taxation: The federal government taxes corporate profits first as corporate income; any part of the remaining profits distributed as dividends to stockholders may be taxed again as income to the stockholder.

earmarking: Allowing a participant in a defined contribution plan to direct the investment of his or her account.

EBITDA: Earnings before interest, tax, depreciation, and amortization expenses. A common metric used to analyze a company's operating profitability before non-operating expenses (such as interest expense) and non-cash charges (such as depreciation). *See also* **EV/EBITDA**.

employee: An individual who provides services to an employer for compensation and whose duties are under the control of the employer.

endowment behavior: An area of behavioral finance that studies the relationship between the investor and his or her investments. All things being equal, or not close to similar, an investor will tend to favor holding and keeping what he or she has over another investment even if the held investment is inferior. This behavior can be devastating for investors, who will justify holding investments that have outlived their usefulness and whose prospects going forward are much poorer than they were in the past. Investors influenced by endowment behavior will hold onto inherited investments even though they would have never bought the investments as part of their investment program on their own. An example is when investors holding stocks, real estate, or other investments that have fallen in price tend to hold onto such investments because they feel entitled or endowed with the prior higher values. Yet those same investors are not likely to buy more of the investment or an equivalent investment after it has fallen similarly, even though its price is better.

enterprise value (EV): One measure of a company's value. The standard EV calculation is market capitalization (number of shares outstanding times the current share price) plus debt and preferred stock minus cash and cash equivalents. In effect, EV measures how much it would cost to actually purchase the (whole) company. Enterprise value is often used when comparing companies with different capital structures. *See also* **EV/EBTIDA**.

equity (stocks): The ownership interest of common and preferred stockholders in a company. Also refers to excess of value of securities over the debit balance in a margin account property. Also, the value of a property that remains after all liens and other charges against the property are paid.

equity investment: A security (usually common stock, convertibles, warrants, or convertible preferred stock) that represents a share of ownership in a business entity (usually a corporation).

ERISA: Employee Retirement Income Security Act of 1974. This is the basic law covering qualified plans and incorporates both the pertinent Internal Revenue Code provisions and labor law provisions.

ESOP: Employee stock ownership plan. A type of defined contribution benefit plan in the United States that buys and holds company stock. ESOPs are often used in closely held companies to buy part or all of the shares of existing owners, but they also are used in public companies. Related to ESOPs are

Section 401(k) plans, which may be used alone or in conjunction with ESOPs to hold company stock. Several features make ESOPs unique as compared with other employee benefit plans. First, only an ESOP is required by law to invest primarily in the securities of the sponsoring employer. Second, an ESOP is unique among qualified employee benefit plans in its ability to borrow money. As a result, leveraged ESOPs may be used as a technique of corporate finance.

estate: All of a person's owned property.

estate planning: A system of planning designed to ensure that your estate will go to whom you want and how you want with confidentiality, limited red tape, and the most favorable tax treatment to benefit your heirs, charities, and other beneficiaries.

estate tax: A tax assessed on the transfer of wealth in an estate.

EV/EBITDA (Equity Value/Earnings Before Interest, Taxes, Depreciation and Amortization): A commonly used valuation ratio to compare companies on an "apples-to-apples" basis. The ratio uses a measure allowing for differences in capital structure (EV) divided by a measure of core operating profitability (EBITDA).

event-driven disposition: Part of an estate planning trust or will that releases assets to a beneficiary based upon an event such as marriage, college graduation, or other milestone. *See also* **age-driven distribution**.

event risk: An unexpected occurrence such as a leveraged buyout that reduces the creditworthiness of a company's debt, causing its bond prices to drop sharply.

exchange traded [mutual] fund: A type of mutual fund that is listed on an exchange and continuously offers and redeems shares at the intra-day price rather than only at the end-of-day price available on open-ended mutual funds.

exclusive benefit rule: Retirement plan fiduciaries must discharge their duties solely in the interest of participants and beneficiaries for the exclusive purpose of providing benefits to participants and beneficiaries and paying administration expenses. *See also* **fiduciary**.

executor: A person named in a will to carry out the provisions of the will.

face value: A bond's face value is ordinarily the amount the issuing company promises to pay at maturity. Face value is not an indication of market value. It is sometimes called par value (insurance). It is also the death benefit or a life insurance policy.

family limited partnership: Often used as an estate planning tool to transfer family property inter-generationally without the matriarch and patriarch losing control prematurely. Percentage ownership is transferred to children and grandchildren without voting rights. The percentage ownership allows for substantial discounting of the property for estate tax purposes.

family of funds: A system of mutual funds managed by the same company that provides the option of switching investments from one type of fund to another with a different risk characteristic either for free or for a small fee.

family trust: A trust that provides income to a spouse and, upon the spouse's death, is automatically disbursed to the children.

Federal Deposit Insurance Corporation (FDIC): A corporation established by federal authority to provide insurance on demand and time deposits in participating banks up to a maximum of $100,000 for each depositor.

fee and commission advisor: An investment or financial advisor who can receive commissions in addition to receiving or charging fees. This advisor usually emphasizes his or her ability to be objective by charging a fee for the advice, and then getting a commission to implement the insurance, investments, and retirement plans that allegedly "you would have to pay anyway." Fee and commission practices are usually not the most professionally managed or ethically driven practices due to the fact of the obfuscation of the conflicts of interest embedded in any practice that can receive commissions. The so-called objective advice is usually found to be designed to line the pocket of the fee-plus-commission adviser. *See also* **contingent differed sales charge, fee only advisor, NAPFA.**

fee-based advisor: A securities licensed financial representative who also is an investment advisor representative. This financial representative can both earn commissions and charge fees to clients.

fee-only advisor: A common term for an investment advisor or financial advisor who believes that commissions taint an advisor's objectivity and, thus, cause his or her advice to be less efficient or more costly. A fee-only advisor refuses any and all commissions or remuneration from anyone other than the investor/client. The National Association of Personal Financial Advisors champions the fee-only approach as the best deal for the consumer.

fiduciary: A person who has the ability to make decisions about a person's well-being or who exercises any discretionary authority or control over the management or disposition of an individual's investments or a retirement plan's assets. Any person who renders advice, management, or assistance in regard to a qualified retirement plan, trust, or corporation is usually considered a fiduciary.

fiduciary duty (board member): The responsibility of the board member to owe the non-profit or for-profit entity an absolute duty of utmost good faith, competent right action, and oversight and to act solely in the entity's best interest. This includes making the appropriate disclosures of all conflicts of interest or other material facts that might impede the ability to be objective or to be competent as a duty bound board member.

fiduciary duty (executor): It is the responsibility of the executor (personal representative) to inventory the estate assets, manage the assets prudently during the period of administration, pay all valid claims and debts against the estate, pay funeral expenses, file estate and income taxes, and distribute the assets pursuant to the decedent's will.

fiduciary duty (investment manager): The legal responsibility for investing money or acting wisely on behalf and in the best interest of the beneficiary; to act responsibly and appropriately on behalf of another party including but not limited to standards of competent right action, foresight, creativity, appropriate conduct, business judgment, prudence, opportunity, and risk management. Retirement plan trustees often delegate the task of the day-to-day management of investment portfolios to a seasoned, capable, disciplined, registered investment advisor with a good track record as part of their fiduciary duty. Managers of charitable entities have a fiduciary duty to the charity, a general partner has a fiduciary duty to the limited partners, and trustees have a fiduciary duty to the beneficiaries of a trust; the obligation also exists to manage assets in the same way a prudent person would manage his or her own assets.

fiduciary duty (trustee): It is the responsibility of the trustee to manage the remaining assets of the trust, collect the income, and disburse income or principal to the beneficiaries as set forth in the trust document. The trustee distributes to the executor amounts necessary to satisfy specific bequests, inheritance and estate taxes, funeral expenses, and claims or debts against the estate. Assets remaining after the payment of these amounts constitute the trust estate. The trust will generally define the powers of the trustee. Most states have adopted the Restatement of the Law of Trusts (Prudent Investor Rule) as the guide for trust administration.

forfeitures: The benefits that a participant loses if he or she terminates employment before becoming eligible for full retirement benefits under a retirement plan. For example, a participant who leaves the service of an employer at a time when he or she will receive only 60% of benefits forfeits the remaining 40%. Under a profit-sharing plan, forfeitures are usually allocated among the remaining participants. Under a defined benefit, money purchase, or target benefit pension plan, the forfeitures are used to reduce employer contributions.

free/commission-based advisor: Some unethical commissioned salespeople charge no fee for their advice saying that it is free, but they expect that financial products will be purchased to compensate for his or her time.

front-end load: The sales fee a mutual fund charges investors to buy shares of the fund. The commission (usually in the range of 3% to 8.5%) is deducted directly from the investor's contribution, to be paid to the broker and for other marketing costs. For instance, a $100,000 investment in a fund with a 5% front-end load would result in $5,000 on load fees and $95,000 in actual fund shares. *See also* **contingent deferred sales load, no-load funds, classes of mutual fund shares**.

frozen plan: A qualified pension or profit-sharing plan that continues to exist even though employer contributions have been discontinued and benefits are no longer accrued by participants. The plan is "frozen" for purposes of distribution of benefits under the terms of the plan.

FSA: Fellow of the Society of Actuaries (pension plans).

fully managed fund: A mutual fund whose investment policy gives its management complete flexibility as to the types of investments made and the proportions of each. Management is restricted only to the extent that federal or state laws require. These funds are usually long-term oriented and seek absolute total returns and are not constrained by indexes, an asset allocation model, or benchmarks. *See also* **absolute total return (mutual) funds**.

general partner: The individual(s) with unlimited liability in a partnership. Usually distinguished from a limited partner in a real estate, hedge fund, or tax-shelter investment. A general partner's obligation is to carry out the duties ascribed to him or her, and the person should have the experience, training, education, and resources to succeed at the task.

gift non-taxable: Anyone can give away tax-free up to $11,000. A married couple may give $22,000. There are no restrictions on who may be a recipient. All gifts between spouses are free of taxes. In addition to these non-taxable gifts, one may choose to use their qualified exclusion as guided by their lawyer or tax advisor. Normally you would use the exclusion amount in a highly leveraged gift such as a qualified personal residence trust. Gifts using the qualified exclusion amount require the filing of a Gift Tax Return Form 709.

gift tax: A tax levied on the transfer of property as a gift. It may be paid by the giver or donor.

gift taxable: Once you have used up your qualified exemption amount, your gifts (with the exclusion of the $11,000 annual exclusion) are subject to gift tax.

group living: An arrangement wherein a group of persons rent or buy a dwelling and share equally in expenses. Sometimes a community sponsors the arrangement and a paid professional supervises the running of the household.

government bonds: Obligations of a government, regarded as the highest grade issues in existence in that country. Safety is naturally dependent on the country of issue.

growth fund: A broad category of aggressive and sometimes speculative mutual funds that have in common the investment objective of longer-term capital growth and capital gains. Usually growth funds are common stock-oriented funds seeking long-term capital growth and future income rather than current income, with little regard to short-term volatility. Growth funds are best suited for investors with time horizons of 6 years or longer using dollar cost averaging. Growth funds can be managed for absolute total returns or designed to model or enhance the returns of a benchmark or an index such as the S&P 500 or an international basket of stocks.

growth investments: Usually include growth stocks, mutual funds, raw land, collectibles, and equities, among others.

growth stock: One of the two general types of common stock. Growth stocks seek selling price increases rather than income in the form of dividends for shareholders by reinvesting earnings to grow the company. *See* **income stock**.

group insurance: Group insurance is usually offered through an employer. The common group insurance benefit is health insurance. As part of the group, an employee is provided coverage, usually after 30 to 60 days of employment, without underwriting such as a medical physical or history. Because the employee is a member of a larger group, coverage is usually provided at a discount. A downside of group insurance is the lack of portability should the employee leave the group. Under most situations, the group insurance ends when employment terminates.

guaranteed renewable: An insurance policy renewable at the option of the insured to a stated age, usually 60 or 65.

hard assets: Investments that are tangible, such as precious metals, gems, art, stamps, and collectibles.

hedge fund: Similar to a private expensive mutual fund, hedge funds pool investors' money to invest. Unlike a mutual fund, a hedge fund is a vehicle typically organized as a private limited partnership that often provides more investment flexibility than most mutual funds do. Some hedge funds have only recently been required to register with the Securities and Exchange Commission. Most are unregulated entities and many are very speculative, largely due to the lack of regulations surrounding these funds. High net-worth individuals and institutions are often the primary investors. Originally managers of hedge funds sought out investments that were not highly correlated with the general market. Today's funds range from "go anywhere" absolute return funds to targeted asset class (such as bank stocks) funds that only invest in one area or that utilize one strategy (buying, shorting, and leveraging a stock portfolio). Fees paid to the fund by its investors often include an annual management fee assessed at 1% to 3% of the assets as well as an incentive fee, which is assessed on annual gains over a certain hurdle mark (this fee is typically 20%).

home sharing: An arrangement in which homeowners are matched with a sharer-renter who shares in living expenses and/or services.

incentive trusts: Part of an estate plan that gives a beneficiary an "incentive" to behave a certain way, in other words, to get a job, stay off drugs, and so on.

income fund: A mutual fund with an investment objective of current income, consistent long-term income, or growing income, rather than capital growth. Bond funds, equity income, and convertible-oriented funds are usually considered income funds.

income stock: One of the two types of common stocks. Income stocks seek current income rather than selling-price increase or capital growth and usually pay out much of their earnings. *See also* **growth stock**.

inefficient market: Markets do not fully reflect all available information causing security prices to be over- or undervalued. Skill used in actively seeking out these pricing deviations will result in market out-performance.

inflation: An economic condition of increasing prices or wages.

integrated plan: A retirement plan that takes into account either benefits or contributions under Social Security. Social Security benefits are used to integrate a defined benefit plan, whereas Social Security contributions are used with defined contribution plans.

intrinsic value or **investment value:** What an investment is really worth independent of its current market price. Intrinsic value is the end product of the fundamental analysis of a company.

investment: The use of money for the purpose of making more money: to gain income or increased capital or both.

investment advisor: A broad term used to describe a professional who is selected to manage investments, usually regulated by the Securities and Exchange Commission.

investment club: A way to join with other novice investors and pool small dollar amounts to buy stocks and at the same time learn more about the stock market.

investment counsel: One whose principal business consists of acting as investment advisor and rendering investment supervisory services.

investment manager: Investment portfolio fiduciary who has the power to manage, acquire, or dispose of investments in the portfolio.

investment options (retirement plan): The different "buckets" or pools of managed or unmanaged investments that can be chosen by retirement plan participants. Each bucket should have its own investment policy statement, ideally with a value-at-risk explanation. Most plans should have an income stock, preferred, and bond-oriented account with a lower value-at-risk percentage of 10% to 20%; a balanced, more equity-oriented account with a variable 20% to 30%; and a mostly equity-oriented account with a higher value at risk.

investor: An individual who attempts to put his assets to work; in other words, to make money and not lose it. Often an investor's concerns are income, safety of investment, and/or capital appreciation.

IRA: Individual Retirement Account.

JD: Doctor of Jurisprudence (attorney).

joint and survivor annuity: An annuity paid for the life of the retirement participant with a survivor annuity for his or her spouse. The survivor annuity must be at least 50%, but not more than 100% of the annuity received by the participant during his or her lifetime. Also, the joint and survivor annuity must be the actuarial equivalent of a single life annuity that would have been paid to the participant.

joint and two thirds survivor annuity: An annuity under which joint annuitants receive payments during a joint lifetime. After the demise of one of the annuitants, the other receives two thirds of the annuity payments in effect during the joint lifetime.

Keogh plan: Slang for *qualified retirement plan*, either a defined contribution plan or a defined benefit plan that is available to self-employed persons and their employees.

land contract: A form of creative finance used in real estate wherein the seller retains legal title to the property until the buyer makes an agreed-upon number of payments to the seller.

large-cap stock: Stocks with the largest market capitalization. Although the exact level can vary, it usually refers to companies having a market capitalization between $10 billion and $200 billion. Sometimes the largest of these stocks are called mega-caps. These are the biggest companies of the financial world. Examples include Toyota, Nestles, Wal-Mart®, Microsoft, Shell Oil®, and General Electric®. Keep in mind that classifications such as *large-cap* or *small-cap* are only approximations that vary from source to source and change over time.

lease: A contract, similar to renting, between owner and user of the asset setting forth conditions upon which the lesser may use the property, stating terms of the lease.

level term: A form of pure protection insurance (term) in which the face value and the premiums remain level for a certain period or for the life of the policy.

leverage investment: Use borrowed capital to finance all or a portion of an investment.

leverage stock: The effect on the per-share earnings of the common stock of a company when large sums must be paid for bond interest or preferred stock dividends or both before the common stock is entitled to share in earnings. Leverage is risky but may be advantageous for the common stock when earnings are good; however, it will work against the common stockholders when earnings decline. Leverage also refers to the amount of debts compared with the income and assets of people or businesses.

limited partner: In this context, a participant in a hedge fund or venture that has been organized as a limited partnership. *See also* **limited partnership**.

limited partnership: A form of business organization in which some partners exchange their right to participate in management for a limitation on their liability for partnership losses. Commonly, limited partners have liability only to the extent of their investment in the venture. To establish limited liability, there must be at least one general partner who is fully liable for all claims against the business. A limited partnership is a popular organizational form for tax-sheltered programs or hedge funds because of the ease with which tax benefits flow through the partnership to the individual partners.

liquidity investment: The ability of the market in a particular security to absorb a reasonable amount of buying or selling at reasonable price changes. Liquidity is one of the most important characteristics of a good, efficiently trading market. Less liquid markets often can have greater fluctuations in price and thus can create enhanced opportunities created by greater price fluctuation, compared to more liquid markets or securities.

listed stock: The stock of a company that is traded on a securities exchange and for which a listing application and a registration statement giving detailed information about the company and its operations have been filed with the Securities and Exchange regulators, unless otherwise exempted, and with the exchange itself.

liquidity (personal): The financial flexibility gained from an estate that has a low debt-to-asset ratio or significant assets that can be turned into liquid cash through a sale or by borrowing against them. Personal liquidity is important because it allows an easy transition between jobs, in disability, or in periods when cash is needed quickly. Often, liquidity is simply provided by a large line of credit.

LLC: Limited Liability Corporation. A business entity that combines the limited liability of a corporation with the partnership treatment for federal tax purposes.

load: A commission sales fee often charged to mutual fund investors who buy load funds. Loads normally vary from about 3% to 8.5% of the total purchase amount. They can be immediate or hidden as a back-out charge where the commission is charged over time, often called a 12b-1 fee for mutual funds. *See also* **no-load funds**.

long: Signifies ownership of securities. "I am long gold," means you own gold (opposite of short).

management fee: The fee paid to the investment manager of an investment partnership, mutual fund, or investment portfolio for managing the assets to achieve the entity's goals. It is usually about one half of 1% to 1.5% of average net assets annually. Not to be confused with a mutual fund's sales charge, 12b-1 fees, trustee fees, brokerage commissions, or other investment management expenses. Management fees are what goes to the investment manager. They vary based on what the manager is supposed to do. If a manager is merely complying with a mandate that requires that he or she models an index or benchmark, the fees are usually very low, since the manager is exercising little skill or expertise or adding little value. Actively managed Global funds seeking *go anywhere* total returns will tend to have higher expenses due to the added research, need for skilled pros, etc.

margin call: A demand upon a customer to put up money or securities with the broker. The call is made when a purchase is made or when a customer's equity in a margin account declines below a minimum standard set by the exchange or by the firm.

market capitalization: The total market value of a publicly traded company. It equals the product of its per share price and the number of shares outstanding. For example, a company selling at $10 per share with 10 million shares outstanding would have a market capitalization, or total market value, of $100 million. *See also* **large-cap stocks, small-cap stocks.**

market multiple: The valuation matrix for different indexes or benchmarks represented as a number price to book: price to cash flow: price to EBTDA and the most followed price to earnings are some of the market multiple's investors follow. For example, the price/earnings ratio (or P/E) for the overall market as measured by the P/E for Standard and Poor's 500 Index or the Dow Jones Index. The market multiple provides an important indicator of the overall level of stock values and is a good indicator of future price performance. Markets sporting high normalized market multiples tend to have poorer future performance than when their normalized market multiple is lower.

market order: An order to buy or sell a stated amount of a security at the current price offered.

market price: In the case of a security, market price is usually considered the last reported price at which the stock or bond sold.

maturity: The date on which a loan or a bond becomes due and is to be paid off.

MBA: Master of Business Administration (advanced business degree).

minimum funding retirement: The minimum amount that must be contributed by an employer who has a defined benefit, money purchase, or target benefit pension plan. The minimum is made up of amounts that go to cover normal costs (for the benefits earned by employees for the current year) plus other plan liabilities, such as past service costs—liabilities for benefits that have been earned for services performed prior to the adoption of the plan. If the employer fails to meet these minimum standards, in the absence of a waiver from the Internal Revenue Service, an excise tax is imposed on the amount of the deficiency.

modern portfolio theory: A theory on how risk-averse investors can construct portfolios in order to optimize market risk for expected returns, emphasizing that risk is an inherent part of higher reward. Also called *portfolio theory* or *portfolio management theory*. According to this theory, it is possible to construct an "efficient frontier" of optimal portfolios offering the maximum possible expected return for a given level of risk. This theory was pioneered by

Harry Markowitz in "Portfolio Selection" (*Journal of Finance.* 1952;7[1]:77–91). There are four basic steps involved in portfolio construction:

(1) security valuation, (2) asset allocation, (3) portfolio optimization, (4) performance measurement.

Modern portfolio theory is a theory and not a way to manage money.

money market fund: A mutual fund that invests in high-quality, short-term debt instruments such as treasury bills, commercial paper, and/or certificates of deposit. Money market fund investors earn a steady stream of interest income that varies with short-term interest rates and generally may be cashed out at any time through checking, credit card sweep, or wire withdrawals.

money purchase pension plan: A defined contribution pension plan in which the employer must contribute a certain percentage of each employee's salary each year, regardless of the company's profit.

mortgage: An instrument by which the borrower (mortgagor) gives the lender (mortgagee) a lien on real estate as security for a loan. The borrower can use the property, and when the loan is repaid, the lien is removed or satisfied.

mortgage bond: A bond secured by a mortgage on a property. The value of the property may or may not equal the value of the so-called mortgage bonds issued against it.

municipal bond: A bond issued by a state or a political subdivision such as a county, city, town, or village. The term also designates bonds issued by state agencies and authorities. In general, interest paid on municipal bonds is exempt from federal income taxes and from state and local income taxes within the state of issue.

mutual fund: A mutual fund is a company that invests in a diversified portfolio of securities. People who buy shares of a mutual fund are its owners or shareholders. Their investments provide the money for a mutual fund to buy securities such as stocks and bonds. A mutual fund can make money from its securities in two ways: a security can pay dividends or interest to the fund or a security can rise in value. A fund can also lose money and drop in value. There are thousands of funds available that are designed for just about any investor or speculator to use as an investment for achieving their investment goals.

NAPFA: National Association of Personal Financial Advisors; fee-only financial advisors with very strict member requirements.

NASD: National Association of Securities Dealers is an association of brokers and dealers in the over-the-counter securities business. The association has the power to expel members who have been declared guilty of unethical practices. Like most securities exchanges worldwide, the NASD is dedicated to, among other objectives, "adopt, administer, and enforce rules of fair practice and rules to prevent fraudulent and manipulative acts and practices, and in general to promote just and equitable principles of trade for the protection of investors."

NASDAQ: National Association of Securities Dealers Automated Quotations; an automated information network that provides brokers and dealers with price quotations on securities traded over the counter.

net asset value: A term usually used in connection with investment companies (mutual funds), meaning net asset value per share. It is common for a mutual fund to compute its assets daily by totaling the market value of all securities owned. All liabilities are deducted, and the balance is divided by the number of shares outstanding. The resulting figure is the net asset value per share.

net change: The change in the price of a security from one period to another.

net return: The total return after taxes, fees, commissions, duties, and inflation earned by the investment over a period of expectation.

new issue: A stock or bond sold for a corporation for the first time. Proceeds may be issued to retire outstanding securities of the company, for new plant or equipment, for additional working capital, or to go to a selling shareholder.

non-cancelable: Policies or contracts that may not be canceled (during a specified term) by the issuer or insurer, but the term *non-can* usually is not applied to disability or health policies unless they are also guaranteed renewable.

nonqualified retirement plan: A retirement plan that is not regulated by a government agency such as the Internal Revenue Service or the Department of Labor, for example. These plans, normally sold by commission insurance agents, are frequently inefficient because of high commissions. They purport to have the following benefits: (1) privacy, (2) no maximum contributions, (3) no tax on gains due to the insurance policies' tax-deferred status, (4) no tax on withdrawals because of loan provisions, and (5) possible estate tax benefits. Beware of nonqualified retirement plans suggested by commission advisors or fee and commission advisors.

normal retirement age: The point at which a participant attains retirement age under a retirement plan. Usually it is age 65; however, it may be a different age (as set forth in the plan) and may also require a stated period of plan participation. Full vesting is required when a participant attains normal retirement age.

no-load fund: A mutual fund that charges no sales fee to buy and sell. No-load funds are usually the best to buy because there are no commission or professional management expenses. Beware: mutual fund associations and regulators have allowed funds to be called no-load while charging 12b-1 marketing expenses. Also, brokers will call funds no-load even when they have significant commission and marketing expenses. *See also* **load, front-end load, back-end load, classes of shares**.

odd lot: An amount of stock less than the established 1.000-, 100-, or 10-share units of trading stocks or certain investments. Often the price is higher for odd lots.

open-end investment company: By definition under the 1940 Act, a highly regulated investment company (mutual funds) that has outstanding redeemable shares. Also generally applied to those investment companies such as mutual funds that continuously offer new shares to the public and stand ready at any time to redeem their outstanding shares.

open-end mutual fund: A mutual fund that allows investors to buy shares directly from the mutual fund company and stands ready to redeem shares whenever shareholders are ready to sell. Open-end funds may issue new shares any time there is a demand for more shares from investors. Shareholders buy and sell shares at the fund's net asset value (plus a possible sales fee), in contrast to a closed-end mutual fund, which trades like stock on a stock exchange. Rather than selling at net asset value, closed-end funds share trade at whatever price the market is willing to pay.

option: A right to buy or sell specific securities or properties at a specified price within a specified time.

ordinary life insurance: A life insurance product also known as *straight life, permanent life,* or *whole life*. Premiums are computed to be paid for life. Usually the last tool to consider in estate planning or insurance planning.

overbought: An opinion as to volume and its relationship to price levels. May refer to a security that has had a sharp rise or to the market as a whole after a period of vigorous buying that, at least in the short term, has left prices too high. Used as a signal to sell.

oversold: The reverse of overbought. A single security or a market that has declined to an unreasonable level. Used as a signal to buy.

over-the-counter (OTC): A market for investments made up of securities dealers who may or may not be members of a security exchange. Over-the-counter ismainly a market made electronically and over the telephone. Thousands of companies have insufficient shares outstanding, stockholders, or earnings to warrant application for listing on a major exchange. Securities of these companies are traded in the over-the-counter market between dealers who act either as principals (ie represent themselves) or as brokers for customers. Today, the OTC market is very sophisticated, and many large companies choose to be listed OTC.

paper profit: An unrealized profit on an unsold investment. Paper profits become realized profits when the security is sold.

partnership: A partnership is usually a contract of two or more persons to unite their property, labor, or skill or for some of them to share the profits and risks.

PBGC: Pension Benefit Guarantee Corporation. A wholly owned government corporation created to administer the termination rules and insuring benefits under the Employee Retirement Income Security Act. The plan is funded with premiums paid by plan sponsors.

PEG ratio: price/earnings-to-growth ratio. One valuation tool used to measure growth stocks. A PEG is calculated by taking the price/earnings ratio divided by the earnings growth rate projected for the company.

penny stocks: Low-priced issues, often highly speculative, selling at $1 to $5 per share. Frequently used as a term of disparagement, although a few penny stocks have developed into investment-caliber issues. Many international companies have low-priced stocks that upon the currency conversion equate to a few cents a share because of the customs of their markets and should not be confused with US- or Canadian-issued (speculative) penny stocks. Just because a stock's share price is low does not mean it is speculative—just because a shares price is high does not mean it is safe. A stock's safety has to do with the company and what it does and with the price you pay for that safety based on its entity value. *See also* **entity value price to entity**.

pension plan: Qualified retirement plans established by an employer for its employees, including profit-sharing plans, stock bonus plans, thrift plans, target benefit plans, money purchase plans, defined benefit plans, and employee stock ownership plans.

plan administrator: The person designated by the plan documentation as administrator. If no designation is made, the plan administrator is the employer. The plan administrator is the person responsible for managing the day-to-day affairs of the plan. The person or corporation choosing a plan administrator must do so with diligence and prudent analysis of the administrator's competencies, systems, and ability to deliver.

plan participant: An employee who has met the age, service, and other requirements of his or her employer's retirement plan. Plan participants are protected by the Employee Retirement Income Security Act, fiduciary protections, and other regulations.

point: In the case of stock, a point means $1. If *ABC* shares rise three points, each share has risen $3. With bonds, a point means $10. A bond is quoted as a percentage of $1,000. In the case of market averages, the word *point* means merely that if, for example, the Dow Jones Industrial Average rises from 10,870 to 10,871, it has risen a point. A point in this average is not equivalent to $1.

pooled income fund: A type of annuity that pools the assets of a number of people, each sharing the income in proportion to ownership.

portfolio: Holdings of securities by an individual or institution. A portfolio may contain international and domestic bonds and stocks, real estate, metals, and commodities. A portfolio is usually constructed around an investment philosophy to achieve specific goals. A bunch of investments does not mean a portfolio.

preferred stock: A senior class of stock with a claim on the company's earnings before payment may be made on the common stock and usually entitled to priority over common stock if the company liquidates. It is usually entitled to dividends at a specified rate when declared by the board of directors, depending on the terms of the issue.

premium: The amount by which a preferred stock or bond may sell above its par value. In the case of a new issue of bonds or stocks, premium is the amount the market price rises over the original selling price.

price/earnings ratio (P/E): The price of a share of common stock divided by its earnings per share for a 12-month period. This is Wall Street's most commonly used ratio to determine a stock's value to investors. A company with a stock price of $20 and earnings per share of $1 has a 20 P/E ($20 divided by $1), whereas a company with a stock price of $10 and the same $1 in earnings per share has a 10 P/E. The higher a stock's P/E, the more expensive the stock is relative to its earnings. Companies that are perceived to grow slowly into the future will tend to have lower P/Es than those that have fast growth expectations. *See also* **PEG ratio**.

price-to-book ratio (PBR): Commonly used valuation ratio that compares a stock's market value with its net assets (assets minus liabilities).

price-to-cash flow (EBIT): Commonly used valuation ratio that compares a stock's market value to its annual cash flow. Because cash flow is not as subject to accounting manipulation as earnings, investors often focus on this ratio when evaluating a stock.

price-NAV ratio (P/NAV): The market price of a closed-end fund divided by its net asset value (NAV). P/NAV serves as a valuation indicator. Closed-end funds selling at a discount will have P/NAV ratios below 100%; those at a premium will have P/NAV ratios in excess of 100%.

product strategy analysis (investing): The comprehensive study of a company's product or service. This involves evaluating the growth prospects, barriers to entry, competitive forces, marketing plans, profitability, sustainability, and so on to pinpoint which products or services have the greatest investment potential.

profit-sharing plan: A type of defined contribution retirement plan whereby employers agree to make discretionary contributions to eligible employees each year.

property and casualty insurance: Insurance coverage to provide for the replacement of or to compensate for property lost, stolen, damaged, or destroyed.

prospectus: A document containing important information that offers a new issue or continuously issued securities like mutual funds to the public. It is required under the Securities Act of 1933. It is a good read for investors and should be reviewed completely when looking at an investment. Mutual funds will have important information as to performance, fees, commissions, benchmark risks, index risks, and general rewards and risks of investing in the fund.

proxy: Written authorization given by a shareholder to someone else to represent him or her and vote at a shareholders' meeting. Investment advisors often act as a client's proxy when voting corporate resolutions to help coordinate the voting and reduce the burden placed on the client in relation to understanding all of the issues addressed at the meeting.

proxy statement: Important information required by the Securities and Exchange Commission to be given to stockholders as a prerequisite to solicitation of proxies for a security, subject to the requirements of Securities Exchange Act.

prudent-man rule: The standard under which a fiduciary must act. The fiduciary is required to act "with the care, skill, prudence, and diligence under the circumstances then prevailing that a prudent man acting in a like capacity and familiar with such matters would use in the conduct of an enterprise of a like character and with like aims." This general rule requires a retirement plan, trust, or investment fiduciary to exercise "care, skill, and prudence," creativity, forward looking analysis, common sense, creativity, and independent thinking in relation to the management of investment assets in a qualified retirement plan, or other funds that are under his or her direction or care. Just because everyone is doing it does not mean it meets this rule. Often investors think they are being prudent just because they have subscribed to some rule of thumb; asset allocation; passive, benchmarking, or an indexing system that may have worked in the past. Prudent investing is about managing risk, and risk is best managed by a disciplined, forward-looking, active, ongoing, **management** process that is global, unencumbered by constraints that could limit a portfolio's returns, or fixed policies that could cause the portfolio to hold speculative investments – due to price or changes in their prospects. Any fiduciary guidelines should benchmark off the fact that the price you pay for an investment is as important as the investment's merits.

put: An option to sell a specified number of shares or quantity of an investment at a specified price within a specified period. The opposite of a call.

QPA: Qualified Pension Administrator (pension plans).

qualified domestic relations order (QDRO): A court order issued under a state's domestic relations law that relates to the payment of child support or alimony or to marital property rights. A QDRO creates or recognizes an alternate payee's right or assigns to an alternate payee the right to receive plan benefits payable to a participant. The alternate payee may be, for example, the participant's spouse, former spouse, or dependent.

qualified pension plan (tax-qualified plan): A plan that meets the requirements of the Internal Revenue Code, generally Section 401(a). The advantage of qualification is that the plan is eligible for special tax considerations. For example, employers and/or participants are permitted to deduct contributions to the plan even though the benefits provided under the plan are deferred to a later date.

quotation: Often shortened to *quote*. The highest bid to buy and the lowest offer to sell a security in a given market at a given time. If you ask your broker for a quote on a stock, he or she may come back with something like "20 and one half to 21." This means that $20.50 is the highest price any buyer wanted to pay at the time the quote was given and that $21 was the lowest price any seller would take at the same time.

rally: A quick rise in the general price level of a market or in an individual investment.

real estate investment trust (REIT): An equity trust that can hold real estate income and growth properties and offer shares that are publicly traded.

redemption fee: Sales fee or back-end load charged by some mutual funds or annuities to shareholders when they sell their shares. Redemption fees are a bad deal if they originate because of commissions. Funds with redemption fees usually have higher overall expenses than true no-load, no 12(b)1, no deferred sales charge, no-commission funds. *See* **back-end load.**

red herring: A preliminary prospectus used to obtain indications of interest from prospective buyers of a new issue of stock.

registered representative: Usually a full-time employee of a broker who has met the requirements of an exchange with regard to background and knowledge of the securities business.

reinvestment risk: One of the risks facing holders of fixed-income securities such as bonds and certificates of deposit during periods of falling interest rates. The risk is that the investor will be forced to reinvest interest or principal payments at lower interest rates. For example, if you have a maturing certificate of deposit that had a relatively high interest rate, you are forced to reinvest at a lower rate if interest rates have fallen.

return: Another term for yield.

reverse mortgage: A financing arrangement for older homeowners to use their equity to remain in their homes. The homeowner borrows from a lending institution an amount equal to 60% to 80% of the home value, and the institution pays out the loan funds monthly for a certain period. At the end of the loan period, the homeowner has to repay the loan, usually by sale of the home. If the homeowner dies before the end of the loan payment period, the house is sold to satisfy the debt. Private reverse mortgages between extremely responsible, well-off children and their parents are useful tools to help parents stay in their homes.

RIA: Registered Investment Advisor (investment, money management). An advisor registered with the Securities and Exchange Commission to give investment advice. The RIA can be anyone. There are no competency requirements for RIAs.

rights: When a company wants to raise more funds by issuing additional securities, it may give its stockholders the opportunity, ahead of others, to buy the new securities in proportion to the number of shares each owns. The piece of paper evidencing this privilege is called a *right*. Because the additional stock is usually offered to stockholders below the current market price, rights ordinarily have a market value of their own and are actively traded. In most cases, they must be exercised within a relatively short period. Failure to exercise or sell rights may result in actual loss to the holder.

risk investing: All investing has risks. There are two main types of risks. The risks imbedded in the individual security investors buy, for example, companies might fail because of competition or poor management. The other risk has to do with the investment style or manager risk. Management risk is imbedded in a manager's skills, biases, philosophy, and style of investing. For example, a manager might be rigidly tied to an asset allocation system that is dependent on indexing. Indexing/asset allocation systems are often based on past investment performance correlations and well-meaning theories such as Modern Portfolio Theory with little influence of price or value in the investing process. Such ridged systems are often championed as "disciplined;" however, the investment world is constantly changing, and any ridged system has of course significant "management risk."

rollover: A method of avoiding the substantial tax bite of a lump sum retirement plan payment, allowing it to be rolled over into an individual retirement account, another retirement plan, or similar vehicle to continue its deferred tax status.

rollover IRA account: An individual retirement account (IRA) that is established to receive a distribution from a qualified plan so that the income tax on the distribution will be deferred.

round lot: A unit of trading or a multiple thereof. On most US exchanges, the unit of trading is 100 shares in the case of stocks and $1,000 par value in the case of bonds. In some inactive stocks, the unit of trading is 10 shares. Global exchanges may have round lots of between 1 and 10,000 shares.

rule of 72: A rough financial formula for calculating the amount of time it takes an investment to double at any rate of return. Divide the rate of return by 72. For example, at 10%, money will double in approximately 7.2 years.

second home: A home that is owned and does not meet the primary residency requirements set forth by the Internal Revenue Service.

segregated account: A separate sub-account within a retirement plan trust consisting of only one plan participant's account balance and not affected by the investment performance of the rest of the plan investments.

SAR/SEP: Salary Reduction/Simplified Employee Pension plan. A salary reduction plan that is available only to companies with 25 or fewer employees that allows employees to contribute into an individual retirement account on a pretax basis. No new SAR/SEPs may be established after 1997, although those created prior to 1997 can continue to be funded.

selling short: An investment management tool whereby the investor sells stock not owned. An often risky technique of borrowing stock in anticipation of a drop in stock value that will bring rewards. Instead of looking for market winners, the short seller looks for losers. Short selling can also be used to hedge a portfolio and reduce a portfolio's overall risk.

simplified employee pension plan (SEP): An easy-to-establish, easy-to-administer, tax-favored retirement plan that takes the form of individual retirement accounts established on behalf of eligible employees (subject to special rules on contributions and eligibility) and funded by the employer.

SIPC excess insurance: Additional brokerage account coverage above the Securities Investor Protection Corporation (SIPC) limit. The amount of excess insurance will vary among brokerage firms.

SIPC insurance: The Securities Investor Protection Corporation (SIPC) offers brokerage account securities coverage up to $500,000 per customer including a $100,000 limit on cash. This protection sets in when a troubled SPIC member firm fails to meet its financial liabilities.

small-cap stock: Refers to stocks with a relatively small market capitalization. The definition of small cap can vary but generally in the USA or larger European markets, it refers to a company with a market capitalization of $300 million to $2 billion. One of the biggest advantages of investing in small-cap stocks is the opportunity to beat institutional investors. Because mutual funds have restrictions that limit them from buying large portions of any one issuer's outstanding shares, some, especially very large billion dollar mutual funds, would not be able to give the small-cap a meaningful position in the fund. To overcome these limitations, the fund would usually have to file with the Securities and Exchange Commission, which means tipping their hand and inflating the previously attractive price.

Keep in mind that classifications such as large-cap or small-cap are only approximations that vary from source to source and change over time. Many feel that anything that is under $100,000,000 in value is small cap, so the definition is generally for a smaller company.

socially conscious investor: An investor who allows his or her values, beliefs (religious, social, or environmental philosophies) to influence investing. Avoiding companies that produce or manufacture tobacco, alcohol, arms, pollution, and/or unethical in management practices or policies and the like is one way such investors exercise their beliefs. Another is to invest in companies that "do good," such as those with good employee relations, that produce alternate energy, or are good corporate citizens. *See also* **values-neutral investing.**

social mutual funds: Mutual funds that are driven not just by profit potential but also by principles and values.

speculator: One who is willing to assume a relatively large risk in the hope of gain. A speculator's principal concern is to increase capital without too much reflection on the possibility of loss or risk. Classical investors tend to take a common sense "whole brained" approach to investing that does not speculate on short-term gains. Naturally all investing is about the future, and we do not know what the future holds, but we know with reasonable certainty that the sun will set in the west and that investors will invest where they will be compensated for taking on risks. A speculator is usually one who does not look at the price in relationship to the value on what he or she buys but merely on its recent past performance.

split: The division of the outstanding shares of a company into a larger number of shares. A 3-for-1 split by a company with 1 million shares outstanding results in 3 million shares outstanding after the split. Each holder of 100 shares before the 3-to-1 split would have 300 shares, although proportionate equity in the company would remain the same; 100 parts of 1 million are the equivalent of 300 parts of 3 million, for example. Stock splits make a company's stock easier to trade by keeping its stock price lower than it would be without the split, thus making it less costly to buy a round lot of shares. Stock splits do not increase a company's value. If a broker calls you and tells you to buy a stock because it is about to split, fire the person and transfer your account immediately.

sponsor: Employer or company that elects to establish a qualified retirement plan and be responsible for the cost of funding and maintaining the retirement trust with contributions and the payment of expenses.

spousal IRA: An individual retirement account (IRA) that is established for the nonworking spouse of an employee and funded with contributions based on the other spouse's earned income. The contribution is limited to $4,000 (2005) for each spouse, plus an additional contribution of $500 if either spouse is age 50 or older.

spread: The difference between the bid price and the offering price.

stock bonus plan: A defined contribution retirement plan that is similar to a profit-sharing plan except that the employer's contributions do not have to be made out of profits, and benefit payments generally must be made in employer company stock.

street name: Securities held under strict guidelines in the name of a broker instead of the customer's name are said to be carried in a street name account. This occurs when the securities have been bought on margin or, when the customer wishes, for convenience and security, to have the security held by a broker.

subchapter S corporation: Business with a legal corporate form that pays income taxes like a sole proprietor.

suitability rule: The rule of fair practice that requires an investment seller to have reasonable grounds for believing that a recommendation to a customer is suitable on the basis of the person's financial objectives, risk tolerance, net worth, and ability to handle risk.

summary annual report: A summary of the financial activity within a qualified plan on any given plan year, that each plan participant is supposed to receive from the plan administrator.

summary plan description (SPD): A detailed summary that should be an easily understood document describing a pension plan's provisions that must be provided to participants and plan beneficiaries.

sustainable management systems (investing): A system for managing sustainable, total return investment portfolios to deliver consistent economic returns over time, through a disciplined intentional approach to management of portfolios.

target benefit plan: A cross between a defined benefit plan and a money purchase retirement plan. Similar to a defined benefit plan in that the annual contribution is determined by the amount needed each year to accumulate a fund sufficient to pay a targeted retirement benefit to each participant on reaching retirement. Similar to a money purchase plan in that contributions are allocated to separate accounts maintained for each participant. *See also* **defined benefit plan** and **money purchase pension plan**.

tax-deductible: Expenses and items that are able to reduce the amount of taxable income. Examples include medical expenses, individual retirement account contributions, charitable deductions, and deductible interest paid.

tax deferral: A method that defers the payment of taxes on income until a future time. The rationale is that while future tax brackets may be higher or lower, tax deferral enables one to compound the tax savings.

tax incentive: Corporate or venture vehicle that includes major tax incentives to invest.

tax-sheltered investment: An investment that has an expectation of economic profit, made even more attractive because of the timing of the profit or the way it is taxed, generally having some or all of the following characteristics: (a) capital gains opportunities, (b) high deductions, (c) deferral of income, (d) depletion, (e) accelerated depreciation, and (f) leverage. The flow-through of tax benefits is a material factor, regardless of whether the entity is organized as a private or public program. Common forms of tax-sheltered investments include cattle breeding, cattle feeding, equipment leasing, oil and gas, and real estate.

tax shelter plan: A slang term used to describe a qualified retirement plan that has been established for the benefit of the owner or specific officers.

tender offer: An offer to buy securities at a specific price. Can be used by a closed-end fund or company to buy back some of its shares because it believes that shares are at bargain levels. Tender offers can also be used by raiders to try to acquire shares of a target company.

time diversification: The idea that the longer securities are held, the lower their risk because good market periods are averaged in with bad ones. However, the opposite can often be true if an investment, due to price to its real value, causes the investment to become speculative in its valuation.

time-sharing: A creative real estate financing technique that allows the use of property on a time-shared basis while building equity for all of the owners. There are two types: right-to-use (membership right) and interval ownership (purchase of a particular week or weeks each year).

top down: An investment strategy whereby the investor looks at broad global economic trends to find the type of industries, countries, and security classes, which seem to be best positioned to perform well in the future and then the top down investor would select individual investments based on that assessment. It is the opposite of a bottom-up strategy in which an investor assesses an individual investment strictly on its own merits, irrespective of the overall economy, or financial climate. Bottom-up and top-down analysis is often used in tandem to make good investment decisions. *See also* **bottom up.**

TPA: Third-party administrator (employee benefits).

trader: Someone who buys and sells for his or her own account for short-term profit.

treasury bills (T-Bills): Short-term US government investments with no stated interest rate, sold at a discount with competitive bidding. For example, a treasury bill may be sold at $9,500 with a value at maturity of $10,000 in 1 year.

treasury bonds: Government bonds issued in $1,000 units (in the USA) with a maturity of 5 years or longer. They are traded on the market like other bonds.

treasury notes: Government bonds, not legally restricted to interest rates, with maturities of 1 to 5 years.

treasury stock: Stock issued by a company but later reacquired. It may be held in the company's treasury indefinitely, reissued to the public, or retired. Treasury stock receives no dividends and has no vote while held by the company.

trust: A fund established under local trust law to hold and administer assets.

trust (estate planning): A trust is a document created during your lifetime that can be revocable or irrevocable, but continues upon your death or disability. Upon death, it becomes irrevocable and provides a successor for yourself or your spouse to manage your assets for a specified period or circumstance. It may include provisions for disabled children, spendthrift family members, tax planning, charitable intent, intergenerational distributions, or the like. The successor trustee may be an individual or corporate trustee. Much like a corporation, it has a life of its own as set forth in the document.

trustee: Individual or entity that assumes and accepts the fiduciary responsibility to safeguard and administer the assets of a trust for the benefit of its beneficiaries.

trustees (retirement): The parties named in the trust instrument or plan authorized to hold the assets of the plan for the benefit of the participants. The trustees may function merely in the capacity of custodian of the assets, or they may also be given authority over the investment of the assets. Their function is determined by the trust instrument or, if no separate trust agreement is executed, under the trust provisions of the plan.

TSA: Slang for tax-sheltered annuity, 403(b) retirement plan available to employees of some schools, hospitals, and other charities. Insurance term for the product used by insurance agents to fund 403(b) plan.

12b-1 fee: A modest to very large fee assessed annually by some mutual funds to cover commissions, advertising, sales, and marketing expenses. The fee is deducted directly from each shareholder's holdings, reducing its return by that amount, and usually represents 0.25% to 1% of net asset value. 12b-1 fees can be up to twice or more of a funds expenses. Beware of these fees. Funds can call themselves no-load and charge 12b-1 fees. See classes of investing

umbrella liability: Insurance coverage in excess of underlying liability policies; provides coverage for many situations excluded by underlying policies and may also include excess major medical expense coverage.

unlisted: A security not listed on a stock exchange.

value-at-risk: A technique that uses the statistical analysis of historical market trends and *volatilities* to estimate a given *portfolio's* potential loss

value investing: An investment philosophy that places primary emphasis on finding bargains through price compared with value as opposed to forecasted earnings growth. Value investors look for companies with good prospects at bargain prices, closed-end funds at attractive discounts, and other investments that seem like bargains be they motels, real estate, bonds, currencies, stocks or something else.

values-neutral investing: Investors who do not allow personal values to influence their investing. Indexes, passive funds, and most mutual funds and thus their companies, are managed under a values-neutral methodology that disregards ethics, violence, exploitation, environmental issues, and sustainable practices. Values-neutral is a value.

variable annuity: An annuity that has the (possible) benefits of higher yield than is available on a fixed annuity by allowing the annuitant to invest in mutual fund-type portfolios (stocks, bonds, etc).

variable rate mortgage: A financing technique in real estate that allows the interest charged on the mortgage to fluctuate with the rise and fall of market interest rates.

vested benefits: Accrued benefits to a participant that are non-forfeitable under the vesting schedule adopted by the plan. Thus, for example, if the schedule provided for vesting at the rate of 10% per year, a participant who has been credited with 6 years of service has a right to 60% of the accrued benefit. If the participant terminates service without being credited with any additional years of service, he or she is entitled to receive 60% of the accrued benefits.

vesting: The non-forfeitable right that a participant has in his or her account balance of a qualified retirement plan trust. This right is accrued based on the number of hours the participant works for the sponsor for a given number of years.

voting right: The right of a common stock shareholder to vote, in person or by proxy, for members of the board of directors and other matters of corporate policy. Most common shares have one vote each. Preferred stock usually has the right to vote when preferred dividends are in default for a specified period. The right to vote may be delegated by the stockholder to another person, for example, the portfolio manager.

warrant: A certificate giving the holder the right to purchase securities at a stipulated price within a specified time limit or perpetually. Sometimes a warrant is offered with securities as an inducement to buy.

when issued: A short form of *when, as, and if issued*. The term indicates a conditional transaction in a security authorized for issuance but has yet to be issued. And when issued, transactions are on an "if" basis, to be settled if and when the actual security is issued and the exchange or National Association of Securities Dealers rules that the transactions are to be settled.

yield: Also known as *income return*. Annual dividends or interest paid by a company expressed as a percentage of the current price. A stock with a current market value of $20 per share that has paid $1 in dividends in the preceding 12 months is said to yield 5% ($1/$20). The current return on a bond or other investment is figured the same way.

yield to call: The rate of return earned by a bondholder when purchasing a bond at the current market price and holding until the call-date. The date on which a bond can be called by its issuer is referred to as the call-date.

yield to maturity: The total return that would be realized if a bond were purchased at its present price and held to maturity. In order to earn the yield to maturity, the investor must also reinvest all interest payments at a rate equal to the yield to maturity. This also assumes that the issuer will make all promised payments on time and in full.

Source: This glossary was compiled and written by Financial and Investment Management Group management team. Contributors include Zach Liggett, Suzanne Stepan, Judy McCorkle, Kevin Russell, Jeff Lokken, Barry Hyman, Jon Mohrhardt, Barry Couturier, Andi Dolan, and Paul Sutherland.

Note: This list is periodically updated at FIMG.NET or UtopiaFunds.NET.

INDEX

Absolute total return (investment) management, 225
Accumulation disorder, 20
Administrator, 225
   plan, 8 245
   third-party, 253
Advisors
   fee-based, 234
   fee-only, 234
Age-driven disposition, 225
Agent, 225
Age-weighted/Class-based plans, 130, 131
Aggressive growth fund, 225
Aloha Medical Mission, 202
Alternative minimum tax (AMT), 225
American Refugee Committee, 202
American Society of Chartered Life (ASCLU), 226
Ameritas, 51
AMT (alternative minimum tax), 225
Annual mutual fund expense ratio, 226
Annual renewable disability insurance (ARDI), 49
Annual renewable term (ART), 226
Annual report, 226
Annuities, 226
   deferred, 140, 141, 229–230
   defined, 142
   disguised, 149
   fixed, 142, 144
   fixed immediate, 140–143
   life insurance and, 141
   questions to ask about, 144
   tax-sheltered, 253
   variable, 140, 142–143, 144
   ways to get out of high-cost, 143
Anxiety, finances and, 19
Arbitrage, 226
ARDI (annual renewable disability insurance, 49
ASCLU (American Society of Chartered Life), 226
Asset, 226
Asset allocation, 159–160, 175–176, 226
   as investment philosophy, 170
   100% funds, 190–191

Asset classes
   balanced total return management style, 188–189
   global equity funds/natural resource funds, 189–190
   income with some growth, 185–186
   long-term fixed income/predictable income, 187–188
   short-term income investments, 185
Assisted living
   planning for, 98–100
   talking about, 100–103
Association insurance, 226
Attributes, for vision statements, 3–4

Back-end load, 226–227
Backups, for computer security, 40
Balanced fund, 227
Balanced indexing, as investment approach, 171
Balanced total return management style asset class, 188–189
Bear markets, 154
Behavioral finance, 227
Beneficiaries, 58
Benefit-guaranteed plans, 112
Boards, sitting on, promises and, 29
Bond, 227
Bond ladder, 227
Bottom-up investment strategy, 171
Bridge to Community, Inc., 202
Browsers, computer security and, 40
Budgeting, advice for, 38. *See also* Family budgeting
Bull markets, 154
Burnout stage, medicine for, 8–11
Buy and hold, as investment strategy, 170
Buying homes, *vs.* renting, 74

Call, 227
Callable, 227
Cannibalizing assets, 227
Canvasback Mission, Inc., 202–203
Capital gain, 228

Capital loss, 228
Cardiostart International, Inc., 203
Career cycles, 4–11
  early enthusiasm stage, 5–6
  happy doctor stage, 6–8
  mid-career burnout stage, 8–11
Cash
  excess, 19
  security and, 16–17
Cash management accounts, 19
Cash-value life insurance, 144, 149–151
CB International, 203
CEBS. *See* Certified employee benefits specialist (CEBS)
Certified employee benefits specialist (CEBS), 228
Certified financial planner (CFP), 228
Certified Insurance Counselor (CIC), 228
Certified Trust and Financial Advisor (CTFA), 229
Charitable gift, 228
Charitable giving, 117–118
  advice for, 118
  large donations, 118–119
Charitable lead trust, 228
Charitable remainder trust, 228
Charles Schwab, 19, 198
Chartered Financial Consultant (ChFC), 228
Chartered Life Underwriter (CLU), 228
Checking accounts, maintaining separate, 19
Children
  advice for finding preschools for, 88
  estate planning and, 120–121
  inheriting wealth and, 94–95
  life insurance on, 61–62
  life insurance trusts for, 59–61
  "problem," 82
  teaching, about money, 89–95
Children's Heartlink, 203
Classes of mutual fund shares, 228
CLU (Chartered Life Underwriter), 228
COLA (cost-of-living adjustment), 228
College
  alternative financing methods for, 85–87
  cashing in retirement savings plans to pay for, 87
  Coverdell Education Savings Accounts for, 83–84
  529 plans for, 80–831
  funding for, net worth and, 87–88
  loans for, 84–85
  saving for, 79–80
  scholarships for, 84
College for Financial Planning, 228
Commission, 228–229
Commitments, determining, 11–13, 14

Commodities, 229
Common sense, xvi
Common stocks, 229
Communication, family budgeting and, 16–17
Compensation, 229
Competitive analysis (investing), 229
Compounding returns, 186
Computer security, checklist for, 40–41
Concern America, 203
Confidentiality, 62–63. *See also* Privacy, financial
Contents, table of, for employee manuals, 25
Contribution limits, for retirement plans, 124, 133
  age-weighted/class-based plan, 130
  defined benefit "traditional pension," 131
  401k, 128
  403(b) plan, 131
  money purchase plan, 130
  profit sharing plan, 129
  Roth IRA, 127
  SEP IRA, 127
  Simple 401k, 128
  Simple IRA, 128
  Solo 401k with profit sharing plan owner only, 129
  traditional IRA, 127
Cost-of-living adjustment (COLA), 228
Coverdell Education Savings Accounts (ESAs), 83–84
Credit cards, maintaining control over, 33
CTFA (Certified Trust and Financial Advisor), 229
Currencies, foreign, keeping, 16–17
Currency risk, 229

Dance of Anger: A Woman's Guide to Changing the Patterns of Intimate Relationships (Lerner), 20
Death insurance. *See* Life
Debt, tax-deductible, 32
Debt management. *See also* Risk management
  illustrations of, 34–37
  for risk reduction, 31
  ten rules for, 32–38
Deferred annuities, 140, 141
  fixed, 229
  variable, 229–230
Deferred sales charge, 230
Defined benefit plans (traditional pensions), 131, 230
Department of Labor (DOL), 231
Depreciation, 230
Director, 230

Disability income insurance
   letter for, 47–48
   overhead expense insurance and, 48–50
   sources for buying, 49
   worksheet for, 46
Disasters, homes and, 71
Discount brokerage firms, working with, 198–200, 230
Discretionary account/authority, 230
Discretionary formula plan, 231
Discrimination, 231
Disguised annuities, 149
Disqualification, 231
Diversification, 160–162
Dividend, 231
Dividend reinvestment plan, 231
Dividend yields, 176–177, 231
Divorce, 42–44
DOCARE International, 204
Doctors. *See* Physicians
Doctors of the World, USA, Inc., 204
Doctors On Call for Service, Inc., 204
Doctors Without Borders, 1, 9–11, 22, 204
Do-it-yourself portfolios
   constructing, 175–177
   formulas for, 177–184
DOL (Department of Labor), 231
Dollar-cost averaging, 231
Double taxation, 231

Earmarking, 232
Earnings before interest, tax, depreciation, and amortization expenses (EBITDA), 232
Education. *See* College
Education culture concept, 81
Education Independent Retirement Accounts (IRAs). *See* Coverdell Education Savings Accounts (ESAs)
E-mail attachments, computer security and, 40
Employee, defined, 232
Employee manuals, 24
   keeping promises in, 24–25
   sample table of contents for, 25
   writing, 24
Employee Retirement Income Security Act (ERISA) (1974), 232
Employee Retirement Security Act, 29–30
Employees
   hiring, 23–24
   terminating, 23

Employee stock ownership plan (ESOP), 232–233
Encryption, WEP, 41
Endowment behavior, xvi, 232
Enterprise value (EV), 232
Equity investment, 232
Equity (stocks), 232
Equity value/earnings before interest, taxes, depreciation and amortization (EV/EBITDA), 223
ERISA. *See* Employee Retirement Income Security Act (ERISA) (1974)
ESAs. *See* Coverdell Education Savings Accounts (ESAs)
ESOP (employee stock ownership plan), 232–233
Esperanca, Inc., 204–205
Estate, 233
Estate planning, 233
   children and, 120–121
   event-driven dispositions, 119–121
Estate plans, intentional, 96–98
Estate tax, 233
EV/EBITDA (equity value/earnings before interest, taxes, depreciation and amortization), 223
Event-driven dispositions, 119–121, 233
EV (enterprise value), 232
Event risk, 233
Excess cash, 19
Exchange trade (mutual) fund, 23
Exclusion rules, for sale of homes, 71–73
Exclusive benefit rule, 233
Executor, 233
Expected return, 153–155

Face value, 233
Family attributes, for vision statements, 3
Family budgeting
   communication and, 17
   as enjoyable process, 17
   for homes, 17
   key to, 16–17
   out-of-control spending and, 19–20
   worksheet for, 18
Family limited partnerships, 233
Family of funds, 234
Family trust, 234
Federal Deposit Insurance Corporation (FDIC), 234
Federal Pell Grant program, 85
Fee-based advisor, 234
Fee-only advisor, 234

Fellow of Society of Actuaries (FSA), 236
Fidelity, 19, 198
Fiduciary obligations
  board member, 28, 234
  Employee Retirement Security Act and, 29–30
  executor, 234–235
  of investment advisors, 165
  investment manager, 235
  trustee, 27–28, 235
Financial and Investment Management (FIM) Group, 170
  investment philosophy of, 172–173
Financial ease, 4
Financial planners, 193–194
Financial planning, xv
Financial plans
  delegating components of, 194–195
  determining, 14
  implementing, 194–195
  sample letter for hiring firms for, 196
  to-do list for, 194
Financial plans, one-page
  estate planning, consultation 1, 97
  estate planning, consultation 2, 102
  stage 1, 21
  stage 2, 26
  stage 3, 56
Firewalls, 40
Firing employees. *See* Termination
529 College Savings plans, 80–83
  vs. Uniform Gifts to Minors Act, 82
Fixed annuities, 142, 144
Fixed immediate annuities, 140–143
Foreign currencies, keeping, 16–17
Forfeitures, 235
401k plans, 124, 129, 225
  simple, 128
  solo, with profit sharing plan owner only, 129
403(b) plans, 124, 131, 225
Free/commission-based advisor, 235
Front-end load, 235
Frozen plan, 235–236
Fully managed funds, 236

General partner, 236
Gifting guidelines, 147
Gift non-taxable, 236
Gift tax, 236
Gift taxable, 236
Global equity funds asset class, 189–190
Global Volunteers, 205

Goals, 11
Government bonds, 236
Gracián, 193
Group insurance, 237
Group living, 236
Growth fund, 236
Growth investment, 237
Growth stock, 237
Guaranteed renewable, 237

Handbooks, employee. *See* Employee manuals
Happy physicians, 6–8
Hard assets, 237
Health Volunteers Overseas, 205
Heart to Heart International, 205
Hedge funds, 144, 162–164, 237
  sample letter to general partner of, 166–168
  SEC and, 164–165
Helps International, 206
Hendricks, Harville, 20
"Hokey-pokey" investment approach, 171
Homes
  budgeting for, 17
  buying *vs.* renting, 74
  determining principal residence, 71–73
  disasters and, 71
  houses *vs.*, 68–69
  investment decisions for, 70
  resalability of, 74
  selling, 71–73, 75, 76
  worksheets for determining size of, 72, 73
Home sharing, 237

If approach, to investing, 152–153
Imago therapy, 20
Immediate life annuities, 140–141
Incentive trust, 237
Income fund, 237
Income protection insurance, 45–51. *See also* Insurance
  beneficiaries and, 58
  letter for, 47–48
  overhead expense insurance and, 48–50
  professional liability insurance, 50–51
  sources for buying, 49
  worksheet for, 46
Income stock, 238
Income with some growth asset class, 185–186
Index funds
  as investment philosophy, 170
  low-cost, 160

Indexing, 175–176
Individual retirement account (IRA) plans, 124, 238
   Roth, 127
   SEP, 127
   simple, 128
   traditional, 127
Inefficient market, 238
Inflation, 238
Insurance. *See also* Life insurance
   association, 226
   beneficiaries and, 58
   cash-value life, 144, 149–151
   coverage checklist, 55
   income protection, 45–51
   low-load term rates, 66–67
   personal liability, 40–41
   for physicians, 40–42
   professional liability, 50–51
   for risk management, 39
   rules for, 59–61
   sales pitches for, 57–58
   sample letter for, 148
   taxes and, 57
Integrated plan, 238
Intentional estate plans, 96–98
International Health Service, 206
International Relief Teams, 206
Interplast, Inc., 206–207
Intrinsic value, 238
Investing
   asset allocation and, 159–160
   asset classes of, 185–190
   common-sense facts about, 155
   decision-making and, 156–159
   determining right way of, 191
   diversification and, 160–162
   do-it-yourself, 175–184
   expected returns and, 153–155
   hedge funds and, 162–168
   if approach to, 152–153
   indexing and, 159–160
   market timing and, 192
   100 # funds, 190191
   perfection and, 191
   philosophy for, 169–171
   sample letter for hiring firms to handle, 197–198
   sustainable portfolios and, 173–175
   working with investment firms and, 198–200
Investment, defined, 238
Investment advisor, 238
Investment Advisors Act (1940), 165
Investment club, 238

Investment counsel, 238
Investment management, sample letter for, 197–198
Investment manager, 238
Investment needs, quantifying, 115
Investment options, 238
Investment philosophy
   of Financial and Investment Management Group, 172–173
   importance of, 169–171
Investments
   tax-favored, 137–138
   tax-sheltered, 137–140
Investment value, 238
Investor, 238
Involuntary termination, 23
IRA. *See* Individual retirement account (IRA) plans

Joint and survivor annuity, 238–239
Joint and two thirds survivor annuity, 239
Jurisprudence, Doctor of (JD), 238

Keogh plan, 239

Land contract, 239
Large-cap stocks, 239
Large-cap stocks, as investment approach, 170–171
Layered fees, 30
Learned helplessness, 94–95
Leases, 239
Lerner, Harriet, 20
Letters, sample
   for disability income insurance, 47–48
   to general partner of hedge funds, 166–168
   for hiring financial planning firms, 196
   for income protection insurance, 47–48
   for insurance, 148
   for investment management, 197–198
Level term, 239
Leveraged long, defined, 163
Leverage investment, 239
Leverage stock, 239
Liability insurance
   personal, 40–41
   professional, 50–51
Life
   key to, 8
   role of money in, 13–15
Life insurance, 51–58, 149–151. *See also* Insurance
   annuities and, 141
   assessing need for, 52
   cash value, 144, 149–151

Life insurance, *continued*
  challenging research on, 53
  on children, 61–62
  as investment, 150
  sources for buying, 51
  taxes and, 57, 149–151
  worksheet, 52–53, 54–55
Life insurance trusts, 59–61
Life planning, long view and, 4
Life satisfaction, 95
Lifestyle attributes, for vision statements, 3
Lifestyles, retirement, visualizing, 107–110
Limited liability corporation (LLC), 240
Limited partner, 239
Limited partnerships, 239–240
Liquidity, 32, 240
Liquidity investment, 240
Listed stock, 240
Load, 240
Loans, for college, 84–85
Logging off, computer security and, 41
Long, defined, 240
Long-term care, retirement and, 117
Long-term fixed income asset class, 187–188
Long view, life planning and, 4
Low Load Insurance Services
  for disability insurance, 49
  for income protection insurance, 45
  for life insurance, 51
Low-load insurance term rates, 66–67

Management fee, 240–241
Margin call, 241
Market capitalization, 241
Market multiple, 241
Market order, 241
Market price, 241
Market timing, 182
Marriage. *See also* Prenuptial agreements
  decisions, 44
  relationships, 15–17
Master of Business Administration (MBA), 241
Maturity, 241
Maturity, mellow, 7
Mega-caps, 170
Mercy Ships, 207
MIMA Foundation, 207
Minimum funding retirement, 241
Mission statements, vision statements for, 2
Modern portfolio theory, 241–242

Money
  developing productive relationships with, 1–2
  role of, in one's life, 13–15
  teaching children about, 89–95
Money market funds, 19, 242
Money purchase plans, 130, 131, 242
Mortgage, 242
Mortgage bond, 242
Municipal bond, 242
Mutual fund groups, working with, 198–200
Mutual funds, 242
  high-load indexed, 144
  open-end, 244

NASDAQ, 243
National Association of Personal Financial Advisors (NAPFA), 242
National Association of Securities Dealers (NASD), 242
Natural resource funds asset class, 189–190
Net asset value, 243
Net change, 243
Net return, 243
New issue, 243
No-load fund, 243
Non-cancelable, 243
Nonqualified retirement plan, 243
Normal retirement age, 243
Northwestern Mutual Life, 49
Northwest Medical Teams International, 207
Nursing care
  planning for, 98–100
  talking about, 100–103

Obligations. *See* Promises
Odd lot, 243
Office buildings, purchasing, 75–77
Offices, considerations for, 75
Old-age care
  planning for, 98–100
  talking about, 100–103
100% funds asset class, 190–191
Online purchases, computer security and, 41
Open-end investment company, 243–244
Open-end mutual fund, 244
Option, 244
Orbis International, 207–208
Ordinary life insurance, 244
OTC (over-the counter), 224
Out-of-control spending, budgeting and, 19–20
Overbought, 244

Overhead expense insurance, 48–50
Oversold, 244
Overspending, consistent, 20–
Over-the-counter (OTC), 244

Paper profit, 244
Partnership, 244
Passports, 65
Passwords, computer security and, 41
PBGC (Pension Benefit Guarantee Corporation), 244
PEG (price/earnings-to-growth) ratio, 244
Penny stock, 245
Pension Benefit Guarantee Corporation (PBGC), 244
Pension plans, information to have available for, 30, 245
Perkins Loan program, 85
Personal attributes, for vision statements, 3
Personal liability insurance, 40–41
Phone calls, privacy and, 63
Physicians
   anxiety over finances and, 19
   career cycles for, 4–11
   as employers, 23–24
   happy, 6–8
   insurance coverage for, 39–42
   solo, 8
   volunteer organizations for, 9–11, 202–208
Physicians for Peace, 208
Plan administrator, 245
Planners, financial, 193–194
Plan participant, 245
Plans. *See* Estate plans; Financial plans
PLUS loans, 84
Points, 245
   paying down interest rate and, 33
Pooled income fund, 245
Portfolios, 245
   constructing do-it-yourself, 175–177
   formulas for do-it-yourself, 177–184
   retirement, managing, 113–115, 126, 153
   sustainable, 173–175
Possessions attributes, for vision statements, 3–4
Predictable income asset class, 188–189
Preferred stock, 245
Premium, 246
Prenuptial agreements, 42–44. *See also* Marriage
   items to include, 43
   keys to, 42
   second marriages and, 42

Preschools, advice for enrolling children in, 88
Price/earning ratio (P/E), 246
Price-NAV ratio (P/NAV), 246
Price-to-book ratio (PBR), 246
Price-to-cash flow (EBIT), 246
Principal residence, determining, 71–73
Priorities, 12–13
Privacy, financial, 62–65
   confidentiality and, 62–63
   phone calls and, 63
   steps for additional, 64–65
Problem children, 82
Product strategy analysis (investing), 246
Professional liability insurance, 50–51
Profit sharing plans, 129, 246
Profit-sharing plans, 124
Project Hope, 208
Promises
   keeping, in employee manuals, 24–25
   sitting on boards and, 29
   as trustee, 27–29
Property and casualty insurance, 246
Prospectus, 246
Proxy, 246
Proxy statement, 247
Prudent-man rule, 247
Put, 247

Qualified domestic relations order (QDRO), 247
Qualified Pension Administrator, 247
Qualified pension plan, 247
Quotation, 247

Rally, 248
Real estate
   as investment, 77–78
   tax shelters and, 77
Real estate investment trust (REIT), 248
Real estate partnerships, 77
Redemption fee, 248
Red herring, 248
Registered Investment Advisor (RIA), 248
Registered representative, 248
Reinvestment risk, 248
Relationships, 43–44
Renting homes, *vs.* buying, 74
Resalability, of homes, 74
Research, challenging, for life insurance, 53

Retirement, 104–107
  budget busters in, 121–122
  calculating income needed for, 113–116
  determining lifestyles for, 116–117
  estimating income needed for, 110–113
  long-term care insurance and, 117
  setting budget based on visualized lifestyle, 110–112
  synergy for, 122–123
  visualizing lifestyle in, 107–110
  worksheet, 105–106, 111–112
Retirement-enhancers, 112
Retirement planning
  cash value life insurance and, 144, 149–151
  first job of, 124
  fixed immediate annuities and, 140–144
  rules of thumb and, 135–136, 145–149
  tax-sheltered investments and, 137–140
  tax strategies and, 136–137
  wealth-destruction products, 144–145
Retirement plans
  comparison of, 127–131
  designing, 125–126
  investment options for, 133–134
  managing portfolios for, 126
  maximum annual contribution limitations for, 124–125, 133
  tax-qualified, 123–134
Retirement portfolios, managing, 113–115
Retirement savings plans, cashing in, to pay for college, 87
Returns, 248
  compounding, 186
Reverse mortgage, 248
RIA (registered Investment Advisor), 248
Rights, 248
Risk investing, 249
Risk management, 38–42. *See also* Debt management
  accepting, 39
  avoiding, 39
  debt and, 31
  insurance for, 39
  minimizing, 39
Rollover, 249
Rollover IRA account, 249
Roth IRA, 127, 134
Round lot, 249
Routers, wireless, computer security and, 41
Rules of thumb
  harmful, 145–149
  retirement planning and, 135–136

Salary Reduction/Simplified Employee Pension Plan (SAR/SEP), 249
Sales pitches, for insurance, 57–58
Scholarships, for college, 84
Schwab direct, 51
Second home, 2497
Second marriages, prenups and, 42
Sector rotate, as investment approach, 170
Securities and Exchange Commission, 164–165
Securities Investor Protection Corporation (SIPC) excess insurance, 250
Securities Investor Protection Corporation (SIPC) insurance, 250
Security, cash and, 16–17
Security patches, for computer security, 40
Segregated account, 249
Selling short, 249
SEP (simplified employee pension) IRA, 127
SEP (simplified employee pension plan), 249–250
Short-term income investments, 185
Simple 401k plan, 128
Simple IRAs, 128
Simplified employee pension plan (SEP), 249–250
Simplified Employ Pension (SEP) IRA, 127
Small-cap stock, 250
social, 250
Socially conscious investor, 250
Social mutual funds, 250
Solo 401k with profit sharing plan owner only, 129
Solo physicians, 8
SPD (summary plan description), 251
Speculator, 250
Spending disorder, 19–20
Split, 251
Sponsor, 251
Spousal IRA, 251
Spread, 251
Stock bonus plan, 251
Stocks
  common, 229
  preferred, 245
Street name, 251
Subchapter S corporation, 251
Subsidized Stafford Loan, 85
Suitability rule, 251
Suitable management systems, 252
Summary annual report, 251
Summary plan description (SPD), 251
Sustainable portfolios, 173–175

Table of contents, sample, for employee manuals, 25
Target benefit plan, 252
Tax-deductible, defined, 252
Tax-deductible debt, 32
Tax deferral, 252
Taxes
  life insurance and, 57, 149–151
  planning process and, 193
Tax-favored investments, 137–138
Tax incentive, 252
Tax-qualified retirement plans, 122, 123–124
Tax-sheltered annuity (TSA), 253
Tax-sheltered investments, 137–140, 252
Tax shelter plans, 252
Tax shelters, real estate as, 77
Tax strategies, 136–137
T-Bills (treasury bills), 253
Templeton, John, 189
Tender offer, 252
Termination
  involuntary, 23
  voluntary, 23
Third-party administrator (TPA), 253
TIAA-CREF, 51
Time diversification, 252
Time-sharing, 252
Timing, market, 182
Top down, 253
Top-down investment approach, 171
TPA (third-party administrator), 253
Trader, 253
Traditional IRA, 127
Treasury bills (T-Bills), 253
Treasury bonds, 253
Treasury notes, 253
Treasury stock, 253
Trustee, 253
Trustees, promises and, 27–28
Trustees (retirement), 253
Trusts, 253
TSA (tax-sheltered annuity), 253
12b-1 fee, 254

UGMA. *See* Uniform Gifts to Minors Act (UGMA)
UGMA (Uniform Gifts to Minors Act), 529 plans *vs.*, 82
Umbrella insurance policies, 40
Umbrella liability, 254
Uniform Gifts to Minors Act (UGMA), 529 plans *vs.*, 82
Unlisted, 254
Unsubsidized Federal Stafford Loan Program, 85
USAA Life, 51
Utopia Funds, 190–191, 200

Vacations, for celebrating retirement, 113
Value-at-risk, 254
Value investing, 254
Values-neutral investing, 254
Variable annuities, 140, 142–143, 144
  reasons not to purchase, 142–143
Variable annuity, 254
Variable rate mortgage, 254
Vested benefits, 254
Vesting, 254
Virus software, for computer security, 40
Vision statements
  attributes to include in, 3–4
  developing, 2–3
Voluntary termination, 23
Volunteer organizations, for physicians, 9–11, 202–208
Voting right, 255

Warrant, 255
Wealth, inheriting, children and, 94–95
Wealth-destruction products, 144–145
WEP (wire equivalent privacy) encryption, 41
Weston, Liz Pulliam, 142–143
When issued, defined, 255
White Coat: Becoming a Doctor at Harvard Medical School (Rothman), 16
Wire equivalent privacy (WEP) encryption, 41
Wireless routers, computer security and, 41
Worksheets
  disability income insurance, 46
  family budgeting, 18
  life insurance, 54–55
  retirement, 105–106
  size of home, 72, 73

Yield, 255
Yield to call, 255
Yield to maturity, 255